W9-CAY-955

TOP TRAILS™
Lake Tahoe

Written by
Mike White

Series edited by
Joseph Walowski

 WILDERNESS PRESS · BERKELEY, CALIFORNIA

Top Trails Lake Tahoe

1st EDITION July 2004
  2nd Printing September 2005

Copyright © 2004 by Mike White

All photos, except where noted, copyright by Mike White
Maps: Mike White and Fineline Maps
Cover design: Frances Baca Design and Andreas Schueller
Interior design: Frances Baca Design
Production and additional interior design: Ben Pease, Pease Press
Book editor: Joe Walowski

ISBN 0-89997-349-3
UPC 7-19609-97349-2

Manufactured in the United States of America

Published by: **Wilderness Press**
               1200 5th Street
               Berkeley, CA 94710
               (800) 443-7227; FAX (510) 558-1696
               info@wildernesspress.com
               www.wildernesspress.com
Visit our website for a complete listing of our books and
for ordering information

Cover photos: Hiking in Bliss State Park, by Lee Foster/Lonely Planet Images (front);
              Aspen leaf, by Mike White (inset)

SAFETY NOTICE: Although Wilderness Press and the author have made every
attempt to ensure that the information in this book is accurate at press time, they are not
responsible for any loss, damage, injury, or inconvenience that may occur to anyone while
using this book. You are responsible for your own safety and health. The fact that a trail is
described in this book does not mean that it will be safe for you. Be aware that trail conditions can change from day to day. Always check local conditions and know your own
limitations.

The Top Trails™ Series

Wilderness Press

When Wilderness Press published *Sierra North* in 1967, no other trail guide like it existed for the Sierra backcountry. The first run of 2800 copies sold out in less than two months and its success heralded the beginning of Wilderness Press. In the past 35 years, we have expanded our territories to cover California, Alaska, Hawaii, the U.S. Southwest, the Pacific Northwest, New England, Canada, and Baja California.

Wilderness Press continues to publish comprehensive, accurate, and readable outdoor books. Hikers, backpackers, kayakers, skiers, snowshoers, climbers, cyclists, and trail runners rely on Wilderness Press for accurate outdoor adventure information.

Top Trails

In its Top Trails guides, Wilderness Press has paid special attention to organization so that you can find the perfect hike each and every time. Whether you're looking for a steep trail to test yourself on or a walk in the park, a romantic waterfall or a city view, Top Trails will lead you there.

Each Top Trails guide contains trails for everyone. The trails selected provide a sampling of the best that the region has to offer. These are the 'must-do' hikes, walks, runs and bike rides, with every feature of the area represented.

Every book in the Top Trails series offers:

- The Wilderness Press commitment to accuracy and reliability
- Ratings and rankings for each trail
- Distances and approximate times
- Easy-to-follow trail notes
- Maps & permit information

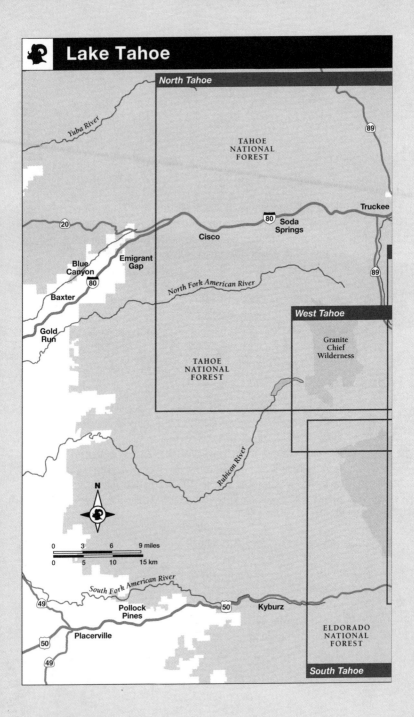

Lake Tahoe

North Tahoe

Yuba River

TAHOE
NATIONAL
FOREST

89

Truckee

20

80 Soda
Springs

Cisco

Blue
Canyon

Emigrant
Gap

80

North Fork American River

Baxter

West Tahoe

Gold
Run

Granite
Chief
Wilderness

89

TAHOE
NATIONAL
FOREST

Rubicon River

N

0   3   6   9 miles

0   5   10   15 km

South Fork American River

49

Pollock
Pines

50

Kyburz

ELDORADO
NATIONAL
FOREST

50

Placerville

49

South Tahoe

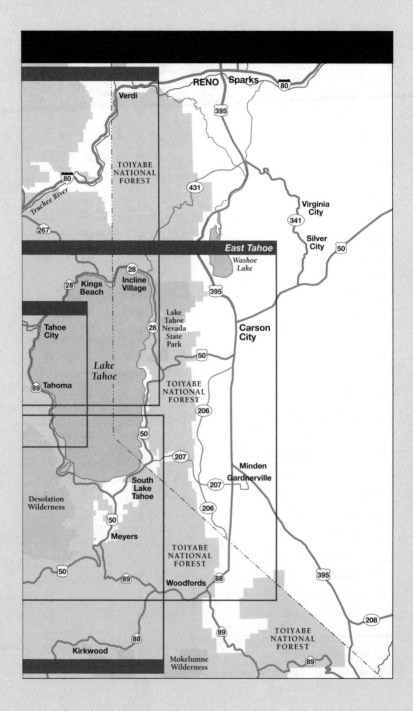

Lake Tahoe Trails

Trail Number and Name	Page	Difficulty 1-2345+	Length in Miles	Type	Hiking	Running	Bicycling	Horses & Handicap	Dogs Allowed	Child Friendly
1. NORTH TAHOE										
1 Mt. Lola & White Rock Lake	29	1	14.4	↗	🚶	🏃	🚴	🐎	🐕	
2 Sagehen Creek	35	1	5.0	↗	🚶	🏃	🚴	🐎	🐕	👪
3 Summit & Warren Lakes	39	1/3/5	15.0	↗	🚶			🐎	🐕	
4 Castle Peak	45	5	9.6	↗	🚶				🐕	
5 Castle & Round Valleys	51	2	9.5	↻	🚶	🏃	🚴	🐎	🐕	👪
6 Loch Leven Lakes	57	4	8.0	↗	🚶	🏃	🚴	🐎	🐕	
7 Mt. Judah Loop	63	3	4.6	↻	🚶	🏃		🐎	🐕	👪
8 PCT: Donner Pass to Squaw Valley	67	5	15.0	↘	🚶			🐎		
9 Granite Chief	75	5/3	10.2	↗	🚶					
10 Five Lakes Basin	81	3	4.0	↗	🚶	🏃			🐕	
11 Mt. Rose	85	3	10.0	↗	🚶	🏃			🐕	
12 Tahoe Meadows	91	1	1.3	↻	🚶			♿		👪
13 TRT: Tahoe Meadows-Brockway Summit	95	5	18.0	↘	🚶	🏃	🚴		🐕	
14 TRT: Tahoe Meadows to Twin Lakes	105	4	19.0	↗	🚶	🏃	🚴	🐎	🐕	
2. WEST TAHOE										
15 TRT: Ward Creek to Twin Peaks	119	3	11.6	↗	🚶	🏃	🚴	🐎	🐕	
16 PCT: Barker Pass to Twin Peaks	123	4	11.2	↗	🚶	🏃	🚴		🐕	
17 Ellis Lake & Ellis Peak	127	4	11.2	↗	🚶	🏃	🚴		🐕	
18 General Creek Trail	131	3	13.0	↗	🚶	🏃	🚴	🐎		👪
19 Sugar Pine Point State Peak	135	1	1.7	↻	🚶			♿		👪
3. SOUTH TAHOE										
20 TYT: Meeks Bay to Tallant Lake	151	4	16.0	↗	🚶	🏃		🐎	🐕	✓
21 D.L. Bliss State Park	157	1	2.0	↻	🚶					👪
22 Rubicon Trail	161	2	5.0	↘	🚶					👪
23 Vikingsholm & Eagle Falls	167	2	2.5	↗	🚶			♿		👪
24 Eagle Lake	173	2	2.0	↗	🚶	🏃			🐕	👪
25 Bayview Trail to Velma Lakes	177	4	10.5	↻	🚶	🏃		🐎	🐕	✓
26 Mt. Tallac	183	5	9.4	↗	🚶	🏃			🐕	✓

TRAIL	Canyon	Mountain	Summit	Stream	Waterfall	Shore	Autumn Colors	Wildflowers	Birds	Wildlife	Cool & Shady	Great Views	Photo Opportunity	Camping	Secluded	Historic	Geology	Steep
1. NORTH TAHOE...continued																		
1	●	●	●	●		●		●				●	●	●	●			
2	●			●			●	●	●	●			●					
3	●	●				●			●			●	●	●				●
4	●	●	●					●				●	●					
5	●	●	●					●		●		●		●		●		●
6	●	●				●		●					●	●				
7		●	●									●						
8		●	●									●	●	●	●			
9	●	●	●	●		●		●			●	●	●					
10	●					●							●					
11		●	●	●	●			●				●	●					
12		●						●	●	●			●					
13		●	●		●	●		●	●			●	●	●	●			
14		●						●	●			●	●	●				
2. WEST TAHOE...continued																		
15	●	●	●	●	●			●				●	●					
16		●	●			●			●			●	●					
17		●	●			●						●	●	●				●
18	●	●		●		●					●	●		●	●			
19						●		●		●	●	●						
3. SOUTH TAHOE...continued																		
20	●	●	●	●		●		●					●	●				
21						●						●	●					
22						●						●	●					
23					●	●					●	●	●			●		
24	●	●		●	●	●							●	●			●	
25	●	●		●		●		●					●	●				
26	●	●	●	●		●		●				●	●					

Lake Tahoe Trails...continued

TRAIL NUMBER AND NAME	Page	Difficulty -12345+	Length in Miles	Type	Hiking	Running	Bicycling	Horses & Handicap	Dogs Allowed	Child Friendly	Permit
3. SOUTH TAHOE...continued											
27 Susie & Heather Lakes, Lake Aloha	189	4	11.8	↗	✓	✓		✓ (Horses)	✓		
28 Triangle-Echo-Angora Loop	195	5	7.2	↻	✓					✓	
29 Echo Lakes to Lake Aloha	201	2-3	12.6	↗	✓	✓		✓ (Horses)	✓		
30 Lake of the Woods to Ropi Lake	207	3-4	13.0	↗	✓	✓		✓ (Horses)	✓		
31 Ralston Peak	213	4	6.0	↗	✓	✓			✓		
32 Horsetail Falls	217	3	3.0	↗	✓						✓
33 Big Meadow to Carson Pass	223	3	10.4	↘	✓	✓		✓ (Horses)	✓		
34 Winnemucca & Round Top Lakes	229	3	4.8	↻	✓	✓		✓ (Horses)	✓		✓
35 Emigrant Lake	235	3	8.2	↗	✓	✓		✓ (Horses)	✓		✓
36 Thunder Mountain	239	3	8.5	↗	✓	✓	✓	✓ (Horses)	✓		
4. EAST TAHOE											
37 TRT: Spooner Summit-Snow Valley Pk.	251	4	12.4	↗	✓	✓	✓	✓ (Horses)	✓	✓	
38 Spooner Lake	255	1	1.8	↻	✓	✓	✓	✓ (Handicap) ✓ (Horses)	✓	✓	
39 Marlette Lake	259	3	10.0	↗	✓	✓	✓	✓ (Horses)	✓		
40 Flume Trail	265	2-3	13.0	↘			✓				
41 TRT: Spooner to South Camp Peak	271	3	10.2	↗	✓	✓	✓	✓ (Horses)	✓		
42 Skunk Harbor	275	3	3.2	↗	✓	✓	✓			✓	
43 TRT: Daggett Pass to Star Lake	279	4	17.6	↗	✓	✓	✓		✓		✓
44 TRT: Armstrong Pass to Star Lake	285	3	11.6	↗	✓	✓	✓	✓ (Horses)	✓		

Legend

USE & ACCESS
- Hiking
- Trail Running
- Mountain Biking
- Horses
- Child Friendly
- Dogs Allowed
- Handicap Access
- Permit Required
- P Parking Fee

TERRAIN
- Canyon
- Mountain
- Summit

WATER
- Stream
- Waterfall
- Lake/Shore

FLORA & FAUNA
- Autumn Colors
- Wildflowers
- Birds
- Wildlife

DIFFICULTY
- 1 2 3 4 5 +
less   more

OTHER
- Cool & Shady
- Great Views
- Photo Opportunity
- Secluded
- Historic
- Geologic Interest
- Moonlight Hiking
- Steep
- Camping

TRAIL	Canyon	Mountain	Summit	Stream	Waterfall	Shore	Autumn Colors	Wildflowers	Birds	Wildlife	Cool & Shady	Great Views	Photo Opportunity	Camping	Secluded	Historic	Geology	Steep
3. SOUTH TAHOE...continued																		
27	✓	⛰		🔀	▮	〰		✻					📷	⛺				
28	✓	⛰	△			〰		✻			🌲	🔭	📷					⛰
29		⛰				〰		✻					📷	⛺				
30		⛰				〰		✻	✦				📷	⛺				
31	✓	⛰	△					✻	✦			🔭	📷			♦		⛰
32	✓			🔀	▮							🔭	📷					P
33	✓	⛰		🔀		〰	🍁	✻	✦	🦌			📷	⛺	♦	⌂		
34	✓	⛰		🔀		〰		✻					📷	⛺		⌂		
35	✓	⛰		🔀		〰		✻			🌲		📷	⛺				
36		⛰	△						✦			🔭	📷					
4. EAST TAHOE...continued																		
37		⛰	△				🍁		✦		🌲	🔭	📷					
38		⛰				〰	🍁	✻	✦	🦌			📷			⌂		P
39	✓	⛰		🔀		〰	🍁	✻	✦	🦌			📷					
40	✓	⛰				〰	🍁					🔭	📷					
41		⛰	△					✻				🔭	📷					
42						〰						🔭	📷			⌂		
43		⛰				〰						🔭	📷	⛺	♦			
44		⛰	△			〰						🔭	📷	⛺				

Contents

CHAPTER 1

North Tahoe

CHAPTER 2

West Tahoe 111

CHAPTER 3

South Tahoe 141

CHAPTER 4

East Tahoe 243

Using Top Trails™

Organization of Top Trails

Top Trails is designed to make identifying the perfect trail easy and enjoyable, and to make every outing a success and a pleasure. With this book you'll find it's a snap to find the right trail, whether you're planning a major hike or just a sociable stroll with friends.

The Region

Top Trails begins with the **Lake Tahoe Map** (pages iv-v), displaying the entire region covered by the guide and providing a geographic overview. The map is clearly marked to show which area is covered by each chapter.

After the Regional Map comes the **Lake Tahoe Trails Table** (pages vi-ix), which lists every trail covered in the guide along with attributes for each trail. A quick reading of the Regional Map and the Trail Table will give a good overview of the entire region covered by the book.

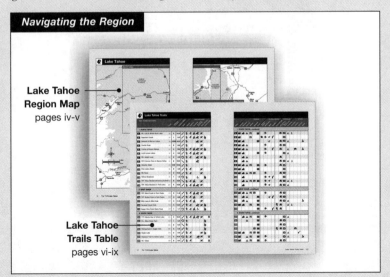

Navigating the Region

Lake Tahoe
Region Map
pages iv-v

Lake Tahoe
Trails Table
pages vi-ix

The Areas

The region covered in each book is divided into Areas, with each chapter corresponding to one area in the region.

Each Area chapter starts with information to help you choose and enjoy a trail every time out. Use the Table of Contents or the Regional Map to identify an area of interest, then turn to the Area chapter to find the following:

- An Overview of the Area, including park and permit information
- An Area Map with all trails clearly marked
- A Trail Feature Table providing trail-by-trail details
- Trail Summaries, written in a lively, accessible style

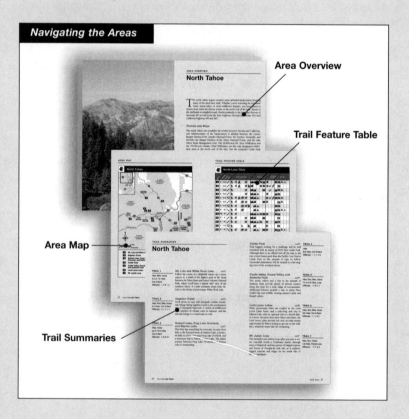

The Trails

The basic building block of the Top Trails guide is the Trail Entry. Each one is arranged to make finding and following the trail as simple as possible, with all pertinent information presented in this easy-to-follow format:

- A Trail Map
- Trail Descriptors covering difficulty, length and other essential data
- A written Trail Description
- Trail Milestones providing easy-to follow, turn-by-turn trail directions

Some Trail Descriptions offer additional information:

- An Elevation Profile
- Trail Options
- Trail Highlights

In the margins of the Trail Entries, keep your eyes open for graphic icons that signal passages in the text.

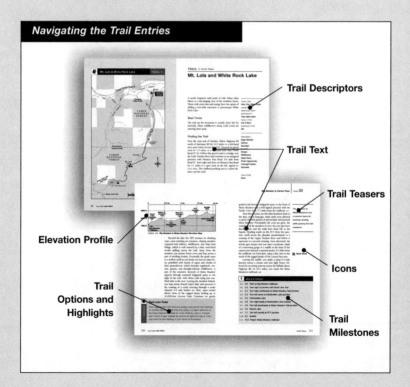

Choosing a Trail

Top Trails provides several different ways of choosing a trail, all presented in easy-to-read tables, charts, and maps.

Location

If you know in general where you want to go, Top Trails makes it easy to find the right trail in the right place. Each chapter begins with a large-scale map showing the starting point of every trail in that area.

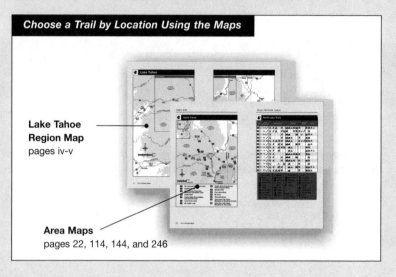

Choose a Trail by Location Using the Maps

Lake Tahoe Region Map
pages iv-v

Area Maps
pages 22, 114, 144, and 246

Features

This guide describes the Top Trails of the Lake Tahoe region. Each trail is chosen because it offers one or more features that make it interesting. Using the trail descriptors, summaries, and tables, you can quickly examine all the trails for the features they offer, or seek a particular feature among the list of trails.

Season and Condition

Time of year and current conditions can be important factors in selecting the best trail. For example, an exposed grassland trail may be a riot of color in early spring, but an oven-baked taste of hell in mid-summer. Wherever relevant, Top Trails identifies the best and worst conditions for the trails you plan to hike.

Difficulty

Each trail has an overall difficulty rating on a scale of 1 to 5, which takes into consideration length, elevation change, exposure, trail quality, etc., to create one (admittedly subjective) rating.

The ratings assume you are an able-bodied adult in reasonably good shape using the trail for hiking. The ratings also assume normal weather conditions—clear and dry.

Readers should make an honest assessment of their own abilities and adjust time estimates accordingly. Also, rain, snow, heat, and poor visibility can all affect the pace on even the easiest of trails.

Choose a Trail by Length, Difficulty, or Features using the Tables

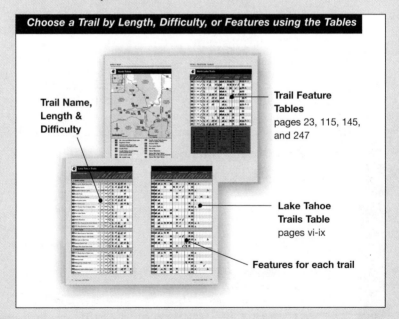

Trail Name, Length & Difficulty

Trail Feature Tables
pages 23, 115, 145, and 247

Lake Tahoe Trails Table
pages vi–ix

Features for each trail

Vertical Feet

This important measurement is often underestimated by hikers and bikers when gauging the difficulty of a trail. The Top Trails measurement accounts for all elevation change, not simply the difference between the highest and lowest points, so that rolling terrain with lots of up and down will be identifiable.

The calculation of Vertical Feet in the Top Trails series is accomplished by a combination of trail measurement and computer-aided estimation. For routes that begin and end at the same spot – i.e. Loop or Out & Back – the vertical gain exactly matches the vertical descent. With a point-to-point route the vertical gain and loss will most likely differ, and both figures will be provided in the text.

Finally, some of Trail Entries in the Top Trails series have an **Elevation Profile**, an easy means for visualizing the topography of the route. These profiles graphically depict the elevation throughout the length of the trail.

Surface Type

Each Trail Entry provides information about the surface of the trail. This is useful in determining what type of footwear or bicycle is appropriate. Surface Type should also be considered when checking the weather – on a rainy day a dirt surface can be a muddy slog; an asphalt surface might be a better choice (although asphalt can be slick when wet).

 Top Trails Difficulty Ratings

1 A short trail, generally level, that can be completed in one hour or less.
2 A route of 1 to 3 miles, with some up and down, that can be completed in one to two hours.
3 A longer route, up to 5 miles, with uphill and/or downhill sections.
4 A long or steep route, perhaps more than five miles or climbs of more than 1000 vertical feet.
5 The most severe, both long and steep, more than 5 miles long with climbs of more than 1000 vertical feet.

Map Legend

Trail	‑ ‑ ‑ ‑ ‑ ‑ ‑		River	———
Other Trail	– – – – – –		Stream	——
			Seasonal Stream	‑·‑·‑·‑·‑
Freeway	▬▬▬▬▬		Body of Water	⬭
Major Road	▬▬▬▬▬		Marsh/Swamp	⸖ ⸖ ⸖
Minor Road	———		Dam	⬤
Tunnel	– – – – –		Peak	▲
Ski Lift/Tramway	⊢•⊢•⊢•⊢			
Railroad	⊢⊢⊢⊢⊢		Park/Forest	▭
Bridge	)(		Boundary	‑·‑·‑·‑
Building	▬ ▮			
Trailhead Parking	**P**		Start/Finish	🚶 start & finish
Picnic	⛱			
Camping	▲		North Arrow	✦ N
Gate	•—•			

Lake Tahoe *from Rubicon Trail (Trail 22)*

Introduction to Lake Tahoe

Tall mountains covered with a thick blanket of conifers surround the breathtakingly blue lake, creating a stunning, alp-like setting, which is famous around the globe. Whether you plumb the depths of Lake Tahoe, climb to the summit of the highest peak, or journey somewhere in between, the Tahoe Basin provides many opportunities to appreciate the grandeur of one of the West's most priceless treasures.

Geography and Topography

The Lake Tahoe Basin presents diverse topography that receives adoration from a devoted tourist base. At an elevation of 6229 feet, Tahoe is the highest lake of its size in the U.S. and, with a depth of 1645 feet (measured near Crystal Bay), is the third deepest lake in North America and tenth deepest lake in the world. The 22-mile-long and 12-mile-wide lake has a 71-mile-long shoreline, with 42 of those scenic miles belonging to California and the remaining 29 owned by Nevada. Lake Tahoe is perhaps best known for the crystal clarity of its waters, which allows visibility of up to 75 feet below the surface. Sixty-three streams flow into Lake Tahoe, but only one, the Truckee River, flows out of the lake, reaching its terminus in the Great Basin, at Pyramid Lake.

Geologists speculate that the landform that would ultimately become the Tahoe Basin we know today was once beneath a shallow ancient sea in the super continent of Pangea. The North American Continental Plate eventually broke away from Pangea and headed west, colliding into the Pacific Ocean Plate, which was drifting east. Extreme pressure and heat were created as the North American Plate rose above the Pacific Plate, producing molten rock that slowly solidified beneath the sedimentary surface into granitic rocks, which were later exposed through faulting.

Faulting fractures in the earth's crust allowed blocks of land to rise and fall, pushing the primarily plutonic rocks of the Sierra Nevada up from the ancient seabed. Two principal faults evolved in the Tahoe area, which produced uplifts that became the main Sierra crest to the west and the Carson Range to the east. In between, the down-thrown fault block formed the deep V-shaped valley of the Tahoe Basin.

Angora Lakes *from Echo Peak (Trail 28)*

A lake began to form at the lowest, southern end of the basin, fed by precipitation and creeks draining the surrounding mountains. The level of the lake rose steadily, until an outlet for the river draining the lake was reached to the north, near the current town of Truckee. Later, a significant lava flow from Mt. Pluto, site of the Northstar at Tahoe resort, dammed the outlet and caused the lake to rise again. Eventually the river was able to cut a new outlet through the volcanic rock, near the present-day Tahoe City. The highest level Lake Tahoe ever reached was an estimated 600 to 800 feet above the current level. Additional volcanic activity occurred at both the south end of the basin, around Carson Pass, and the north end of the basin, near Donner Pass.

Although a regional ice sheet was absent, in theory the last Ice Age put the finishing touches on the Tahoe Basin. Separate rivers of ice followed some of the existing V-shaped stream channels, carving them into classic U-shaped canyons. Glacial action scoured several of the canyons on the west side of the basin, uncovering the classic granite bedrock associated with the Sierra Nevada today. In the process, some of the area's most picturesque lakes were formed, including Donner, Cascade, Fallen Leaf, and Echo Lakes, as well as scenic Emerald Bay on Tahoe's southwest shore. Because the Sierra crest creates a rain-shadow effect which limits the amount of pre-cipitation, minimal glaciation occurred from the Carson range to the east. Without the glacial scouring on the west side of the Tahoe Basin, the topog-raphy of the Carson Range is primarily granitic soils rather than the classic Sierra granite bedrock. While the west side of the Tahoe Basin is sprinkled with an abundance of tarns, lakes, and ponds, the east side is nearly devoid of such features. Additional glacial activity influenced the area when ice dams formed across the Truckee River canyon and broke several times, producing floods that further shaped the canyon, depositing debris downstream as far away as present-day Reno.

Flora

Since the area ranges in elevation from 6229 feet at lake level to 10,881 feet at the summit of Freel Peak, you can expect to encounter a wide range of flora on trails within the Tahoe Basin. The mountains and hills surrounding the beautiful shoreline of Lake Tahoe are carpeted with conifers. Although it's hard to believe at first glance, these trees belong almost exclusively to a second growth forest, as the basin was nearly denuded to provide timber and fuel for Virginia City and the surrounding mines during the heyday of the Comstock Lode. Although the varied vegetation defies strict classification, the following zones provide a general overview of Tahoe's flora.

The **upper montane zone**, the largest zone in the basin and containing the widest variety of plant types, runs from lake level to about 8000 feet. The upper montane zone can be grouped into six distinct divisions. Up to around 7000 feet, the **white fir forest** is named for the dominant member of a mixed forest, which also includes incense cedar, sugar pine, Jeffrey pine, and ponderosa pine, as well as red fir at the upper limits. Preferring a moist habitat, the white fir forest can form dense stands with little ground cover, or more open stands allowing deciduous trees and shrubs to thrive, including quaking aspen, willow, maple, currant, gooseberry, thimbleberry, and honeysuckle. Above the white fir forest, the **red fir forest** extends to about 8500 feet. Unlike the white fir forest, red fir is found in exclusive stands, usually on cool northern or eastern exposures. The red fir forest is generally dense, allowing very little ground cover, which when present is composed primarily of shade-loving flowers and plants. The **Jeffrey pine forest** occupies drier slopes than those preferred by the white and red fir forests. Spanning elevations from lake level to approximately 8000 feet, open Jeffrey pine forests intermix in the lower realms with sugar pine, ponderosa pine, white fir, and incense cedar. Those conifers are replaced by western white pine, ponderosa pine, and red fir toward the upper limits.

On southern exposures, light stands of Jeffrey pine forest oftentimes intermix with Sierra juniper or with open areas of **montane chaparral**. The drought-tolerant montane chaparral community spans elevations across the spectrum of the upper montane zone into the subalpine zone, typically occupying dry slopes with a southern exposure. This community incorporates several common shrubs, including huckleberry oak, tobacco brush,

Fallen Leaf Lake

rabbitbrush, manzanita, chinquapin, and sagebrush. Along the eastern fringe of the Carson Range, mountain mahogany and juniper trees may dot the slopes of the montane chaparral community. Areas of sufficient ground-water produce the **montane meadow** community. Similar to the montane chaparral community, montane meadows span the realm of the upper montane zone into the subalpine zone. The wetter environment allows grasses, rushes, and sedges to thrive, along with several species of water-loving wild-flowers. The last of the five classifications within the upper montane zone is the **riparian** community. With the additional moisture provided by perennial streams, lush foliage along the banks includes deciduous trees and shrubs such as aspen, cottonwood, willow, alder, creek dogwood, and mountain ash. Smaller plants and colorful wildflowers are also common in creek-side environments.

Above the upper montane zone, the **subalpine zone** begins around 8000 feet and continues upward to timberline, which, depending on a number of variables, starts anywhere from 9000 to 10,000 feet in the Tahoe Sierra. With characteristically poor soils and a harsh climate, where snow covers the ground for nine months of the year, the prolific forests below give way to isolated stands of conifers and the open terrain of meadows and talus slides. Red firs, lodgepoles pines, and junipers may extend into this zone in some areas, with lodgepole pines often rimming the shoreline of subalpine lakes. Despite the sporadic appearance of these trees from the lower realm, the two conifer species most closely associated with the subalpine zone are mountain hemlock and whitebark pine. Nearing timberline, dwarfed and wind-battered whitebark pines become the only conifers able to survive the conditions of this harsh environment. Shrubs and plants in this zone also take on a diminished stature, hugging the ground in order to eke out an existence. Common plants include heathers and laurels. Where seeps and rivulets provide moist soils, a short-lived but stunning display of colorful wildflowers delights passersby. Rock outcroppings may provide equally delightful displays of plants and flowers.

Above timberline, at the extreme upper elevations of the Tahoe Basin, is the **alpine zone**. Although there is some debate among botanists as to whether the Tahoe area has a well-defined alpine zone, only the backcountry traveler who reaches the summit of some of the basin's highest peaks will be able to observe the area in question. The vegetation within this zone appears to be a combination of tundra species from the north and desert species from the east. Whatever their origin, these plants are generally compact, low-growing perennials that grow rapidly and flower briefly, with most of their growth occurring below ground. Low-growing shrubs, such as low sagebrush and short-stemmed stenotus, share the extreme conditions and poor soils of the alpine region with an assortment of wildflowers. The uppermost slopes of Mt. Rose and Freel Peak provide some of the best opportunities in the Tahoe Sierra to experience the flora of the alpine zone.

Fauna

Along with a wide variety of plants, the Lake Tahoe Basin is home to a varied community of fauna. While traveling the trails around Lake Tahoe, with alert eyes you may be able to spot several different species of animals.

The largest mammal in the region is the omnivorous **black bear**, which ranges in color from black to cinnamon. Some members of Tahoe's black bear population, particularly near developed communities on the west shore, have become quite pesky in seeking food from garbage cans, dumpsters and campgrounds. However, most bears you might see in the backcountry remain timid, and are wary of human encounters. Although bears here are not nearly the nuisance that bears are in the backcountry of Yosemite, Kings Canyon, or Sequoia national parks, backpackers should still obey Bear Safety Guidelines (page 6).

More likely to be seen along the trail than a bear in the Tahoe Sierra is the **mule deer**, so named for its floppy ears. Mule deer prefer varied terrain with an ample food supply, mainly leaves from trees and shrubs, along with grasses, sedges, and other herbs. Watch for mule deer around dusk in grassy meadows, or during the day in open forest where browse is plentiful. Deer

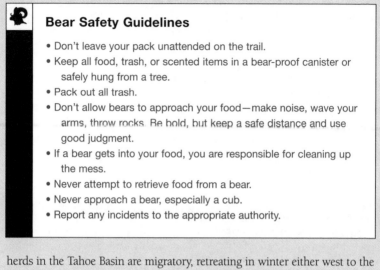

Bear Safety Guidelines

- Don't leave your pack unattended on the trail.
- Keep all food, trash, or scented items in a bear-proof canister or safely hung from a tree.
- Pack out all trash.
- Don't allow bears to approach your food—make noise, wave your arms, throw rocks. Be bold, but keep a safe distance and use good judgment.
- If a bear gets into your food, you are responsible for cleaning up the mess.
- Never attempt to retrieve food from a bear.
- Never approach a bear, especially a cub.
- Report any incidents to the appropriate authority.

herds in the Tahoe Basin are migratory, retreating in winter either west to the foothills or east to the Carson Valley. Since extinction of the grizzly bear and wolf from the Sierra, the mule deer's only natural predator is the mountain lion.

Although present in the greater Tahoe area, **mountain lions**, also known as cougars, are rarely seen by humans. Ranging in length from 6.5 to 8 feet and weighing as much as 200 pounds, mountain lions are primarily nocturnal, patrolling a vast range. Although mule deer are their principal food source, mountain lions will stalk smaller mammals as well. At an average weight of 20 pounds, the **bobcat** is the mountain lion's smaller cousin. Also nocturnal and equally reclusive, bobcats prefer a diet of rodents. You're much more likely to hear their blood-curdling scream during the night than see bobcats in the wild.

The highly adaptable **coyote** is often seen loping across the meadows and through the woodlands of Lake Tahoe. From backcountry campsites spread around the Tahoe Basin, backpackers frequently hear the coyote's nighttime chorus of howls and yelps. Although many area residents are familiar with the coyote, they fail to realize that it is omnivorous, preferring a diet of small rodents, but also dining on berries and plants when such prey is unavailable.

Other common, medium-sized mammals of Lake Tahoe include martens, marmots, raccoons, porcupines, red fox, weasels, and badgers. Hikers frequently see Douglas squirrels, California ground squirrels, golden-mantled ground squirrels, western gray squirrels, western flying squirrels, and chipmunks. Smaller rodents include pikas, voles, shrews, mice, moles, and pocket gophers.

Eastern Sierra meadows *along Sagehen Creek (Trail 2)*

At dusk, backpackers camped around one of Tahoe's backcountry lakes are almost guaranteed a visit from a handful of **bats** searching the skies for the evening's first course of insects. Mid-summer visitors will be comforted to know that large helpings of mosquitoes are on the bats' menu.

The skies above the Lake Tahoe Basin are home to hundreds of bird species. While hiking around the shore of Lake Tahoe or the banks of rivers and creeks, keep your eyes peeled for **bald eagles** and **ospreys**, although they are not particularly common. **Red-tailed hawks** are raptors more frequently seen patrolling the skies. **Great horned owls** are primarily nocturnal, but may be seen napping on a tree limb during the day. A walk along Tahoe's trails without seeing a **Clark's nutcracker**, **mountain chickadee**, or **Steller's jay** is hard to imagine. Numerous songbirds fly around the Tahoe Basin, but a fine treat would be the sighting of a **mountain bluebird** flitting about a subalpine meadow or perched on the branch of a young lodgepole pine near the edge.

Amphibians and reptiles are common residents of the area. The most frequently seen species include **Pacific tree frog**, **western fence lizard**, and the common **garter snake**. Although possible, encountering a western rattlesnake in the Lake Tahoe Basin is extremely unlikely.

Insects are abundant members of the Lake Tahoe community. Unfortunately, the mosquito gains the most attention. Thankfully, depending on elevation and the rate at which the previous winter's snowpack melts, the peak of the mosquito season lasts for just a few weeks in the backcountry, usually through the last weeks of July into the first week of August.

The lakes and streams of the Tahoe Basin teem with fish, where anglers can ply their craft in search of brook, brown, cutthroat, and rainbow trout.

Along with these trout, Lake Tahoe itself is home to a couple of introduced species, **Mackinaw**, also known as lake trout, and **Kokanee salmon**. Although biologists theorize that Mackinaws in Lake Tahoe may reach weights as high as 50 pounds, the record catch so far is 37 pounds, 6 ounces. Landlocked cousins of the sockeye salmon, Kokanee salmon were introduced to Lake Tahoe in 1944. The Taylor Creek Stream Profile Chamber at the Lake Tahoe Visitor Center provides an excellent opportunity for viewing the annual spawning migration of the Kokanee each autumn, usually coinciding with the locally renowned Kokanee Festival, held the first week of October.

When to Go

Although Lake Tahoe is considered a year-round recreation destination, those wishing to hike snow-free trails will have wait until the **summer hiking season**, when the previous winter's snowpack has melted and the customarily pleasant weather has settled into the region. Trails begin to shed their winter mantle at lake level as early as mid-to-late April, with the snow line progressively receding up the mountainside until the highest elevations are clear, usually no later than mid-July. The **wildflower bloom** generally begins in earnest a couple of weeks after snowmelt, which varies, depending on such factors as elevation, exposure, and temperature.

On a par with many locations in the desert Southwest, the Lake Tahoe Basin has a 93% probability of sunshine for any day from June through August. However, unlike the desert Southwest, mild summer temperatures rarely exceed 80°F. With the moderating influences of both the lake's 193-square-miles surface area and the dense forests surrounding the lake, nighttime temperatures stay mild during the summer months as well, with lows ranging from the high 30s in June to the low 40s in July and August. Precipitation during the summer is generally light at lake level, with averages of .69 inch for June, .26 inch for July, and .31 inch for August. Most of that falls during thunderstorms, which can be intense at higher elevations in the mountains. Unlike the Rocky Mountains, the Tahoe Sierra may experience summers of little or no thunderstorms, or a run of days when they're fairly frequent. Hikers should always be prepared for an afternoon cloudburst and to beat a hasty retreat from higher elevations when lightning is threatening.

Warm, dry weather often lingers through the waning days of summer and occasionally through the end of September and into October. The Tahoe area is usually blessed during **autumn**, when temperatures are cooler but still pleasant enough for hiking. In October, when **fall color** adorns the meadows and stream canyons of the Tahoe Basin, the average high temperature is 57°F and, although the average precipitation for the month climbs

Shirley Lake (*Trail 9*)

to 1.9 inches, there is still an 84% chance of having a sunny day. Usually in November a Pacific storm brings the first significant snowfall to the mountains, encouraging hikers to trade in their boots for skis or snowshoes.

Since Lake Tahoe is such a popular summer destination, many of the trails are heavily used during the height of the tourist season. Weekends between Memorial Day and Labor Day can be particularly crowded, especially on the southwest side of the lake. When contemplating a trip for June, July, or August, plan on hiking during the week. If a weekday adventure is out of the question, try to arrive early on the weekends to secure a parking spot and to beat the hordes up the trail. Desolation Wilderness has long been one of the most visited wilderness areas in the United States, resulting in quotas and fees for overnight users. Although the number of dayhikers is not limited, trailhead registration is required for entry into the wilderness. While Lake Tahoe can be a bit of a human zoo during the summer at some localities, a good percentage of the backcountry sees light to moderate use.

Fall provides some of the finest trail experiences of the year. After Labor Day weekend the Tahoe area sees a diminishing number of tourists, a trend that continues as the days progress, until ski season begins. With good weather the norm and fewer people competing for space on the trail, hikers can experience the grandeur of the Tahoe backcountry in uncrowded fashion.

Trail Selection

Several criteria were used to arrange this assortment of Tahoe's 44 best trails. Only the premier hikes, runs, and rides were included, based upon beautiful scenery, ease of access, quality of trail, and diversity of experience. Some of the trails selected are highly popular, while others may see infrequent use. Anyone fortunate enough to complete all the trips in this guide would have a comprehensive appreciation for the natural beauty of one of the West's most scenic recreational havens.

About 70% of the trails included in this guide are classified as out-and-back trips, requiring you to retrace your steps back to a trailhead. The remaining percentage is roughly distributed between point-to-point, loop, and partial-loop trips.

Key Features

Top Trails-series books contain information about "features" for each trail. Although primarily a mountainous region, the Lake Tahoe Basin has such outstanding diversity that it offers at least a little of each feature, including sandy beaches. Lakes, streams, and waterfalls occur in abundance, as do high summits with spectacular vistas and rugged canyons. A plethora of verdant meadows are graced with scenic wildflower displays, and numerous aspen groves provide plenty of autumn color. All these features combine to make Lake Tahoe and the surrounding topography a photographer's paradise. About the only feature that suffers in the Lake Tahoe region is solitude, due in some part to the abundance of these other attributes.

Multiple Uses

All the trails in this guide are suitable for **hiking**, with the exception of the Flume Trail (Trip 40). Even though hikers are permitted to use it, the Flume Trail is so popular with mountain bikers that hikers should yield their rights to the two-wheeled crowd. Although all the trails are equally legal for runners, some have been determined impractical for such use.

Lake Tahoe, has become one of the West's premier Meccas for **mountain bikers**. Mountain biking is not permitted on sections of the Pacific Crest Trail, or in the wilderness areas around Lake Tahoe, which currently include Mt. Rose, Granite Chief, Desolation, and Mokelumne wildernesses. If two proposed wilderness areas become reality, this ban may extend to areas around Castle Peak and Meiss Meadows. Other trails—though they may be administratively classified as multi-use trails—have been excluded from prospective use by mountain bikes because of unsuitable terrain or conditions.

Equestrians will find plenty of trails within the Lake Tahoe Basin to ride. A handful of trails have been restricted from equestrian use by governmental agencies, primarily for environmental concerns or a high probability of conflict between horses and humans. Others are not recommended for horses because of unsuitable terrain.

Trail Safety

Elevations in the Lake Tahoe Basin vary from 6229 feet at lake level to 10,881 feet at the summit of Freel Peak. Although these elevations are not considered extreme by mountaineering standards, people living near sea level who recreate at the higher elevations may experience symptoms of **altitude sickness.** These include headache, fatigue, loss of appetite, shortness of breath, nausea, vomiting, drowsiness, dizziness, memory loss, and loss of mental acuity. Untreated, altitude sickness can lead to acute mountain sickness, which is more serious and requires immediate medical attention.

To avoid altitude sickness, acclimatize slowly, drink plenty of fluids, and eat a diet high in carbohydrates prior to the trip. A rapid descent generally alleviates any symptoms if they develop. A severe case of altitude sickness is unlikely at elevations around Lake Tahoe, although not impossible.

Less atmosphere to filter the sun's rays at higher altitudes increases the risks of exposure to the **sun.** Wear an appropriate sunblock on exposed areas, and reapply as necessary. Sunglasses will protect the eyes, which is especially important in areas where the sun reflects off snowfields or the granite bedrock that is prevalent on the west side of the basin.

Dehydration is another potential hazard while recreating in the backcountry of Lake Tahoe. Carry and drink plenty of fluids while on the trail. Any water gathered from streams or lakes should be filtered or treated. Some of the trails in the Tahoe area, particularly in the Carson Range, have long, waterless stretches, so plan on packing extra water in those areas.

Although the weather in the mountains around Lake Tahoe is predictably fair, conditions can change rapidly at any time. Be sure to pack appropriate clothing to endure any change in the weather. Even if the day is fair, temperatures can be radically different at lake level than at the summit of a windswept peak like Mt. Tallac or Freel Peak. Dousing thunderstorms can leave the ill-prepared wet, cold, and potentially hypothermic; snowfall has occurred at Lake Tahoe during every month of the year.

Mosquitoes can be a major irritant for recreationists during midsummer, when long pants, long-sleeved shirts and mosquito netting are good apparel choices. Application and reapplication of an insect repellent with plenty of DEET should keep the winged pests at bay. Such measures are a good deterrent against ticks as well, although they are generally much less of a nuisance. There is a remote possibility, however, that a tick could infect you with Lyme disease or Rocky Mountain spotted fever. Inspect your body for bites at least once a day and check your clothes for any unwanted travelers. If bitten by a tick, use a pair of tweezers to firmly grasp the pest and use gentle traction for its removal, making sure that the head is not left behind. After successful removal, wash the area thoroughly with antibacterial soap and water and apply an antibiotic ointment. Consult a physician if flu-like symptoms, headache, rash, joint pain, or fever develop.

Camping and Permits

Plenty of camping opportunities exist around the greater Lake Tahoe area. The hard part may be securing a spot, as many of the campgrounds are extremely popular during the summer months, especially on weekends. Reservations are recommended between Memorial Day weekend and Labor Day weekend. The Forest Service manages the bulk of public campgrounds in the greater Lake Tahoe area. California State Parks and Nevada State Parks manage several excellent campgrounds as well. South Lake Tahoe and Tahoe City each offer a public campground. In addition, there are a number of private campgrounds, including popular Camp Richardson, on the southwest shore.

Desolation Wilderness is the one area in the Tahoe Basin that requires dayhikers to secure a permit. Self-registration is available at most trailheads. Otherwise, permits can be obtained from the Lake Tahoe Visitor Center near Fallen Leaf Lake.

Wilderness permits are required for backpackers entering Desolation Wilderness or Mokelumne Wilderness. More specific information on these permits is provided in the chapter on trails in South Tahoe. Backpackers using the Pacific Crest Trail or Tahoe Rim Trail must use portable gas stoves (no campfires) and obtain a campfire permit for their use. At the time of research, wilderness permits are not required for overnight use of Granite Chief Wilderness or Mt. Rose Wilderness.

On the Trail

Every outing should begin with proper preparation, which usually takes just minutes. Even the easiest trail can turn up unexpected surprises. People seldom think about getting lost or suffering an injury, but unexpected things can and do happen. Simple precautions can make the difference between a miserable outcome — or merely a good story to tell afterwards.

Use the Top Trails ratings and descriptions to determine if a particular trail is a good match with your fitness and energy level, given current conditions and time of year.

Have a Plan

Choose Wisely The first step to enjoying any trail is to match the trail to your abilities. It's no use overestimating your experience or fitness — know your abilities and limitations, and use the Top Trails Difficulty Rating that accompanies each trail.

Prepare and Plan

- Know your abilities
- Leave word about your plans
- Know the area and the route

Leave Word About your Plans The most basic of precautions is leaving word of your intentions with family or friends. Many people will hike the backcountry their entire lives without ever relying on this safety net, but establishing this simple habit is free insurance.

It's best to leave specific information — location, trail name, intended time of travel — with a responsible person. However, if this is not possible or if plans change at the last minute, you should still leave word. If there is a registration process available, make use of it. If there is a ranger station or park office, check in.

Review the Route Before embarking on any trail, be sure to read the entire description and study the map. It isn't necessary to memorize every detail, but it is worthwhile to have a clear mental picture of the trail and the general area.

If the trail and terrain are complex, augment the trail guide with a topographic map; Top Trails will point out when this could be useful. Maps as well as current weather and trail condition information are often available from local ranger and park stations.

Trail Essentials

- **Dress to keep cool, but be ready for cold**
- **Plenty of water**
- **Adequate food**

Carry the Essentials

Proper preparation for any type of trail use includes gathering the essential items to carry. The checklist will vary tremendously by trail and conditions.

Clothing When the weather is good, light, comfortable clothing is the obvious choice. It's easy to believe that very little spare clothing is needed, but a prepared hiker has something tucked away for any emergency from a surprise shower to an unexpected overnight in a remote area.

Clothing includes proper footwear, essential for hiking and running trails. As a trail becomes more demanding, you will need footwear that performs. Running shoes are fine for many trails. If you will be carrying substantial weight or encountering sustained rugged terrain, step up to hiking boots.

In hot, sunny weather, proper clothing includes a hat, sunglasses, long-sleeved shirt and sunscreen. In cooler weather, particularly when it's wet, carry waterproof outer garments and quick-drying undergarments (avoid cotton). As general rule, whatever the conditions, bring layers that can be combined or removed to provide comfort and protection from the elements in a wide variety of conditions.

Water Never embark on a trail without carrying water. At all times, particularly in warm weather, adequate water is of key importance. Experts recommend at least 2 quarts of water per day, and when hiking in heat a gallon or more may be more appropriate. At the extreme, dehydration can be life threatening. More commonly, inadequate water brings fatigue and muscle aches.

For most outings, unless the day is very hot or the trail very long, you should plan to carry sufficient water for the entire trail. Unfortunately, in North America natural water sources are questionable, generally loaded with various risks: bacteria, viruses and fertilizers.

Sierra Nevada and southern Lake Tahoe *from Daggett Pass area*

Water Treatment If it's necessary to make use of trailside water, you should filter or treat it. There are three methods for treating water: boiling, chemical treatment, and filtering. Boiling is best, but often impractical — it requires a heat source, a pot, and time. Chemical treatments, available in sporting goods stores, handle some problems, including the troublesome Giardia parasite, but will not combat many man-made chemical pollutants. The preferred method is filtration, which removes Giardia and other contaminants and doesn't leave any unpleasant aftertaste.

If this hasn't convinced you to carry all the water you need, one final admonishment: be prepared for surprises. Water sources described in the text or on maps can change course or dry up completely. Never run your water bottle dry in expectation of the next source; fill up when water is available and always keep a little in reserve.

Food

While not as critical as water, food is energy and its importance shouldn't be underestimated. Avoid foods that are hard to digest, such as candy bars and potato chips. Carry high energy, fast-digesting foods: nutrition bars, dehydrated fruit, gorp, jerky. Bring a little extra food — it's good protection against an outing that turns unexpectedly long, perhaps due to weather or losing your way.

Less than Essential, But Useful Items

Map and Compass (*and the know-how to use them*) Many trails don't require much navigation, meaning a map and compass aren't always as essential as water or food — but it can be a close call. If the trail is remote or infrequently visited, a map and compass should be considered necessities.

A hand-held GPS (Global Positioning Satellite) receiver is also a useful trail companion, but is really no substitute for a map and compass; knowing your longitude and latitude is not much help without a map.

Cell Phone Most parts of the country, even remote destinations, have some level of cellular coverage. In extreme circumstances, a cell phone can be a lifesaver. But don't depend on it; coverage is unpredictable and batteries fail. And be sure that the occasion warrants the phone call — a blister doesn't justify a call to search and rescue.

Gear Depending on the remoteness and rigor of the trail, there are many additional useful items to consider; pocket knife, flashlight, fire source (water-proof matches, light, or flint), and a first-aid kit.

Every member of your party should carry the appropriate essential items described above; groups often split up or get separated along the trail. Solo hikers should be even more disciplined about preparation, and carry more gear. Traveling solo is inherently more risky. This isn't meant to discourage solo travel, simply to emphasize the need for extra preparation. Solo hikers should make a habit of carrying a little more gear than absolutely necessary.

Trail Checklist

- Leave no trace
- Stay on the trail
- Share the trail
- Leave it there

Trail Etiquette

The overriding rule on the trail is "**Leave No Trace**." Interest in visiting natural areas continues to increase in North America, even as the quantity of unspoiled natural areas continues to shrink. These pressures make it ever more critical that we leave no trace of our visit.

Never Litter If you carried it in, it's easy enough to carry it out. Leave the trail in the same, if not better condition than you find it. Try picking up any litter you encounter and packing it out — it's a great feeling! Just one piece of garbage and you've made a difference.

Stay on the Trail Paths have been created, sometimes over many years, for many purposes: to protect the surrounding natural areas, to avoid dangers, and to provide the best route. Leaving the trail can cause damage that takes years to undo. Never cut switchbacks. Shortcutting rarely saves energy or time, and it takes a terrible toll on the land, trampling plant life and hastening erosion. Moreover, safety and consideration intersect on the trail. It's hard to get truly lost if you stay on the trail.

Share the Trail The best trails attract many visitors and you should be prepared to share the trail with others. Do your part to minimize impact. Commonly accepted trail etiquette dictates that **bike riders yield to both hikers and equestrians**, **hikers yield to horseback riders**, **downhill hikers yield to uphill hikers**, and **everyone stays to the right**. Not everyone knows these rules of the road, so let common sense and good humor be the final guide.

Leave it There Destruction or removal of plants and animals, or historical, prehistoric or geological items, is certainly unethical and almost always illegal.

Getting Lost If you become lost on the trail, stay on the trail. Stop and take stock of the situation. In many cases, a few minutes of calm reflection will yield a solution. Consider all the clues available; use the sun to identify directions if you don't have a compass. If you determine that you are indeed lost, stay on the main trail and stay put. You are more likely to encounter other people if you stay in one place.

CHAPTER 1

North Tahoe

North Tahoe

The north Tahoe region contains some splendid backcountry, boasting many of the area's best trails. Whether you're searching for expansive vistas, serene lakes, or vivid wildflower displays, you have plenty to choose from amid the diverse terrain at the north end of the lake. Access to the trailheads is straightforward, thanks primarily to the four-lane freeway of Interstate 80, as well as the Mt. Rose Highway (Nevada State Route 431) and California highways 89 and 267.

Permits and Maps

The north Tahoe area straddles the border between Nevada and California, and administration of the backcountry is divided between the Carson Ranger District of the Toiyabe National Forest, the Truckee, Sierraville, and Nevada City Ranger Districts of the Tahoe National Forest, and the Lake Tahoe Basin Management Unit. The 28,000-acre Mt. Rose Wilderness and the 19,050-acre Granite Chief Wilderness are the only designated wilderness areas at the north end of the lake, but the proposed Castle Peak Wilderness would add another 18,000 acres. Currently, permits are not required for either day or overnight trips.

Maps of the north Tahoe region are available at Forest Service ranger stations in Nevada City, Grass Valley, Sierraville, Truckee, Sparks, and Carson City. The best maps for trail use are the USGS 7.5-minute topographic quadrangles. Specific maps for the trails covered in this section are listed in the Appendix.

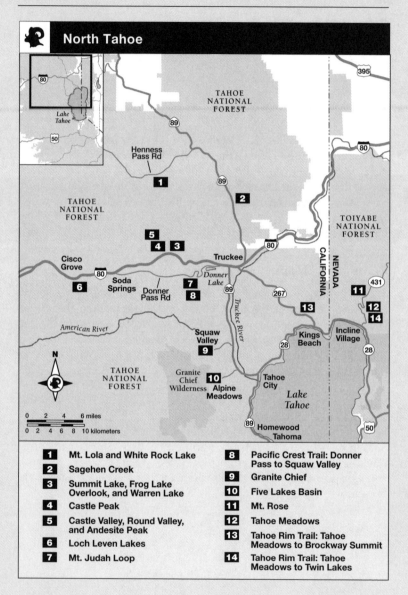

North Tahoe

1 Mt. Lola and White Rock Lake	**8** Pacific Crest Trail: Donner Pass to Squaw Valley
2 Sagehen Creek	**9** Granite Chief
3 Summit Lake, Frog Lake Overlook, and Warren Lake	**10** Five Lakes Basin
4 Castle Peak	**11** Mt. Rose
5 Castle Valley, Round Valley, and Andesite Peak	**12** Tahoe Meadows
6 Loch Leven Lakes	**13** Tahoe Rim Trail: Tahoe Meadows to Brockway Summit
7 Mt. Judah Loop	**14** Tahoe Rim Trail: Tahoe Meadows to Twin Lakes

TRAIL FEATURE TABLE

North Lake Trails

Trail	Difficulty	Length	Type	Uses & Access	Terrain	Flora & Fauna	Other
1	4	14.4	↗	Hiking, Trail Running, Mountain Biking, Horses, Dogs Allowed	Canyon, Mountain, Summit, Stream, Lake/Shore	Wildflowers	Great Views, Photo Opportunity, Camping, Secluded
2	1	5.0	↗	Hiking, Trail Running, Mountain Biking, Horses, Dogs Allowed, Child Friendly	Canyon, Stream	Wildflowers, Birds, Wildlife	Photo Opportunity
3	3	15.0	↗	Hiking, Horses, Dogs Allowed	Canyon, Mountain, Lake/Shore	Birds	Great Views, Photo Opportunity, Camping, Steep
4	5	9.6	↗	Hiking, Dogs Allowed	Canyon, Mountain, Summit	Wildflowers	Great Views, Photo Opportunity
5	3	9.6	↺	Hiking, Trail Running, Mountain Biking, Horses, Dogs Allowed, Child Friendly	Canyon, Mountain, Summit	Wildflowers	Wildlife, Great Views, Camping, Historic, Steep
6	4	8.0	↗	Hiking, Trail Running, Mountain Biking, Horses, Dogs Allowed	Canyon, Mountain, Lake/Shore	Wildflowers	Photo Opportunity, Camping
7	3	4.6	↺	Hiking, Trail Running, Horses, Dogs Allowed, Child Friendly	Mountain, Summit		Great Views
8	5	15.0	↘	Hiking, Horses	Mountain, Summit		Great Views, Photo Opportunity, Camping, Secluded
9	5	10.2	↗	Hiking	Canyon, Mountain, Summit, Stream, Lake/Shore	Wildflowers	Great Views, Photo Opportunity, Cool & Shady
10	3	4.0	↗	Hiking, Trail Running	Canyon, Mountain		Photo Opportunity
11	3	10.0	↗	Hiking, Trail Running, Dogs Allowed	Mountain, Summit, Stream, Waterfall	Wildflowers	Great Views, Photo Opportunity
12	5	1.3	↺	Hiking, Handicap Access, Child Friendly	Mountain	Wildflowers, Birds, Wildlife	Photo Opportunity
13	5	18.0	↘	Hiking, Trail Running, Mountain Biking, Dogs Allowed	Mountain, Summit, Waterfall, Lake/Shore	Wildflowers, Birds	Great Views, Photo Opportunity, Camping, Secluded
14	4	19.0	↗	Hiking, Trail Running, Mountain Biking, Horses, Dogs Allowed	Mountain	Wildflowers, Birds	Great Views, Photo Opportunity, Camping

USE & ACCESS
- Hiking
- Trail Running
- Mountain Biking
- Horses
- Child Friendly
- Dogs Allowed
- Handicap Access
- Permit Required
- P Parking Fee

TERRAIN
- Canyon
- Mountain
- Summit

WATER
- Stream
- Waterfall
- Lake/Shore

FLORA & FAUNA
- Autumn Colors
- Wildflowers
- Birds
- Wildlife

DIFFICULTY
- 1 2 3 4 5 +
- less   more

OTHER
- Cool & Shady
- Great Views
- Photo Opportunity
- Secluded
- Historic
- Geologic Interest
- Moonlight Hiking
- Steep
- Camping

North Tahoe

Castle Peak 45

Peak baggers looking for a challenge will be well rewarded with an ascent of 9103-foot Castle Peak. Although there is no official trail all the way to the top, a boot-beaten path from the Pacific Crest Trail at Castle Pass to the summit is easy to follow. Successful summiteers will be rewarded with a far-ranging view of the northern Sierra.

TRAIL 4

Hike
9.6 miles, Out & Back
Difficulty: 1 2 3 4 **5**

Castle Valley, Round Valley, and Andesite Peak 51

Two scenic valleys and a trip to the summit of Andesite Peak provide plenty of diverse scenery along this loop for a wide range of recreationists. Additional bonuses include a visit to rustic Peter Grubb Hut and wildlife viewing around Castle and Round valleys.

TRAIL 5

Hike, Run, Bike, Horse
9.6 miles, Loop
Difficulty: 1 2 **3** 4 5

Loch Leven Lakes 57

Three picturesque lakes are cradled in the Loch Leven Lakes basin, and a mile-long side trip to Salmon Lake adds an optional visit to a fourth lake. At a lower elevation than most Tahoe area lakes, the Loch Leven Lakes provide not only an early season opportunity for hikers itching to get out on the trail, but a relatively warm lake for swimming.

TRAIL 6

Hike, Run, Bike, Horse
8.0 miles, Out & Back
Difficulty: 1 2 3 **4** 5

Mt. Judah Loop 63

Hikers, runners, and equestrians would be hard pressed to find a shorter and less difficult trail in the Tahoe Sierra that affords such impressive views. Don't expect much solitude or any water along this route, which initially follows a segment of the Pacific Crest Trial.

TRAIL 7

Hike, Run, Bike, Horse
4.6 miles, Loop
Difficulty: 1 2 **3** 4 5

Tahoe Meadows
Whole Access Trail 91

A short nature trail samples some of the highlights of Tahoe Meadows, a large subalpine clearing carpeted with wildflowers and teeming with life. The wide, pleasantly graded trail is well suited to wheelchair-bound naturalists and families with young children.

TRAIL 12

Hike; Handicap Access
1.3 miles
Loop
Difficulty: **1** 2 3 4 5

Tahoe Rim Trail: Tahoe Meadows
to Brockway Summit 95

Several miles of this section of the Tahoe Rim Trail cross south-facing volcanic slopes at or just below the crest of an exposed ridge. Here are some of the most panoramic Lake Tahoe views available anywhere in the basin. The 18-mile distance, combined with a lack of access from connecting trails, ensure that you'll have most of the trail to yourself, at least in the middle of the route.

TRAIL 13

Hike, Run, Bike
18.0 miles
Point to Point
Difficulty: 1 2 3 4 **5**

Tahoe Rim Trail:
Tahoe Meadows to Twin Lakes 105

After an initial climb from Tahoe Meadows, this part of the Tahoe Rim Trail closely follows the crest of the Carson Range, offering fine views of Lake Tahoe to the west and the Great Basin to the east. A number of connecting roads and trails present plenty of trip alternatives, especially for mountain bikers.

TRAIL 14

Hike, Run, Horse,
Bike (even days only)
19.0 miles, Out & Back
Difficulty: 1 2 3 **4** 2

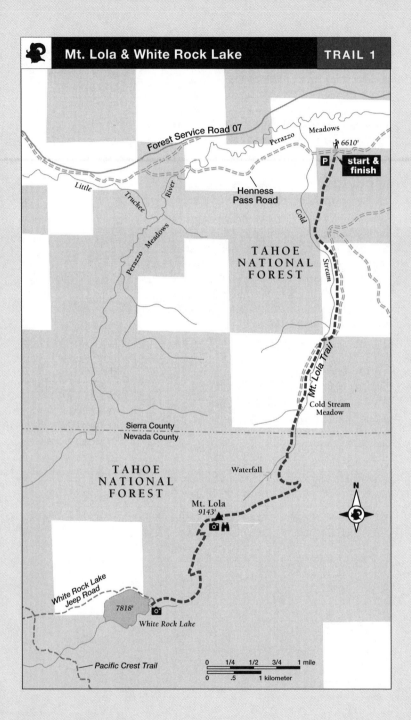

Mt. Lola & White Rock Lake

TRAIL 1

Forest Service Road 07

Perazzo Meadows

6610'

Little

Truckee

River

Perazzo Meadows

Henness Pass Road

start & finish

P

TAHOE NATIONAL FOREST

Cold Stream

Mt. Lola Trail

Sierra County
Nevada County

Cold Stream Meadow

TAHOE NATIONAL FOREST

Waterfall

N

Mt. Lola
9143'

White Rock Lake Jeep Road

7818'

White Rock Lake

Pacific Crest Trail

| 0 | 1/4 | 1/2 | 3/4 | 1 mile |

| 0 | .5 | 1 kilometer |

Mt. Lola and White Rock Lake

A nearly forgotten trail north of Lake Tahoe takes hikers to a far-ranging view of the northern Sierra. Those with extra time and energy have the option of adding a 2-mile extension to picturesque White Rock Lake.

Best Times

The trail up the mountain is usually snow free by mid-July, when wildflowers along Cold Creek are entering their peak.

Finding the Trail

Near the west end of Truckee, follow Highway 89 north of Interstate 80 for 14.5 miles to a left-hand turn onto Forest Service Road 07. Proceed on paved road for 1.5 miles, to a left-hand turn onto Forest Road 07-10. Follow this gravel road to a bridge over the Little Truckee River and continue to an unsigned junction with Henness Pass Road, 0.6 mile from Road 07. Turn right and drive on Henness Pass Road for 3.1 miles to a spur road on the left, signed MT LOLA TRAIL. The trailhead parking area is a short distance up this road.

Logistics

Although the Mt. Lola Trail is closed to all motor vehicles, a 4WD road closely parallels the trail through Coldstream Valley. In addition, White Rock Lake is accessible to 4WD vehicles via a road on the west side of the lake.

TRAIL USE
Hike, Run, Bike, Horse
LENGTH
14.4 miles, 8 hours
VERTICAL FEET
±2550
DIFFICULTY
– 1 2 3 **4** 5 +
TRAIL TYPE
Out & Back
SURFACE TYPE
Dirt

FEATURES
Dogs Allowed
Canyon
Mountain
Summit
Stream
Shore
Wildflowers
Great Views
Photo Opportunity
Camping
Secluded

FACILITIES
None

At 9143 feet, Mt. Lola is the highest summit between the Tahoe Basin and Lassen Park.

Trail Description

▶1 Single-track trail leads away from the trailhead on a moderate climb through mixed forest of western white pines, lodgepole pines, and white firs. At 0.6 mile, hop across a small seasonal stream lined with a tangle of alders and young aspens and continue the climb toward the mouth of Coldstream Canyon. Where the single-track trail merges with an old roadbed, you head upstream high above the level of the creek. Gaps in the mixed forest allow enough sunlight for an understory of tobacco brush, pinemat manzanita, and currant. Farther up the canyon the trail eventually draws closer to Cold Creek before intersecting a well-traveled road, 2.2 miles from the trailhead.

Walk along the road to a substantial wood bridge that spans the stream, and soon encounter a fork in the road. Take the left-hand fork and head upstream a short way to the resumption of single-track trail on the left, which is unsigned but marked by a series of metal diamonds. Within a stone's throw of the road to the right and the creek to the left, you continue upstream on mildly graded trail beneath mixed forest until breaking out into the open at Coldstream Meadow. Dotted with clumps of willow and carpeted with a variety of grasses and wildflowers, the meadow lends a pastoral feel to the surroundings. A spur road near the far end of the meadow leads to a campsite in a copse of trees that's sure to lure overnighters.

 Camping

Just beyond the spur to the campsite, the route follows the main road briefly until single-track trail resumes where the road bends sharply toward a crossing of Cold Creek. You proceed upstream for a while on mildly graded trail, hopping over a pair of tiny rivulets along the way. As the canyon narrows, the grade of the ascent increases and the trail draws

White Rock Lake *from Mt. Lola*

nearer to the diminishing stream, crossing to the east bank at 3.8 miles from the trailhead.

You climb more steeply up the canyon after the creek crossing, reaching a faint use-trail after 0.25 mile that soon leads to a view of a short waterfall, where the braided stream courses through moss-covered channels and tumbles picturesquely down a slanted rock face. Beyond the fall, the trail angles away from Cold Creek and ascends into the realm of mountain hemlocks. After a prominent switchback, the trees part enough to allow a glimpse of the upper slopes of Mt. Lola and, as you follow the winding trail up the northeast ridge of the peak, other landmarks spring into view, including Independence Lake to the east and Castle Peak to the south. Reaching the summit, the incredible 360° view is ample reward for the toil of the ascent. ▶2 Scores of peaks are visible from Mt. Lola, including Lassen Peak, Sierra Buttes, Mt. Rose, and Freel Peak. You'll also see verdant plains such as Sierra Valley and Martis Valley, and many bodies of water, such as Stampede, Boca, and Prosser reservoirs. An old wooden sign reading MT. LOLA, ELEV. 9143 FT. marks the top, along with some low brick pillars, a few rock enclosures, and a metal army box holding the sum-

Stream

Summit

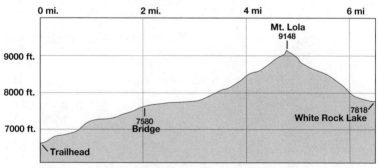

TRAIL1   Mt. Lola & White Rock Lake Elevation Profile

mit register. A short walk to the southern lip of the summit area reveals the shimmering surface of White Rock Lake, a mere 1.25 miles southwest of Mt. Lola.

To reach White Rock Lake, weave your way down the trail on the southwest ridge of the volcanic mountain amid low-growing shrubs, scattered wildflowers, and a few stunted pines farther down the ridge. After a couple of switchbacks, you make a descending traverse across the head of a canyon, through scattered western white pines, mountain hemlocks, and firs. Briefly descend the cleft of a seasonal drainage until the trail merges with a steep, rocky old road that leads you down to a junction east of the lake. The left-hand branch leads across the seasonal inlet to pleasant campsites along the stream bank. Veer to the right and follow the road past a large meadow to the east shore of White Rock Lake, ▶3 where shady conifers line the shoreline and dramatic rock cliffs provide a rugged backdrop. Several decent campsites are spread around the lakeshore.

White Rock Lake boasts a number of tiny islands close to the shoreline, which provide swimmers with excellent slabs for sunbathing.

≋ Shore

🚶	MILESTONES	
▶1	0.0	Start at trailhead
▶2	5.2	Summit of Mt. Lola
▶3	7.2	White Rock Lake

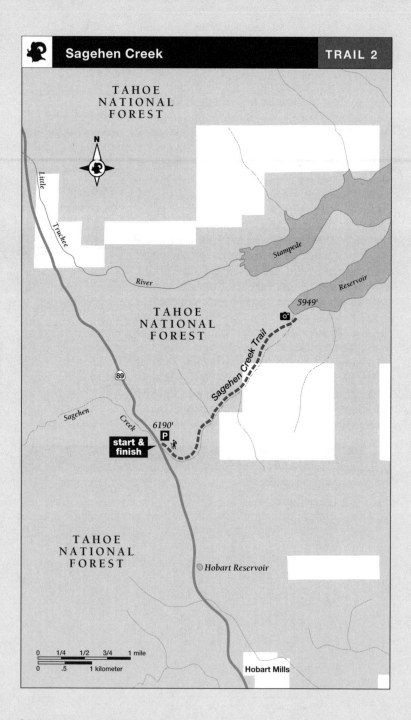

TAHOE
NATIONAL
FOREST

N

Little

Truckee

Stampede

River

Reservoir

5949'

TAHOE
NATIONAL
FOREST

Sagehen Creek Trail

89

Sagehen

Creek

6190'

P

start &
finish

TAHOE
NATIONAL
FOREST

Hobart Reservoir

0   1/4   1/2   3/4   1 mile

0   .5   1 kilometer

Hobart Mills

Sagehen Creek

Wildflower season reaches a dramatic crescendo in early summer along Sagehen Creek, where a short, easy trail provides access for young and old alike. Those who hike all the way to the end of the trail will have the bonus of a nice view of Stampede Reservoir.

Best Time

June is the best time to view the extensive fields of wildflowers along the creek and to see Stampede Reservoir without a bathtub ring. Mid-October is when aspens and shrubs are ablaze with fall colors.

Finding the Trail

From Interstate 80 near the town of Truckee, travel north on California Highway 89 for 6.8 miles to a dirt parking area on the right, just past a highway bridge over Sagehen Creek.

Logistics

Although the trailhead is unmarked, the start of the well-worn trail is easy to locate.

Trail Description

▶1 Head downstream on the north side of Sagehen Creek along the edge of a mixed forest of lodgepole pines, Jeffrey pines, white firs, incense cedars, and junipers. Lush riparian vegetation fills the creek bottom to your right, along with a wide variety of

---

TRAIL USE
Hike, Run, Bike, Horse
LENGTH
5.0 miles, 1 hour
VERTICAL FEET
±225'
DIFFICULTY
– **1** 2 3 4 5 +
TRAIL TYPE
Out & Back
SURFACE TYPE
Dirt

FEATURES
Dogs Allowed
Child Friendly
Canyon
Stream
Autumn Colors
Wildflowers
Birds
Wildlife
Photo Opportunity

FACILITIES
None

Sagehen Creek

wildflowers, including lupine, aster, paintbrush, mule ear, corn lily, senecio, penstemon, and buttercup. Wild rosebushes alongside the trail provide delicate pink blossoms and a sweet fragrance in midsummer. Meadowlands farther downstream beckon skilled botanists and curious youngsters alike to leave the trail and explore the lush surroundings.

Eventually, the trail veers to the northeast and moves a little farther away from the creek. You stroll through a forest of mostly lodgepole pines, where, in early summer, a bounty of mule ears carpets the slopes with a stunning display of yellow that stretches for quite a distance. Careful observation of the hillside above reveals that this area has seen past logging and at least one forest fire. Two miles from the trailhead you traverse a grassy clearing, cross a small rivulet, and emerge into a broad meadow filled with sagebrush and grasses that borders the southeast arm of Stampede Reservoir. The trail follows a raised finger of ground above the sometimes boggy meadow to a small copse of pines, where an old timber beam provides a way across the main channel of Sagehen Creek. The trail continues alongside the creek for a short distance before disappearing for good in the meadowland. Rimmed by pine-dotted hills, the sapphire blue waters of Stampede Reservoir stretches out in front of you. ▶2

> The short, easy trail along Sagehen Creek provides access to one of the finest wildflower displays in the greater Tahoe area.

🏃 **MILESTONES**

▶1   0.0   Start at trailhead
▶2   2.5   Stampede Reservoir

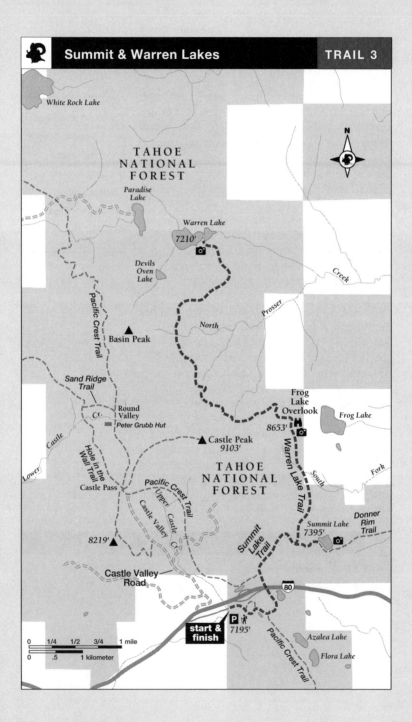

White Rock Lake

TAHOE
NATIONAL
FOREST

Paradise
Lake

Warren Lake
7210'

Devils
Oven
Lake

Creek

Pacific Crest Trail

North

Prosser

▲ Basin Peak

Sand Ridge
Trail

Frog
Lake
Overlook

Frog Lake

Round
Valley

8653'

Cr.

Peter Grubb Hut

Castle

▲ Castle Peak
9103'

Warren Lake Trail

Hole in the
Wall Trail

Lower

Castle Pass

TAHOE
NATIONAL
FOREST

South

Fork

Pacific Crest Trail

Upper

Castle
Valley

Cr.

Donner
Rim
Trail

Summit Lake
7395'

8219' ▲

Summit
Lake
Trail

Castle Valley
Road

80

0   1/4 1/2 3/4   1 mile

0   .5   1 kilometer

start &
finish   7195'

Pacific Crest Trail

Azalea Lake

Flora Lake

Summit Lake, Frog Lake Overlook, and Warren Lake

Two scenic lakes and a spectacular vista point are the principal attractions of this hike, which is within the proposed Castle Peak Wilderness. The hike to Summit Lake is an easy 2-mile stroll, whereas the trip to Warren Lake is another story —over the course of 7.5 miles you gain and lose nearly 4,500 feet of elevation. In between, Frog Lake Overlook provides a grand vista of the Donner Pass region. With three such worthwhile goals, you can tailor your trip to fit your individual needs and schedule.

Best Time

Mid-July through August is the best time for hiking on snow-free trails, although, following winters of heavy snowfall, the trail across the upper basin of North Fork Prosser Creek may see lingering snowbanks well into summer.

Finding the Trail

West of Donner Summit, take the Castle Peak/Boreal Ridge Road exit from Interstate 80. Drive to the frontage road on the south side of the freeway and proceed east 0.3 mile to the Pacific Crest Trail parking area. The large parking lot has trailer parking, pit toilets, and running water in season.

TRAIL USE
Hike, Horse
LENGTH*
VERTICAL FEET*
DIFFICULTY*
*See table below
TRAIL TYPE
Out & Back
SURFACE TYPE
Dirt

FEATURES
Dogs Allowed
Canyon
Mountain
Lakes
Birds
Great Views
Photo Opportunity
Camping
Steep

FACILITIES
Restrooms
Picnic Tables
Water

🚶 DESTINATIONS	LENGTH	VERTICAL FEET	DIFFICULTY
Summit Lake	4 miles, 2 hours	±450'	– **1** 2 3 4 5 +
Frog Lake Overlook	8 miles, 5 hours	±1700'	– 1 2 **3** 4 5 +
Warren Lake	15 miles, 10 hours	±2225'	– 1 2 3 4 **5** +

Logistics

Avoid the temptation to shorten your trip by beginning at the westbound Donner Summit Rest Area parking lot. Vehicles parked there longer than a couple of hours are subject to fines.

Trail Description

►1 From the parking lot follow a well-signed gravel path to a stone bridge over a seasonal stream and continue on dirt track through lodgepole pines, western white pines, and white firs. Soon encounter a junction with the Glacier Meadow Loop, ►2 where you veer right and continue eastbound toward the Pacific Crest Trail. After a short distance you come to a second junction with the Glacier Meadow Loop, ►3 where you veer to the right again. Pass by a shallow pond, where mountain hemlocks join the mixed forest, and then make a short descent to the Pacific Crest Trail junction, near the edge of a grass- and willow-filled meadow, 0.5 mile from the trailhead. ►4

Head north on the PCT around the fringe of the meadow and pass through a pair of large culverts, underneath the eastbound and westbound lanes of Interstate 80. Beyond the culverts you make a moderate climb to the crossing of a seasonal creek and then come to a well-signed, four-way junction, 1 mile from the trailhead. ►5

Following signed directions for Summit and Warren lakes, turn right and proceed on a mild to moderate climb through alternating stretches of mixed forest and open areas sprinkled with granite slabs and boulders. At 1.7 miles, just past a small meadow covered with corn lilies, you come to a junction of the Warren and Summit lakes trails. ►6

To visit **Summit Lake**, follow the right-hand trail out of the forest and across the slopes of a granite ridge carpeted with pinemat manzanita, where views temporarily open up of the Donner Summit

Nearly 18,000 acres of land surrounding Castle Peak have been targeted for inclusion in the wilderness system as the Castle Peak Wilderness.

Lake

Frog Lake from Overlook

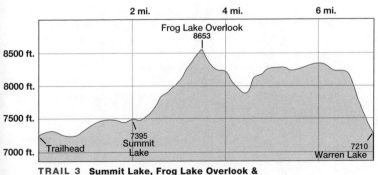

TRAIL 3 Summit Lake, Frog Lake Overlook &
Warren Lake Elevation Profile

region. Eventually the trail heads back into the forest and leads you onward to the shoreline of serene Summit Lake. ►7 Except for some cliffs at the north end, the lake is surrounded by trees and edged with shrubs.

From the Summit and Warren lakes junction ►8, head north on a steep climb up a forested hill toward the top of a volcanic ridge directly west of peak 7888. Before you reach the top, the forest gives way to shrub-covered slopes, which allows for fine views of the surrounding terrain. Beyond this point the stiff ascent temporarily abates as you stroll through a clearing and drop to a crossing of a tributary of South Fork Prosser Creek. All too soon you resume the steep climb toward a saddle just west of peak 8653, hopping over several more small creeks on the way. Nearing the saddle, a short use-trail branches away from the Warren Lake Trail

Steep

Cross-Country Routes

Several use-trails and cross-country routes in the Castle Peak backcountry provide numerous diversions. About 0.8 mile before Warren Lake, a use-trail leaves the Warren Lake Trail at a low ridge, northbound for Devils Oven Lake. From there, cross-country routes proceed to Warren and Paradise lakes. A fine loop trip returns to the trailhead by heading west from Paradise Lake on a jeep road for 1.1 miles and then following the PCT south for 8.3 miles.

Peak baggers may be tempted by a route that exits the use-trail to Devils Oven Lake a short distance from the junction with the Warren Lake Trail and then ascends Basin Peak. Following a usetrail along the crest of the ridge between Basin and Castle peaks may also be rewarding. From the summit of Castle Peak, proceed along the west ridge to a connection with the PCT at Castle Pass (see Trip 4, page 45).

OPTIONS

and ascends rocky slopes to the top of this peak. Standing at the edge of **Frog Lake Cliff**, ►9 you have a dramatic view straight down into privately owned Frog Lake, as well as west toward Castle Peak and east to the distant Carson Range.

Indefatigable super-hikers may elect to continue their journey to **Warren Lake**, although a reasonable assessment of the trip will lead most recreationists to conclude that a visit to the lake is best done as a 2-3 day backpack. From the saddle, follow the trail on a winding descent across mostly open slopes dotted with conifers. At 4.4 miles reach the crest of a minor ridge and a faint junction with an old trail from the vicinity of Frog Lake. Veer west and continue the descent for 0.6 mile to the bottom of Coon Canyon. From there follow an undulating 1.5-mile traverse around the head of North Fork Prosser Creek basin to a saddle due south of Warren Lake. Beyond the saddle the trail plummets over 1000 feet in a mile to reach the south shore of Warren Lake. ►10

Most hikers will be more than satisfied with the scenic aerie of Frog Lake Overlook as their day's goal.

🚶 MILESTONES

►1	0.0	Start at PCT trailhead
►2	0.2	Veer right at Glacier Meadow Loop junction
►3	0.3	Veer right at Glacier Meadow Loop junction
►4	0.5	Turn left (north) at PCT junction
►5	1.0	Turn right (northeast) at Summit Lake Trail junction
►6	1.7	Turn right (east) at Warren Lake Trail junction
►7	2.0	Summit Lake
►8	2.3	Return to Warren Lake junction, turn right (north)
►9	4.0	Frog Lake Overlook
►10	7.5	Warren Lake

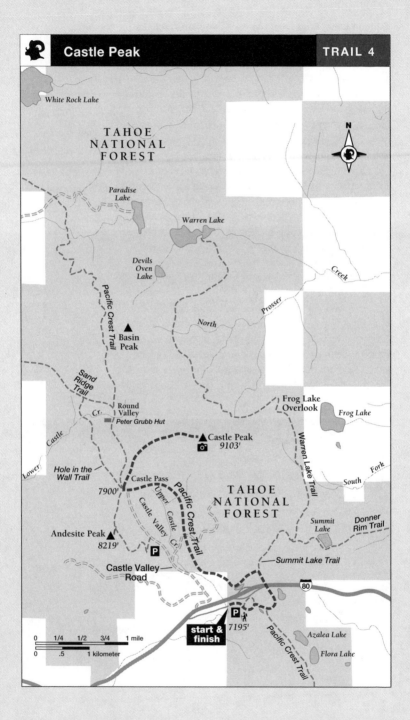

Castle Peak   TRAIL 4

White Rock Lake

TAHOE
NATIONAL
FOREST

Paradise
Lake

Warren Lake

Devils
Oven
Lake

Creek

Pacific Crest Trail

Prosser

North

Basin
Peak

Sand
Ridge
Trail

Round
Valley
Cr.
Peter Grubb Hut

Frog Lake
Overlook

Frog Lake

Castle

Castle Peak
9103'

Lower

Hole in the
Wall Trail

Castle Pass

7900'

Upper
Castle
Valley
Cr.

Pacific Crest Trail

Warren Lake Trail

South
Fork

TAHOE
NATIONAL
FOREST

Andesite Peak
8219'

Summit
Lake

Donner
Rim Trail

Summit Lake Trail

Castle Valley
Road

80

0   1/4   1/2   3/4   1 mile
0   .5   1 kilometer

start &
finish

7195'

Pacific Crest Trail

Azalea Lake

Flora Lake

Castle Peak

A climb to one of North Tahoe's highest summits provides summiteers with an expansive view of the northern Sierra, which on clear days includes distant Lassen Peak in the north and the coastal hills to the west.

Best Time

Mid-July to early September is the prime time for an ascent. A favorite winter ascent of backcountry skiers and snowshoers, most of the lingering snow banks across the trail have disappeared by mid-July.

Finding the Trail

West of Donner Summit, take the Castle Peak/Boreal Ridge Road exit from Interstate 80. Drive to the frontage road on the south side of the freeway and proceed east 0.3 mile to the Pacific Crest Trail parking area. The large parking lot has trailer parking, pit toilets, and running water in season.

Logistics

Two alternatives will shorten the trip. The first option is to park near the start of the Castle Valley Road, just north of the Interstate 80 ramps, and walk the road to Castle Pass. With a high-clearance vehicle, the second option drives the Castle Valley Road to a parking area near the Hole in the Wall trailhead. From there a shorter hike along the road leads to Castle Pass.

TRAIL USE
Hike

LENGTH
9.6 miles, 3 hours

VERTICAL FEET
±2205'

DIFFICULTY
− 1 2 3 4 **5** +

TRAIL TYPE
Out & Back

SURFACE TYPE
Dirt

FEATURES
Dogs Allowed
Canyon
Mountain
Summit
Wildflowers
Great Views
Photo Opportunity

FACILITIES
Restrooms
Picnic Tables
Water

Trail Description

Castle Peak and the neighboring mountains are mostly volcanic in nature, offering an abundance of interesting ramparts and turrets.

▶1 From the parking lot follow a well-signed gravel path to a stone bridge over a seasonal stream and continue on dirt track through lodgepole pines, western white pines, and white firs. Soon encounter a junction with the Glacier Meadow Loop, ▶2 where you veer right and continue eastbound toward the Pacific Crest Trail. After a short distance you come to a second junction with the Glacier Meadow Loop, ▶3 where you veer to the right again. Pass by a shallow pond, where mountain hemlocks join the mixed forest, and then make a short descent to the Pacific Crest Trail junction, near the edge of a grass- and willow-filled meadow, 0.5 mile from the trailhead. ▶4

Head north on the PCT around the fringe of the meadow and pass through a pair of large culverts, underneath the eastbound and westbound lanes of Interstate 80. Beyond the culverts you make a moderate climb to the crossing of a seasonal creek and then come to a well-signed, four-way junction, 1 mile from the trailhead. ▶5

Remaining on the Pacific Crest Trail, you proceed straight ahead at the four-way junction, following signed directions to Castle Pass. The PCT rises and then drops to the north shore of a small pond, where you should veer right at an unmarked Y-junction with a path bound for the Donner Summit Rest Area.

Beyond the unmarked junction, you follow mildly graded trail through mixed forest, toward Castle Valley. Eventually the trail brings you alongside the creek for a brief time and then travels just east of the verdant meadows of Castle Valley. Use trails branch away from the PCT at various points, headed toward the creek and meadows. At 2.3 miles from the trailhead you cross a well-traveled dirt road, and then continue upstream through Castle Valley, hopping over lushly lined tributaries along

Castle Peak

Cross-Country Routes

Ambitious peak baggers can double-summit by following a boot-beaten path from Castle Peak along the north ridge to the top of 9017-foot Basin Peak. On the way back, dropping west from the ridge about halfway between Castle and Basin Peaks to head cross-country to a connection with the PCT in Round Valley provides an easier alternative to a return over Castle Peak.

the way. Nearing the head of the valley, the PCT
bends to the west on an ascending traverse to a
signed three-way junction with a trail from the
Castle Valley Road. ►6 From there, a short but stiff
climb brings you to Castle Pass and a junction with
a trio of paths, 3.3 miles from the trailhead. ►7

At Castle Pass take the use trail to the right,
which ascends the west ridge of Castle Peak. As you
climb the rocky ridge the conifers diminish, allowing you increasingly good views of Castle Peak
ahead and other peaks and landmarks scattered
around the Donner Pass region. A steep, zigzagging
ascent heads around to the north side of the mountain, where switchbacks then lead you toward the
summit. After a rocky stretch of climbing, a splendid view greets you at the top of the 9103-foot
peak. ►8 Clear days offer a 360° view, all the way to
Lassen Peak in the north, Mt. Diablo and the coastal
hills to the west, the peaks of Desolation Wilderness
to the south, and the Carson Range to the east.
Don't forget to pack along a map of the area to help
you identify the numerous landmarks visible from
the summit.

▲ **Summit**

🚶 MILESTONES

►1 0.0 Start at PCT trailhead
►2 0.2 Veer right at Glacier Meadow Loop junction
►3 0.3 Veer right again at Glacier Meadow Loop junction
►4 0.5 Turn left (north) at PCT junction
►5 1.0 Proceed straight ahead (west) at Summit Lake Trail junction
►6 3.2 Veer right at Castle Valley Road junction
►7 3.3 Castle Pass—Leave PCT and turn right on use trail
►8 4.8 Summit of Castle Peak

View *from Castle Peak*

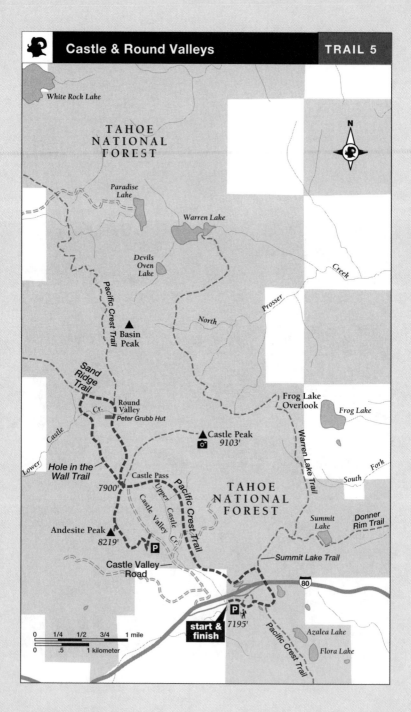

White Rock Lake

TAHOE
NATIONAL
FOREST

N

Paradise
Lake

Warren Lake

Devils
Oven
Lake

Creek

Pacific Crest Trail

Prosser

North

Basin
Peak

Sand
Ridge
Trail

Round
Valley

Frog Lake
Overlook

Frog Lake

Castle

Cr.

Peter Grubb Hut

Lower

Castle Peak
9103'

Warren Lake Trail

Hole in the
Wall Trail

Castle Pass

7900'

Pacific Crest Trail

Upper

Castle

Cr.

Castle Valley

South

Fork

TAHOE
NATIONAL
FOREST

Summit
Lake

Donner
Rim Trail

Andesite Peak
8219'

P

Castle Valley
Road

Summit Lake Trail

80

P

start &
finish

7195'

Pacific Crest Trail

Azalea Lake

Flora Lake

| 0 | 1/4 | 1/2 | 3/4 | 1 mile |
| 0 | | .5 | | 1 kilometer |

Castle Valley, Round Valley, and Andesite Peak

Although most of this route travels outside the proposed Castle Peak Wilderness, plenty of pleasant terrain is encountered along the way, including two picturesque meadows and an excellent view from atop Andesite Peak. Both Castle and Round meadows offer the chance to see raptors in search of prey or deer browsing the tender foliage. Throw in Peter Grubb Hut for a bit of Tahoe Sierra history and you have the makings of a fine adventure.

Best Time

Mid-July through September provides snow-free hiking.

Finding the Trail

West of Donner Summit, take the Castle Peak/Boreal Ridge Road exit from Interstate 80. Drive to the frontage road on the south side of the freeway and proceed east 0.3 mile to the Pacific Crest Trail parking area. The large parking lot has trailer parking, pit toilets, and running water in season.

Logistics

With a pair of durable vehicles you can arrange a shuttle and shave off 1.6 miles of hiking, by driving the Castle Valley Road to within 0.1 mile of the Hole in the Wall trailhead. With a high-clearance vehicle you may be able to get all the way to the trailhead. Trip length with shuttle is 8.0 miles.

TRAIL USE
Hike, Run, Bike, Horse
LENGTH
9.6 miles, 6.5 hours
VERTICAL FEET
1700'
DIFFICULTY
– 1 2 **3** 4 5 +
TRAIL TYPE
Loop
SURFACE TYPE
Dirt

FEATURES
Dogs Allowed
Child Friendly
Canyon
Mountain
Summit
Wildflowers
Wildlife
Great Views
Historic
Camping
Steep

FACILITIES
Restrooms
Picnic Tables
Water

Trail Description

The shuttle option is tempting but be sure you have the proper vehicle.

►1 From the parking lot follow a well-signed gravel path to a stone bridge over a seasonal stream and continue on dirt track through lodgepole pines, western white pines, and white firs. Soon encounter a junction with the Glacier Meadow Loop, ►2 where you veer right and continue eastbound toward the Pacific Crest Trail. After a short distance you come to a second junction with the Glacier Meadow Loop, ►3 where you veer to the right again. Pass by a shallow pond, where mountain hemlocks join the mixed forest, and then make a short descent to the Pacific Crest Trail junction, near the edge of a grass- and willow-filled meadow, 0.5 mile from the trailhead. ►4

Head north on the PCT around the fringe of the meadow and pass through a pair of large culverts, underneath the eastbound and westbound lanes of Interstate 80. Beyond the culverts you make a moderate climb to the crossing of a seasonal creek and then come to a well-signed, four-way junction, 1 mile from the trailhead. ►5

Remaining on the Pacific Crest Trail, you proceed straight ahead at the four-way junction, following signed directions to Castle Pass. The PCT rises and then drops to the north shore of a small pond, where you should veer right at an unmarked Y-junction with a path bound for the Donner Summit Rest Area.

Beyond the unmarked junction, you follow mildly graded trail through mixed forest, toward Castle Valley. Eventually the trail brings you alongside the creek for a brief time and then travels just east of the verdant meadows of Castle Valley. Use trails branch away from the PCT at various points, headed toward the creek and meadows. At 2.3 miles from the trailhead you cross a well-traveled dirt road, and then continue upstream through Castle Valley, hopping over a number of lushly lined tribu-

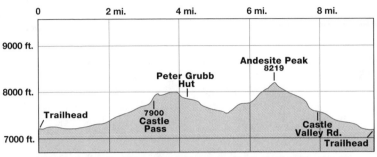

TRAIL 5 **Castle & Round Valleys, Andesite Peak Elevation Profile**

taries along the way. Nearing the head of the valley, the PCT bends to the west on an ascending traverse to a signed three-way junction with a trail from the Castle Valley Road. ▶6 From there, a short but stiff climb brings you to Castle Pass and a junction with a trio of paths, 3.3 miles from the trailhead. ▶7

    Steep

At Castle Pass, proceed north on the Pacific Crest Trail, on a traverse across a lightly forested slope. After about a half-mile you begin a moderate,

Peter Grubb Hut

OPTIONS

Peter Grubb Hut was built in the 1930s and was the northernmost in a series of six huts patterned after hut systems in the Swiss Alps that were planned for the Tahoe Sierra along the crest between Donner and Echo passes. Although only four of the six huts were built, the ones that were have provided overnight shelter at a nominal cost for back-country skiers and hikers for several decades. For more information or to make a reservation, contact the Sierra Club at this address: Clair Tappan Lodge, PO Box 36, Norden, CA 95724. (530) 426-3632

switchbacking descent toward Round Valley. Nearing the floor of the valley, a short use-trail leads to Peter Grubb Hut, ►8 4.2 miles from the Pacific Crest trailhead. The hut is complete with a wood-burning stove and firewood, gas stove and cooking utensils, table and chairs, a loft with sleeping platforms, and a detached outhouse. Interesting old photos and memorabilia cover the walls and provide a sample of the area's history.

Historic

The PCT crosses Lower Castle Creek north of the hut and leads to a Y-junction with the Sand Ridge Trail a short way farther, where you leave the PCT and turn left (east). ►9 A winding descent through a mixed forest of western white pines, red firs, and lodgepole pines follows, leads across some lushly lined streams and below a striking granite cliff to another Y-junction with the Hole in the Ground Trail, 0.6 mile from the previous junction. ►10

Turn left (south) at the junction, on a moderately graded, winding descent through mixed forest, to a small, willow-filled meadow bordered with wildflowers, and proceed to a crossing of Lower Castle Creek. Beyond the crossing you make a moderately steep, winding climb toward the crest of a hill and then follow gently rising trail toward the vicinity of Castle Pass, where you reach a junction with a short connecting trail to the PCT, 6 miles from the trailhead. ►11

Great Views

Continue to climb toward the north ridge of Andesite Peak. Where you gain the crest of the ridge, Castle Peak and Valley burst into view. Follow the crest toward Andesite Peak, reaching a Y-junction with the 0.1-mile spur trail to the summit, 6.5 miles from the trailhead. ►12 The short climb to the top of Andesite Peak is rewarded by a fine 360° view. ►13

From the summit of Andesite Peak, return to the junction. ►14 Follow the Hole in the Wall Trail on a switchbacking descent across a forested hillside toward Castle Valley below. The forest parts temporarily to allow one more view of Castle Peak and the Carson Range to the east. You're soon back into the forest, where a series of switchbacks leads you down the hillside to the floor of the valley and a junction with the Castle Valley Road at 7.9 miles. ▶15 Near a couple of trailhead signs, a small patch of dirt provides parking for any high-clearance vehicles that make it this far up the road.

Without a vehicle at the trailhead you should head southeast and follow a rough and rocky section of the road for about 0.1 mile to a second parking area suitable for sedans. Without a vehicle parked here you must continue down the valley all the way to the end of the Castle Valley Road, walk the paved access road below Interstate 80 to the frontage road on the south side, and follow that road back to the trailhead. ▶16

🚶	MILESTONES	
▶1	0.0	Start at PCT trailhead
▶2	0.2	Veer right at Glacier Meadow Loop junction
▶3	0.3	Veer right again at Glacier Meadow Loop junction
▶4	0.5	Turn left (north) at PCT junction
▶5	1.0	Proceed straight ahead (west) at Summit Lake Trail junction
▶6	3.2	Veer right at Castle Valley Road junction
▶7	3.3	Castle Pass, proceed north on PCT
▶8	4.2	Peter Grubb Hut
▶9	4.4	Turn left (west) at junction with Sand Ridge Lake Trail
▶10	5.0	Turn left (south) at junction with Hole in the Wall Trail
▶11	6.0	Proceed straight ahead (south) at junction with Castle Pass lateral
▶12	6.5	Junction with trail to Andesite Peak
▶13	6.6	Andesite Peak
▶14	6.7	Junction with trail to Andesite Peak
▶15	7.9	Turn right (southeast) onto Castle Valley Road
▶16	9.6	Return to PCT trailhead

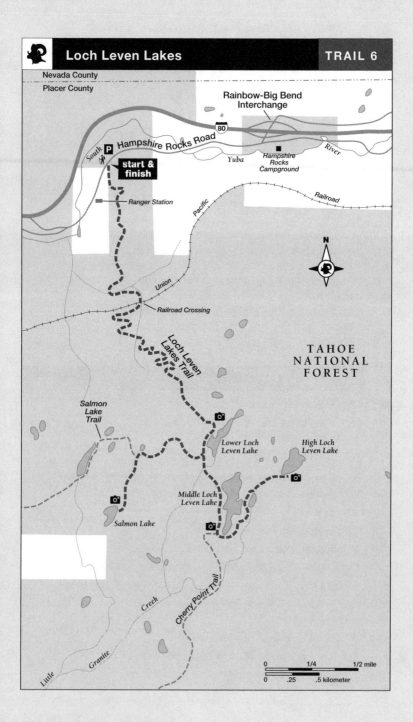

Loch Leven Lakes

TRAIL 6

Nevada County
Placer County

Rainbow-Big Bend
Interchange

South Hampshire Rocks Road

P start & finish

Yuba

Hampshire
Rocks
Campground

River

Ranger Station

Pacific

Railroad

Union

Railroad Crossing

Loch Leven Lakes Trail

TAHOE
NATIONAL
FOREST

N

Salmon
Lake
Trail

Lower Loch
Leven Lake

High Loch
Leven Lake

Middle Loch
Leven Lake

Salmon Lake

Cherry Point Trail

Creek

Granite

Little

| 0 | 1/4 | 1/2 mile |

| 0 | .25 | .5 kilometer |

Loch Leven Lakes

The Loch Leven Lakes provide hikers itching for summer an early-season opportunity to reach a trio of picturesque lakes nestled into a granite basin. A pleasant side trip to Salmon Lake increases the total of lakes to four. Swimmers will appreciate the relatively warm waters and scads of slabs and islands for sunbathing, while anglers can test their skills on the stocked trout that inhabit the lakes.

Best Time

A low-elevation trail by Tahoe Sierra standards, the Loch Leven Lakes Trail is usually snow free by mid- to late June, when wildflowers along the lower section of trail are at their glorious peak. Cool but pleasant weather usually persists into November.

Finding the Trail

Take the Rainbow Road/Big Bend exit from Interstate 80 and follow Hampshire Rocks Road westbound for 0.9 mile to the trailhead parking area on the right-hand shoulder. The trail begins on the opposite side of the road from the parking lot.

Logistics

The alignment of the Loch Leven Lakes Trail is incorrectly shown on the USGS Cisco Grove quadrangle. The map on page 56 shows the true route.

TRAIL USE
Hike, Run, Bike, Horse
LENGTH
8.0 miles, 4 hours
VERTICAL FEET
±1710'
DIFFICULTY
− 1 2 3 **4** 5 +
TRAIL TYPE
Out & Back
SURFACE TYPE
Dirt

FEATURES
Dogs Allowed
Canyon
Mountain
Lakes
Wildflowers
Photo Opportunity
Camping

FACILITIES
Restrooms

Lower Loch Leven Lake

Trail Description

 Canyon

▶1 An old wood sign marked LOCH LEVEN LAKES is all that delineates the start of a trail that climbs over a shrub- and boulder-covered hillside of exposed granite slabs beneath widely scattered conifers. A short, winding descent takes you briefly into a stand of white firs and lodgepole pines with a lush understory before the climbing resumes across mostly open terrain with nice views of Cisco Butte and the South Yuba River canyon. Soon the trail leads back into a grove of trees with a small pond that turns into little more than a quagmire by late summer. Beyond the pond, cross another stretch of shrubs and granite slabs before dropping through another forested section to a bridge across an alder-lined stream. Beyond the bridge a steep quarter-mile climb leads to the twin tracks of the Union Pacific Railroad, 1.25 miles from the trailhead. ▶2 As you cross the two sets of tracks pay close attention to traffic, especially coming toward you from the uphill direction, as trains descending from Donner Pass move swiftly and relatively quietly.

Find the continuation of the trail on the far side of the tracks and resume climbing through a mixed forest of incense cedars, white firs, and Jeffrey, lodgepole, and western white pines. Soon you reach the first of many switchbacks that will eventually transport you out of the South Yuba River canyon and into the lakes basin. Approaching Loch Leven Summit, the high point of the climb, the gradient mercifully eases and you follow a slight descent into

OPTIONS

Side Trip to Salmon Lake

From Lower Loch Leven Lake, follow the unsigned side trail right on a rising and winding climb across grass- and flower-covered slopes for 0.3 mile, followed by a gradual descent through alternating sections of granite slabs and light forest. Just before the lake, you reach a junction with a trail heading west to the Salmon Lake trailhead on Huysink Lake Road. ▶4 Veer left at the junction and continue another 0.2 mile to Salmon Lake. Although smaller and not as scenic as the Loch Leven Lakes, elliptical Salmon Lake is rimmed by low granite humps, scattered trees, and clumps of shrubs and grasses. Backpackers will find more solitude than at Loch Leven but far fewer campsites. This side trip adds 1.8 miles to the main trail.

Lake

the lakes basin until a short, steep, and rocky section of trail brings you to the first of the lakes. An old sign heralds your arrival at the west shore of Loch Leven Lake, 2.75 miles from the trailhead. ►3 Passable campsites are scattered around the lake and gently sloping granite slabs are sure to lure swimmers and sunbathers. Continue along the west side of Lower Loch Leven Lake to an unsigned junction with a lateral to Salmon Lake. (See Side Trip to Salmon Lake.)

From the Salmon Lake junction, ►4 a brief descent followed by a short climb leads to Middle Loch Leven Lake, where a number of pleasant campsites will lure overnighters. At the far end of the lake is a junction with the Cherry Point Trail, which heads southwest toward North Fork American River. ►5

Photo Opportunity

Turn left at the junction and follow the trail around the lower end of the middle lake, ascend a rock cleft, and then climb over granite slabs to the upper lake. ►6 High Loch Leven Lake is perhaps the most picturesque of the lakes, with heather-rimmed shores bordered by granite cliffs and stands of conifers. Fine campsites above the southeast shore will certainly appeal to those backpackers willing to hike all the way to the last lake in the chain.

🚶 MILESTONES

- ►1 0.0 Start at trailhead
- ►2 1.25 Union Pacific Railroad Tracks
- ►3 2.75 Lower Loch Leven Lake
- ►4 2.9 Proceed straight ahead (south) at Salmon Lake junction
- ►5 3.3 Veer left (east) at Cherry Point Trail junction
- ►6 4.0 High Loch Leven Lake

Middle Loch Leven Lake

Rainbow Lodge

Halfway between the trailhead and the freeway, Rainbow Lodge provides an excellent watering hole or eatery after a trip to Loch Leven lakes. Fine bed-and-breakfast packages are available for those looking for an overnight adventure. Call (800) 500-3871 or visit the website at www.rainbowlodge.net for more information.

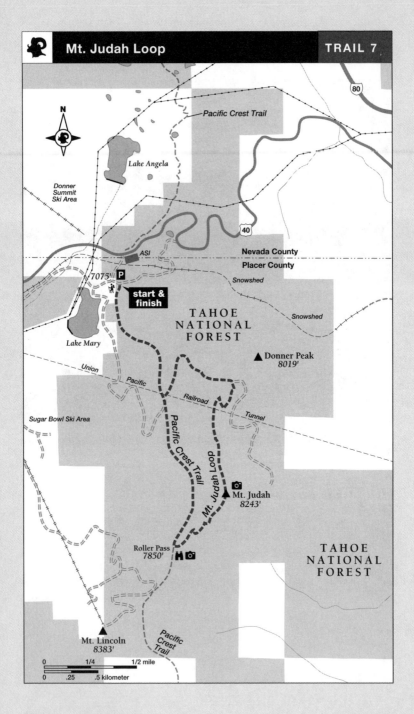

Pacific Crest Trail

Lake Angela

Donner
Summit
Ski Area

80

40

ASI

Nevada County

Placer County

7075' P

start &
finish

Snowshed

Snowshed

TAHOE
NATIONAL
FOREST

Lake Mary

▲ Donner Peak
8019'

Union

Pacific

Railroad

Tunnel

Sugar Bowl Ski Area

Pacific Crest Trail

Mt. Judah Loop

▲ Mt. Judah
8243'

Roller Pass
7850' H ◙

TAHOE
NATIONAL
FOREST

Pacific
Crest
Trail

▲ Mt. Lincoln
8383'

0   1/4   1/2 mile

0   .25   .5 kilometer

Mt. Judah Loop

With minimal effort, hikers can reach some of the grandest views available in the northern Tahoe Sierra, via the 4.6-mile Mt. Judah Loop. The rugged terrain around Donner Pass is impressive, and the trail affords many excellent vista points along the way to the awe-inspiring view from the summit of Mt. Judah. The section of the loop that connects with the Pacific Crest Trail was constructed in the 1990s, but despite its recent origin, the Mt. Judah Loop has justifiably become a very popular hike, so don't anticipate a high degree of solitude. Be sure to pack plenty of water, as none is available en route.

TRAIL USE
Hike, Run, Horse
LENGTH
4.6 miles, 2.5 hours
VERTICAL FEET
±1165'
DIFFICULTY
− 1 2 **3** 4 5 +
TRAIL TYPE
Loop
SURFACE TYPE
Dirt

Best Time

The trail is generally snow free from mid-July to October, although early in the season lingering snowbanks may cover the forested sections of trail, particularly following winters of heavy snows.

FEATURES
Dogs Allowed
Child Friendly
Mountain
Summit
Great Views

Finding the Trail

From Interstate 80 take either the Donner Lake or Soda Springs exit and drive approximately 4 miles on Donner Pass Road (Old Highway 40) to Donner Pass. Near the pass, just west of Alpine Skills International, turn south onto an old road, observing Pacific Crest Trail signs. After a short distance turn left and immediately reach the trailhead, where you'll find very limited parking.

FACILITIES
None

Logistics

Although the Mt. Judah Loop is outside of a designated wilderness, mountain bikes are not allowed on the Pacific Crest Trail.

Trail Description

▶1 After a narrow swath of lush vegetation filled with flowers and ferns, a series of short switchbacks leads you on a climb of a pine- and fir-dotted granite headwall. Beyond the switchbacks, follow the trail across a hillside carpeted with huckleberry oak, where views of the Donner Pass region improve with each step (the lake directly below you is Lake Mary). After a while, pass through a stand of red firs before breaking back out into the open at a crossing of a ski slope. In this clearing, 0.9 mile from the trailhead, you encounter a junction between the PCT and the north end of the Mt. Judah Loop. ▶2

Remaining on the PCT, you pass below a chairlift for the Sugar Bowl Ski Area, and then cross an old road, 0.1 mile from the junction. Reenter forest beyond the road, where mountain hemlocks begin to intermix with the red firs, and, in early summer, mule ears provide bursts of color. Reach the south junction of the Mt. Judah Loop at 1.8 miles from the trailhead. ▶3

Leave the PCT and follow the loop trail on a winding ascent of Mt. Judah's southwest ridge, reaching the top of the peak at 0.5 mile from the junction. At the time of research, a large cairn with metal flagpole and tattered flags marked the summit. ▶4 The marvelous view includes such landmarks as Donner Lake, Martis Valley, and the Carson Range to the east; Castle Peak, Mt. Lola, and the Sierra Buttes to the north; Sugar Bowl, Summit Valley, and Lake Van Norden to the west; and the continuation of the Sierra crest to the south.

 Great Views

From the top of Mt. Judah, descend a bare ridge to a saddle and then start climbing again toward the north summit. The trail veers east away from this slightly lower peak, although a short use-trail branching away from the main trail provides an easy way to the top. Traverse the east side of the ridge before a descent leads through a mixed forest around the nose of the ridge to a three-way junction at a saddle between Mt. Judah and Donner Peak, 3.1 miles from the trailhead. ▶5

With extra time and energy you could follow a use-trail from the saddle, northeast to the base of Donner Peak's multiple summit pinnacles. However, from there you'll need some basic rock-climbing skills to scramble up exfoliating slabs to top of the easiest summit.

From the junction, bend left and follow the course of an old road for 0.4 mile on a steady descent around the north side of the mountain to the resumption of single-track trail. Heading southwest, you continue the descent into a thickening forest until reaching the ski slope and the north junction of the PCT, 3.7 miles from the trailhead. ▶6 From there, retrace your steps 0.9 mile along the PCT to the trailhead. ▶7

Unless you're an expert climber, avoid Donner Peak's highest pinnacle, as the climbing is difficult and the exposure is significant.

△ Summit

🚶 MILESTONES

▶1 0.0 Start at trailhead
▶2 0.9 Proceed straight ahead (south) at north loop junction
▶3 1.8 Turn left (northeast) at south loop junction
▶4 2.3 Summit of Mt. Judah
▶5 3.1 Veer left (west) at three-way junction
▶6 3.7 Turn right (north) at north loop junction
▶7 4 .6 Return to trailhead

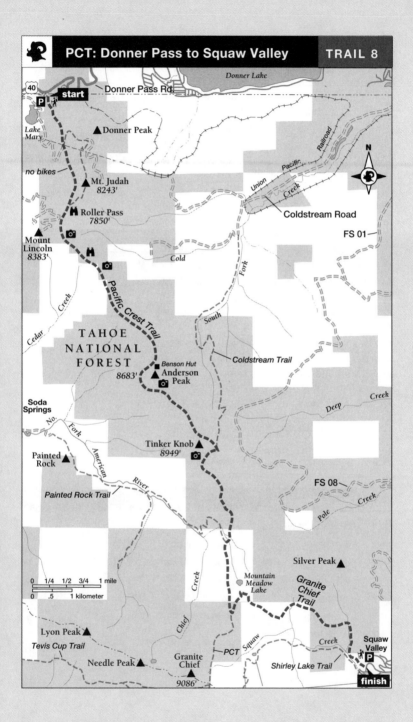

Pacific Crest Trail: Donner Pass to Squaw Valley

This section of the Pacific Crest Trail lives up to its name, offering some of the finest views in the Tahoe area from a several-mile stretch of trail that stays on or near the actual crest of the range. The 15-mile distance may be daunting to casual hikers, but experienced hikers in good condition will find the well-maintained PCT a rewarding challenge.

Best Time

The views from the trail are impressive anytime between mid-July and October. Early in the season snowbanks may cover some of the forested sections of the trail, particularly following winters of heavy snows.

Finding the Trail

START: From Interstate 80 take either the Donner Lake or Soda Springs exit and drive approximately 4 miles on Donner Pass Road (Old Highway 40) to Donner Pass. Near the pass, just west of Alpine Skills International, turn south onto an old road, observing Pacific Crest Trail signs. After a short distance turn left and immediately reach the trailhead, where you'll find very limited parking.

END: From Highway 89, about 8.5 miles south of Truckee and 5 miles north of Tahoe City, head west on Squaw Valley Road for 2.25 miles and park in the large parking area on the right, across from the fire station and the Olympic Village Inn.

TRAIL USE
Hike, Horse
LENGTH
15.0 miles, 8-10 hours
VERTICAL FEET
+3000'/-3800'
DIFFICULTY
– 1 2 3 4 **5** +
TRAIL TYPE
Point to Point
SURFACE TYPE
Dirt

FEATURES
Mountain
Summit
Great Views
Photo Opportunity
Camping
Secluded

FACILITIES
None

Trail Description

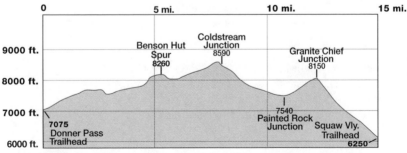 Great Views

▶1 After a narrow swath of lush vegetation filled with flowers and ferns, a series of short switchbacks leads you on a climb of a pine- and fir-dotted granite headwall. Beyond the switchbacks, follow the trail across a hillside carpeted with huckleberry oak, where views of the Donner Pass region improve with each step (the lake directly below you is Lake Mary). After a while, pass through a stand of red firs before breaking back out into the open at a crossing of a ski slope. In this clearing, 0.9 mile from the trailhead, you encounter a junction between the PCT and the north end of the Mt. Judah Loop. ▶2

Remaining on the PCT, you pass below a chairlift for the Sugar Bowl Ski Area, and then cross an old road, 0.1 mile from the junction. Reenter forest beyond the road, where mountain hemlocks begin to intermix with the red firs, and, in early summer, mule ears provide bursts of color. Reach the south junction of the Mt. Judah Loop at 1.8 miles from the trailhead. ▶3

Remaining on the Pacific Crest Trail, continue south from the junction for a short distance to a hemlock-shaded saddle known as **Roller Pass**, where a metal post bears a historical marker complete with a plaque and a quotation from Nicholas

TRAIL 8   PCT: Donner Pass to Squaw Valley Elevation Profile

Mts. Lincoln & Disney *from Pacific Crest Trail*

Carriter, a member of the ill-fated Donner Party. In September of 1846 the pioneers winched their wagons up to this spot with the aid of oxen. A short spur trail leads east from the saddle to the lip above the steep wall of Emigrant Canyon and to a vista that will certainly increase your admiration for these rugged pioneers and their dogged determination in getting their wagons out of the deep canyon and up to the pass.

Away from Roller Pass, the PCT closely follows the Sierra crest through light forest. Soon the trees diminish, and a nearly continuous stream of awesome views begins as you traverse the east slope of Mt. Lincoln. In the middle of nowhere, an old wood sign marked MT. LINCOLN points toward the summit, but all evidence of a former trail has vanished. If your desire is to scale this peak, an easier way to the summit can be found farther south, where a use-trail leaves the PCT to follow the southeast ridge to the top.

 Summit

Anderson Peak *from Pacific Crest Trail*

As you continue, the Sierra crest seems to stretch out ahead forever, while to the west the gash created by the North Fork American River seems too deep to be real. For the next several miles this section of the PCT is a prototypical crest trail, as the path stays high, either directly on or very near the apex of the range. Heading away from Mt. Lincoln, the PCT descends across an open volcanic slope, which during mid-summer is covered in a sea of yellow from multitudinous mule ears. A pair of long-legged switchbacks takes you through a stand of western white pines, red firs, and mountain hemlocks before you emerge back out into the open across shrub-covered slopes. You reach the bottom of the 0.75-mile descent from Mt. Lincoln at a 7500-foot saddle overlooking Coldstream Valley to the east and Cedar Creek canyon to the west.

From the saddle you ascend lunar-like slopes, where only small tufts of vegetation and a few mule ears seem capable of taking root in the porous volcanic soils. Eventually tobacco brush, currant, and sagebrush regain a foothold, as you progress toward the next high point, Anderson Peak, which from the trail presents a dramatic foreground profile. Cross a hillside covered with muddy-looking lava flows, follow a pair of switchbacks, and then pass below peak 8374 on the way to the base of Anderson Peak, where you'll encounter a use-trail branching away from the PCT, 5.3 miles from the trailhead. ►4

Following this unsigned path away from the PCT will take you up the north ridge of Anderson Peak in ten minutes or so to Benson Hut, one of four historic huts operated by the Sierra Club. Unless you're caught in a life-threatening storm, advanced reservations are required for use of the hut (see sidebar). Peak baggers can continue on a use-trail beyond the hut, which leads across a talus slope and then climbs steeply to the summit of Anderson Peak, where they'll enjoy another superb vista.

⚠ Camping

Away from the spur-trail junction to Benson Hut, the PCT skirts the west side of Anderson Peak well below the summit and follows a mile-long, gently ascending course southeast toward Tinker Knob. As you hike, tiny, drought-tolerant wildflowers cheer you onward. Just below Tinker Knob, where the PCT veers sharply east, you reach the high point

Benson Hut

Backpackers will find a dearth of campsites along this route — the only reasonable sites are the pair of basins just north of the crossing of the North Fork American River. However, overnighters may be able to obtain Spartan lodging in the Benson Hut by contacting the Sierra Club at this address: Clair Tappan Lodge, PO Box 36, Norden, CA 95724. (530) 426-3632

> If you wish to reach the summit of Tinker Knob, leave the trail where the PCT veers sharply east, and make the easy scramble over fractured rock to the top of the 8949-foot peak.

of the route between Donner Pass and Squaw Valley.

Begin your 2-mile descent from Tinker Knob to the North Fork American River by turning east on a descending trail below the north face of Tinker Knob. After 0.25 mile reach the junction with the Coldstream Trail near Tinker Knob Saddle, 8.2 miles from the trailhead. ▶5 The 6-mile Coldstream Trail offers an alternate route to a remote trailhead in Coldstream Valley, but access through Donner Memorial State Park and across private land is not always guaranteed.

From Tinker Knob Saddle, you drop steeply via switchbacks into the canyon of a tributary to the North Fork American River. After 0.6 mile the grade eases, as you follow a descending traverse well below the crest, hopping over a pair of spring-fed streams along the way. Enter a basin where waterless campsites are available and continue to a smaller basin with both water and at least one campsite, 0.3 mile farther. Beyond the second basin a steeper descent takes you past rock outcrops to a crossing of the North Fork American River and a junction with Painted Rock Trail at 10.7 miles from the trailhead. ▶6

From the Painted Rock junction, a series of switchbacks lead you up to the crest of a ridge to good views of Granite Chief to the south and Needle and Lyon peaks to the southwest. The USGS Granite Chief quad shows the old alignment of the trail that used to follow the headwaters of the North Fork upstream to Mountain Meadow Lake. The PCT was subsequently rerouted, as the land around the lake is privately owned and also is used by the University of California as an Ecological Study Area. Follow this newer section of trail to a junction, about 0.4 mile directly southwest of the lake and 12.2 miles from the trailhead, where the Granite Chief Trail heads northeast. ▶7

 Great Views

Leave the PCT at the junction and head northeast on the Granite Chief Trail, following a winding descent through a thick forest of mountain hemlocks and red firs. Switchbacks lead into a tributary canyon of Squaw Creek, where patches of flowerfilled meadow periodically interrupt the forest. Break out into the open, as you leave the trees and descend a series of sloping, granite benches that afford fine views of the Squaw Valley area. Locating the route of the trail over these granite benches may be difficult at times, but ducks and old paint marks on rocks may help guide you.

 Wildflowers

About 1.5 miles from the PCT junction, you make an easy crossing of a perennial stream and continue the descent, through alternating stretches of light forest and granite slabs. Cross a marshy hillside fed by seeps and then follow switchbacks to the easy crossing of another Squaw Creek tributary, which you then follow downstream through thickening vegetation. Nearing the valley floor, a number of intersecting paths combined with a lack of signs create a mildly confusing conclusion to your journey, but fortunately all paths lead to the large parking lot at Squaw Valley. ▶8

𝕏 MILESTONES

▶1	0.0	Start at trailhead
▶2	0.9	Proceed straight ahead (south) at north loop junction
▶3	1.8	Proceed straight ahead (south) at south loop junction
▶4	5.3	Spur trail to Benson Hut
▶5	8.2	Proceed straight ahead (south) at Coldstream Trail junction
▶6	10.7	Proceed straight ahead (south) at Painted Rock Trail junction
▶7	12.2	Turn left (northeast) at Granite Chief Trail junction
▶8	15.0	Squaw Valley parking lot

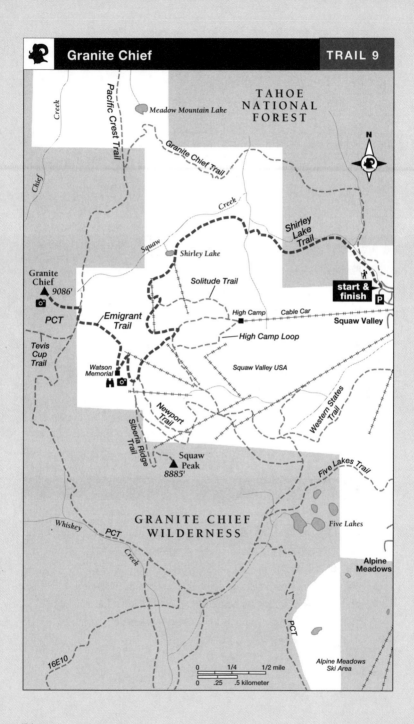

Creek

Pacific Crest Trail

Meadow Mountain Lake

TAHOE
NATIONAL
FOREST

Granite Chief Trail

Chief

Creek

N

Squaw

Shirley Lake

Shirley
Lake
Trail

Granite
Chief
▲ 9086'

start &
finish
P

PCT

Emigrant
Trail

Solitude Trail

High Camp

Cable Car

Squaw Valley

Tevis
Cup
Trail

High Camp Loop

Watson
Memorial

Squaw Valley USA

Newport
Trail

Siberia Ridge Trail

Western States Trail

▲ Squaw
Peak
8885'

Five Lakes Trail

Whiskey

PCT

Creek

GRANITE CHIEF
WILDERNESS

Five Lakes

Alpine
Meadows

PCT

16E10

| 0 | 1/4 | 1/2 mile |
| 0 | .25 | .5 kilometer |

Alpine Meadows
Ski Area

Granite Chief

At 9006 feet, Granite Chief is the centerpiece of the surrounding Granite Chief Wilderness, directly west of Squaw Valley USA. An excellent view from the summit is available from two different approaches requiring two different levels of commitment. The first alternative follows a stiff climb from Squaw Valley along Squaw Creek, past Shirley Lake, and over the Sierra crest to the base of the peak. The second utilizes the aerial cable car from Squaw Valley to High Camp, greatly reducing the effort and time involved to reach the summit. Whichever way you choose, the view from the top is excellent and the scenery along the way is quite rewarding as well.

TRAIL USE
Hike
LENGTH
10.2 miles, 4-6 hours
VERTICAL FEET
±3425'
DIFFICULTY
− 1 2 3 4 **5** +
TRAIL TYPE
Out & Back
SURFACE TYPE
Dirt, Paved

FEATURES
Canyon
Mountain
Summit
Stream
Lake
Birds
Great Views
Photo Opportunity
Cool & Shady

FACILITIES
None

Best Time

Although the route is usually snow free from mid-July through mid-October, wildflowers are typically at their peak from late July to mid-August.

Finding the Trail

From Highway 89, about 8.5 miles south of Truckee and 5 miles north of Tahoe City, head west on Squaw Valley Road for 2.25 miles into the center of Squaw Valley. Turn right on Squaw Peak Road and continue to the lower intersection with Squaw Peak Way and park in the wide shoulder. If you opt for the cable car route, simply park in the main parking lot of Squaw Valley and take the short walk to the cable car building.

Logistics

High Camp offers the possibility of a high-class adventure. After the climb of Granite Chief, hikers can swim in the pool, revive at the spa, dine at one of the cafes or restaurants, or sip a cold one in the bar.

Parking is not available at the Shirley Lake trailhead, near the upper intersection between Squaw Peak Road and Squaw Peak Way. While taking the cable car up to High Camp will save 2.5 miles of hiking and nearly 2000 feet of elevation gain, you'll have to cough up $17 for the ride. However, if you walk all the way from the bottom of Squaw Valley, you can ride the cable car from High Camp back to Squaw Valley for free.

Trail Description

►1 From the parking area follow a short dirt path that leads to the actual trailhead, which is near the upper intersection of Squaw Peak Road and Squaw Peak Way. Find the continuation of the path along the left-hand bank of Squaw Creek, which is sheltered by red firs, and lodgepole and Jeffrey pines. Lacking a single designated route, multiple paths follow a moderately steep course upstream past shrubs and around boulders. At some point you'll probably come to the realization that this trail evolved from repeated use and wasn't the result of a trail builder's thoughtful design. Entering a shady forest, thimbleberry and bracken fern carpet the canyon floor, while the tumbling creek drops over short rock steps and into picturesque pools.

 Cool & Shady

Leave the forest cover to climb steeply over boulders and slabs, where blue paint marks help to keep you on route. After hopping across a side stream you reenter mixed forest, as western white

Squaw Valley Cable Car

OPTIONS

The Squaw Valley cable car makes it possible to opt out of ascending or descending, and shortens the length by half, to 5.0 miles, three hours.

Squaw Peak

pines join the previously mentioned conifers.
Continue the stiff climb alongside the creek, which
is lined with lush vegetation and wildflowers in season. The grade temporarily abates as you reach the
top of an open bench and enjoy a limited view of the
surroundings before returning to a climb through
the trees. Eventually the trail veers away from Squaw
Creek and leads to a log crossing of an alder-lined
tributary stream, 1.25 miles from the trailhead.

Beyond the stream crossing you climb over an
extensive area of granite slabs and boulders with
intermittent stretches of dirt trail. The open terrain
allows views of the canyon and Squaw Valley below,
as well as the supports and cables for the passing
cable cars on your left. The grade eases a bit above
the slabs and you follow a mild ascent through scattered forest and around granite humps. A short
descent then leads to the shoreline of diminutive
and shallow Shirley Lake, 2.2 miles from the trailhead. ▶2 Lodgepole pines and mountain hemlocks
on the near shore and meadows and shrubs on the

Granite Chief

far shore rim the lake. An area of granite cliffs lends an alpine ambience to the lake.

The trail heads south from the lake and makes a steep climb via switchbacks under a chairlift and across wildflower carpeted slopes to Shirley Lake Road. Proceed along this road past the junction of the Solitude Trail, at 2.8 miles. ►3 Continue on a steep climb, which zigzags beneath the Shirley Lake Express chairlift for 0.4 mile, to a signed junction with the High Camp Loop Trail. ►4 Those who elected to ride the cable car join the description at this point, having walked 0.3 mile from High Camp along the north side of the loop trail.

 Wildflowers

Following signed directions toward Emigrant Peak, Siberia Ridge, and Newport, turn right on the High Camp Loop Trail and climb along the dirt road toward the Sierra crest. In early season the open slopes surrounding the route are extensively carpeted with mule ears, lupines, and other wildflowers. Soon you reach another junction, where the loop trail bends to the left but you veer to the right. ▶5 Pass above the Shirley Lake Express chairlift and then below the Emigrant chairlift on the way to signed junction "D." ▶6

At junction "D," turn right, obeying signs for Squaw Peak and Emigrant Peak, and climb a short distance to junction "E." ▶7 Turn right and follow the Emigrant Trail to the crest of the ridge and the site of the Watson Monument. ▶8

📷 **Photo Opportunity**

From the monument, descend along the ridge to a saddle and a signed junction at a hairpin turn. ▶9 Turn right and follow this trail for a short distance to a three-way junction with the Pacific Crest Trail. ▶10 Following signed directions for Granite Chief, you veer right and climb to the crest of the east ridge of Granite Chief. ▶11 Leave the PCT at the top of the ridge and follow a use trail for 0.3 mile to the summit. ▶12 Views from the top of Granite Chief are quite rewarding, including the Desolation peaks to the south, Castle Peak and the terrain around Donner Pass to the north, and a part of Lake Tahoe to the east.

🚶 **MILESTONES**

▶1 0.0 Start at trailhead
▶2 2.2 Shirley Lake
▶3 2.8 Continue straight ahead at Solitude Trail junction
▶4 3.2 Turn right at High Camp Loop Trail junction
▶5 3.3 Continue straight ahead at Newport junction
▶6 3.7 Turn right at Siberia Ridge junction
▶7 3.8 Turn right at Emigrant junction
▶8 4.0 Watson Memorial
▶9 4.4 Turn right at junction in saddle
▶10 4.6 Turn right at PCT junction
▶11 4.7 Leave PCT at southeast ridge of Granite Peak
▶12 5.1 Summit of Granite Chief

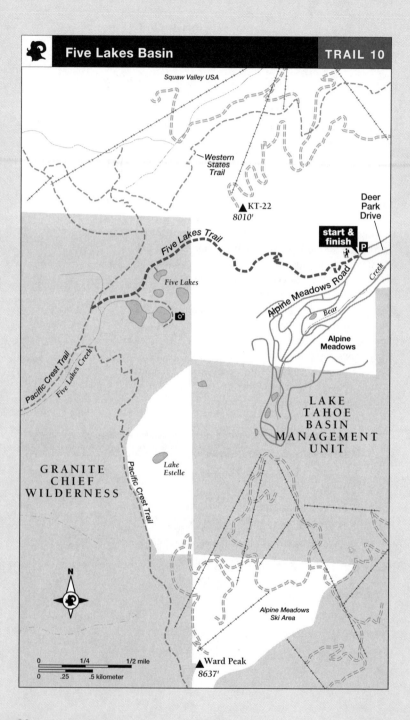

Squaw Valley USA

Western
States
Trail

▲ KT-22
8010'

Deer
Park
Drive

Five Lakes Trail

**start &
finish**

🅿

Alpine Meadows Road

Bear

Creek

Five Lakes

📷

Alpine
Meadows

Pacific Crest Trail

Five Lakes Creek

LAKE
TAHOE
BASIN
MANAGEMENT
UNIT

GRANITE
CHIEF
WILDERNESS

Pacific Crest Trail

*Lake
Estelle*

N

*Alpine Meadows
Ski Area*

0   1/4   1/2 mile

0   .25   .5 kilometer

▲ Ward Peak
8637'

Five Lakes Basin

A short but steep climb leads to a forested basin holding five serene, forest-rimmed lakes which are well suited for an afternoon of sunbathing, picnicking, fishing, or just relaxing. Since the lakes are only an hour away don't expect to be alone, particularly on weekends.

Best Time

Snow leaves the trail by mid-July and usually returns after October.

Finding the Trail

Approximately 10 miles south of Truckee and 4 miles north of Tahoe City, leave Highway 89 and follow Alpine Meadows Road for 2.1 miles to the trailhead, which will be on the right-hand side of the road, opposite an intersection of Deer Park Drive. Park along either shoulder of the road, as conditions allow.

Logistics

Due to overuse, camping is not allowed in the Five Lakes Basin.

Trail Description

►1 Leave the trailhead and begin a moderate climb across shrub-covered slopes carpeted with a dense tangle of manzanita, snowberry, and huckleberry oak, and dotted with a few Jeffrey pines and white firs. Views of the canyon and the Alpine Meadows

TRAIL USE
Hike, Run
LENGTH
4.0 miles, 2-3 hours
VERTICAL FEET
±1000'
DIFFICULTY
– 1 2 **3** 4 5 +
TRAIL TYPE
Out & Back
SURFACE TYPE
Dirt

FEATURES
Dogs Allowed
Canyon
Mountain
Lakes
Photo Opportunity

FACILITIES
None

View from Five Lakes Trail

Easy access to the Pacific Crest Trail beyond the Five Lakes Basin provides hikers possessing extra time and energy with plenty of opportunities for further wanderings.

Ski Area improve with the subsequent gain in elevation, as you continue up the open, south-facing hillside. Higher up the slope a series of switchbacks leads to an arcing ascent that takes you across a granitic ridge, where stunted western white pines and Jeffrey pines eke out an existence in the inhospitable surroundings. This section of the climb feels very alpine thanks to the granitic rock and the vertical exposure. The grade momentarily eases, but all too soon you resume climbing, crossing the Granite Chief Wilderness boundary near a stand of red firs, 1.4 miles from the trailhead. ▶2

Past the boundary the steep climb moderates for good and you stroll through moderate forest cover, soon encountering a short use-trail heading southwest to the first of the forest-rimmed lakes. A short distance farther, at 1.9 miles, is a three-way junction, where the left-hand trail heads toward the largest lake. ▶3

Largest of the Five Lakes

🚶 **MILESTONES**

▶1 0.0 Start at trailhead
▶2 1.4 Granite Chief Wilderness boundary
▶3 1.9 Junction to largest lake trail

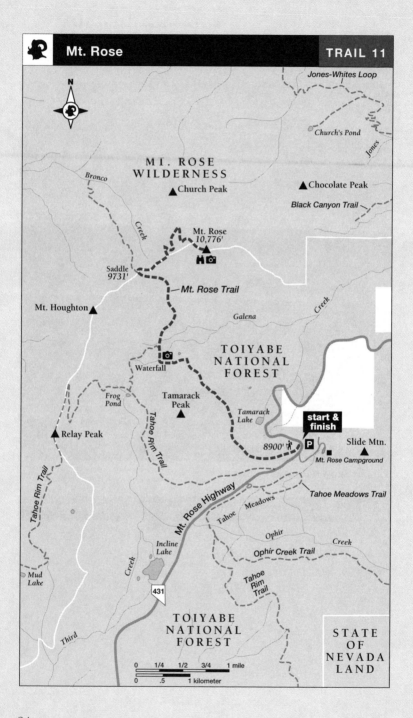

Jones-Whites Loop

Church's Pond

Jones

MT. ROSE
WILDERNESS

Bronco

Creek

▲ Church Peak

▲ Chocolate Peak

Black Canyon Trail

Mt. Rose
10,776'

Saddle
9731'

Mt. Rose Trail

Galena

Creek

Mt. Houghton ▲

TOIYABE
NATIONAL
FOREST

Waterfall

Frog
Pond

Tamarack
Peak
▲

Tamarack
Lake

start &
finish

▲ Relay Peak

8900'

Slide Mtn.
▲

Mt. Rose Campground

Tahoe Rim Trail

Tahoe Meadows Trail

Mt. Rose Highway

Tahoe Meadows

Incline
Lake

Tahoe

Ophir

Creek

Ophir Creek Trail

Creek

Mud
Lake

Tahoe
Rim
Trail

431

Third

TOIYABE
NATIONAL
FOREST

STATE
OF
NEVADA
LAND

0   1/4   1/2   3/4   1 mile

0   .5   1 kilometer

Mt. Rose

The route to the summit of Mt. Rose may be the most popular trail in the state of Nevada, as evidenced by the full trailhead parking lot on summer weekends. The attractions of this trip are many, including spectacular views of Lake Tahoe from the summit, a delightful display of wildflowers in the Galena Creek drainage, and a chance to scale the third-highest peak in the Tahoe Basin—the highest Tahoe summit with a maintained trail.

TRAIL USE
Hike, Run
LENGTH
10 miles, 6 hours
VERTICAL FEET
+2425'
DIFFICULTY
– 1 2 **3** 4 5 +
TRAIL TYPE
Out & Back
SURFACE TYPE
Dirt

FEATURES
Dogs Allowed
Mountain
Summit
Stream
Waterfall
Wildflowers
Great Views
Photo Opportunity

FACILITIES
Restrooms
Campground

Best Time

Although the trail is usually snow free in early July, mid-July to mid-August is the best time to view the wildflower display along Galena Creek. Generally, the trail stays open through October, but autumn days may see an inversion layer over the Truckee Meadows that allows only a hazy view of Reno and Sparks.

Finding the Trail

Finding the Trail: From Reno, take Highway 395 to the Mt. Rose Highway (State Route 431) and travel west to the Mt. Rose Summit (8911 feet) and the new trailhead which, at the time of research, the Forest Service had scheduled for completion in 2004. From Incline Village, the parking area is 8 miles east of the 28/431 junction. The old Mt. Rose trailhead is 0.3 mile west of the summit, where the route of the Tahoe Rim Trail now follows the access road to Relay Ridge.

Tahoe Meadows and Lake Tahoe *from Mt. Rose Trail*

Trail Description

 Wildflowers

►1 From the parking lot at Mt. Rose Summit, follow new trail on an ascending traverse above the Mt. Rose Highway, across a sagebrush- and grass-covered hillside dotted with boulders and sprinkled with lodgepole and whitebark pines. Mule ears and lupines add dashes of purple and yellow to the slopes in early to mid-summer. As you continue the climb, the pines become even more widely scattered, which allows for fine views of the upper end of Tahoe Meadows and Lake Tahoe rimmed on the far shore by towering peaks. Eventually the trail veers away from the highway and enters light forest on the way to a saddle between Tamarack Peak on your left and Peak 9201 on your right.

Beyond the saddle the gently rising trail slices across the eastern flank of Tamarack Peak, where mountain hemlocks begin to intermix with the pines. Gaps in the trees permit periodic glimpses of meadow-rimmed Tamarack Lake, 400 feet below, and the reddish-gray, volcanic summit of Mt. Rose looming above the treetops.

Near the 1.5-mile mark the climbing ends and you begin a mild descent across steep slopes on the northeast side of Tamarack Peak. After the crossing of a seasonal stream, proceed across a forested bench before continuing the descent across another steep hillside. Soon the pleasant sound of running water propels you onward toward a waterfall. Reach the floor of Galena Creek canyon at 2.3 miles from the trailhead and stand below this scenic gem, where multiple ribbons of water spill picturesquely down dark rock walls. Downstream, an expansive meadow provides a fine foreground view for the massive hulk of Mt. Rose.

Waterfall

Away from the fall you cross the creek and skirt the base of a rock-strewn hill, opposite a willow- and flower-lined creek and lush meadow to the right. A moderate climb leads away from the creek and meadow and winds uphill to the crossing of a small tributary stream. A short walk from the stream brings you to a junction with the old section of the Mt. Rose Trail, 2.5 miles from the trailhead. ►2

From the junction, curve around and cross another tributary of Galena Creek, where an uninterrupted climb to the summit begins. During peak season, a brilliant display of wildflowers mixes with a lush assemblage of shrubs near the creek, where the variety of flowers includes lupine, paintbrush, angelica, larkspur and mule ears. Leaving the luxuriant vegetation behind, the trail makes a moderate ascent of a dry hillside before turning into a narrow, steep canyon. Climb the slender cleft, twice crossing a seasonal creek, to the wilderness boundary,

Mt. Rose

150 yards below a saddle southwest of Mt. Rose. A short climb leads up to the saddle and a trail junction amid some weather-beaten whitebark pines, 3.6 miles from the trailhead. ▶3 A sign indicates: MT. ROSE SUMMIT to the right (east) and BIG MEADOWS straight ahead (northwest) toward Bronco Creek.

To reach the summit of Mt. Rose, head through scattered whitebark pines along a narrow ridge toward the gray volcanic mass of Mt. Rose. At the end of the ridge, the grade increases and you begin the first of five switchbacks up the west slope of the peak, where views of the surrounding countryside improve with each step. From the switchbacks, the trail makes an ascending traverse around to the northwest side of the mountain, where low-growing alpine plants soon replace the stunted pines. Another series of switchbacks climbs up the rocky slopes, while the actual summit lies just out of view. As you approach what seems to be the top, one more set of three short switchbacks brings you to the summit ridge, from where a short jaunt leads to the top. ▶4

Improvements at the summit consist of a trail register and rock walls piled high to restrain the notorious winds that frequent the area. If you happen to arrive under calm conditions, count your blessings. Views are impressive in all directions. On normal days the Sierra Buttes are visible to the north, above and beyond the Little Truckee River reservoirs of Prosser, Boca and Stampede. Lake Tahoe is the preeminent gem, encircled by an impressive ring of peaks, including Pyramid Peak and Mt. Tallac above the southwest shore and Jobs Peak, Jobs Sister and Freel Peak in the Carson Range. Reno/Sparks and the rest of the Truckee Meadows are clearly visible from the summit as well.

On extremely clear days you can see north all the way to the Cascade volcanoes of Lassen Peak and Mt. Shasta.

△ Summit

🚶	**MILESTONES**
▶1	0.0 Start at trailhead
▶2	2.5 Turn right at junction of old Mt. Rose Trail
▶3	3.6 Turn right at junction of Bronco Creek Trail
▶4	5.0 Summit of Mt. Rose

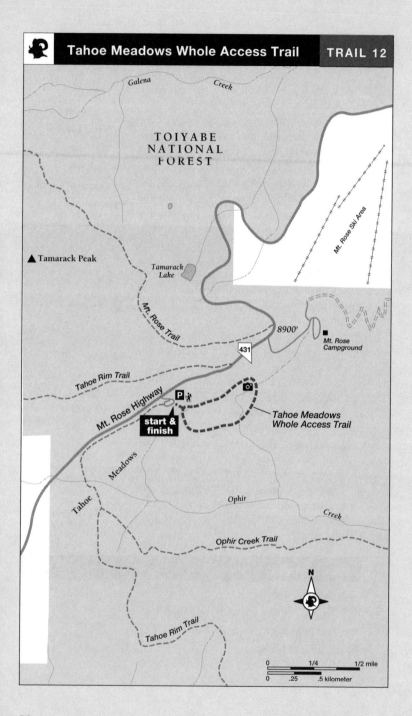

Galena   Creek

TOIYABE
NATIONAL
FOREST

Mt. Rose Ski Area

▲ Tamarack Peak

Tamarack
Lake

Mt. Rose Trail

8900'

431

Mt. Rose
Campground

Tahoe Rim Trail

Mt. Rose Highway

P

start &
finish

Tahoe Meadows
Whole Access Trail

Meadows

Tahoe

Ophir

Creek

Ophir Creek Trail

N

Tahoe Rim Trail

0		1/4		1/2 mile
0	.25		.5 kilometer	

Tahoe Meadows
Whole Access Trail

The Tahoe Meadows Whole Access Trail is a wheel-chair-accessible trail providing a fine opportunity to experience a part of verdant, subalpine Tahoe Meadows. Not only will the wheelchair bound enjoy this loop, but families with small children will appreciate the wide, gently graded, 1.3-mile long path as well. The trail loops around the northeast finger of 8700-foot Tahoe Meadows, exposing hikers to a lush meadowland environment full of plants, wildflowers, and trickling streams, bordered by a light forest of lodgepole pines. Slide Mountain and Mt. Rose provide a fine backdrop to the scenery-rich meadows.

TRAIL USE
Hike
LENGTH
1.3 miles, 0.75 hours
VERTICAL FEET
±100'
DIFFICULTY
– **1** 2 3 4 5 +
TRAIL TYPE
Loop
SURFACE TYPE
Dirt

Best Time

Snow usually clears out of Tahoe Meadows by the end of June, allowing vivid wildflower displays from mid-July through August. Without the flowers, the hiking season still continues, until the first significant snowfall in early November.

FEATURES
Handicap Accessible
Child Friendly
Mountain
Wildflowers
Birds
Wildlife
Photo Opportunity

Finding the Trail

From Reno, take Highway 395 to the Mt. Rose Highway (State Route 431) and travel west to the Mt. Rose Summit (8911 feet) and continue 0.7 mile to the Tahoe Rim trailhead parking lot on the south side of the highway, where you'll find restrooms and running water. From Incline Village, the parking area is about 7.3 miles east of the 28/431 junction.

FACILITIES
Restrooms
Picnic Tables
Water

Trail Description

▶1 From the parking lot, head east on a wide, rock-lined path for 0.1 mile to a junction. ▶2 Pedestrians are encouraged to turn right at the junction, following a counter-clockwise loop around the northeast finger of Tahoe Meadows. Proceed across a long wooden bridge over a marshy stretch of ground to the far edge of the meadow and then veer northeast along the fringe, passing in and out of shady stands of lodgepole pine. Around the east edge of the meadow, a series of short wooden bridges takes you across marshy areas and gurgling tributaries of Ophir Creek. As the loop bends around toward the trailhead, a short lateral leads onto a low hummock of granite, from where you have a fine view of the sprawling meadow from a slightly elevated vantage. Back on the main trail, you follow the course of an abandoned road along the north fringe of the meadow to the junction. ▶3 From here, make the easy climb back to the parking lot. ▶4

大	MILESTONES

▶1	0.0	Start at trailhead
▶2	0.1	Turn right at junction
▶3	1.2	Continue straight at junction
▶4	1.3	Return to trailhead

Tahoe Meadows

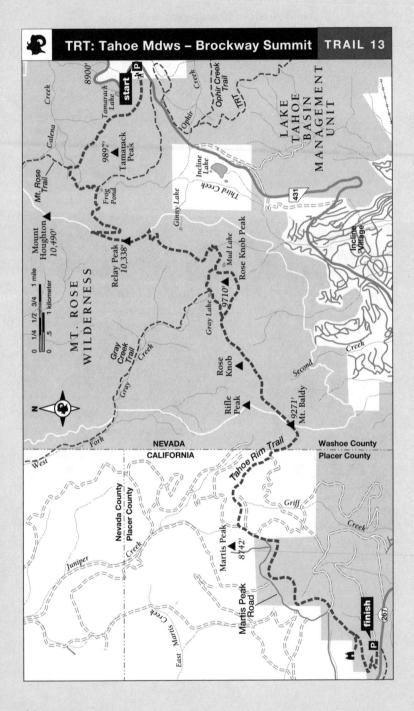

Tahoe Rim Trail: Tahoe Meadows to Brockway Summit

The section of the Tahoe Rim Trail between Tahoe Meadows and Brockway Summit was the last link of the 164-mile trail to be completed before the official opening in 2002. Offering some of the route's finest views, as well as the trail's high point atop Relay Peak (10,338 feet), one wonders how we got along without this part of the trail for so long. The 18-mile distance at relatively high altitude is a difficult one-day hike, but a reasonable expectation of solitude in the middle section is a fine tradeoff for those who are up to the task. Backpackers will find good campsites at Gray Lake, a half-mile off the TRT near the midpoint of the trip.

Best Time

Wildflowers are at their peak from mid-July to mid-August, but the spectacular views are always in season during the usually snow-free months of July through October.

Finding the Trail

START: From Reno, take Highway 395 to the Mt. Rose Highway (State Route 431) and travel west to the Mt. Rose Summit (8911 feet) and the new trailhead that the Forest Service was hoping to complete in 2004. From Incline Village, the parking area is 8 miles east of the 28/431 junction.

END: From Highway 28 in Kings Beach or Interstate 80 near Truckee, proceed on California Highway 267 to the TRT parking area, 0.5 mile south of

TRAIL USE
Hike, Run, Bike
LENGTH
18 miles, 9 hours
VERTICAL FEET
+2900'/-4850'
DIFFICULTY
- 1 2 3 4 **5** +
TRAIL TYPE
Point to Point
SURFACE TYPE
Dirt, Paved

FEATURES
Dogs Allowed
Mountain
Summit
Waterfall
Lake
Wildflowers
Birds
Great Views
Photo Opportunity
Camping
Secluded

FACILITIES
Restrooms
Campground

Brockway Summit, and 2.8 miles from the junction with Hwy 28 in Kings Beach. A steep dirt road (FS 16N56) on the west side leads quickly up to a small parking area. (No facilities).

Trail Description

▶1 From the parking lot at Mt. Rose Summit, follow new trail on an ascending traverse above the Mt. Rose Highway, across a sagebrush- and grass-covered hillside dotted with boulders and sprinkled with lodgepole and whitebark pines. Mule ears and lupines add dashes of yellow and purple to the slopes in early to mid-summer. As you continue the climb, the pines become even more widely scattered, which allows for fine views of the upper end of Tahoe Meadows and Lake Tahoe rimmed on the far shore by towering peaks. Eventually the trail veers away from the highway and enters light forest on the way to a saddle between Tamarack Peak on your left and Peak 9201 on your right.

Beyond the saddle the gently rising trail slices across the eastern flank of Tamarack Peak, where mountain hemlocks begin to intermix with the pines. Gaps in the trees permit periodic glimpses of meadow-rimmed Tamarack Lake, 400 feet below, and the reddish-gray, volcanic summit of Mt. Rose looming above the treetops.

■ **Waterfall**

Near the 1.5-mile mark the climbing ends and you begin a mild descent across steep slopes on the northeast side of Tamarack Peak. After the crossing of a seasonal stream, proceed across a forested bench before continuing the descent across another steep hillside. Soon the pleasant sound of running water propels you onward toward a waterfall. Reach the floor of Galena Creek canyon at 2.3 miles from the trailhead and stand below this scenic gem, where multiple ribbons of water spill picturesquely down dark rock walls.

Upper Galena Creek meadows

Downstream, an expansive meadow provides a fine foreground view for the massive hulk of Mt. Rose.

Away from the fall you cross the creek and skirt the base of a rock-strewn hill, opposite the willow- and flower-lined creek and lush meadow to the right. A moderate climb leads away from the creek and meadow and winds uphill to the crossing of a small tributary stream. A short walk from the stream brings you to a junction with the old section of the Mt. Rose Trail, 2.5 miles from the trailhead. ▶2

Until the next single-track section of the TRT is built, you must turn left at the junction and head steeply uphill on the old trail, following a jeep road through scattered lodgepole pines. The trail curves around the head of the canyon, crosses another branch of nascent Galena Creek, and then climbs over a low saddle to a junction with the service road for Relay Peak, 3.25 miles from the trailhead. ▶3

Turn right from the junction and follow the service road across piped, spring-fed Third Creek and then begin a steep ascent of the slope below Relay Ridge. Near the base of the tramway tower that services the facilities on the ridge, you follow the road around a sharp bend, and after 0.5 mile double back sharply to switchback up the hillside. As you gain the crest near a plethora of electronic equipment, Boca, Stampede and Prosser reservoirs spring into view, as does the town of Truckee, backdropped nicely by Donner Lake, as well as the mountainous terrain around Donner Summit.

 Summit

Entering the Mt. Rose Wilderness, you now follow single-track trail south-southwest along Relay Ridge on a stiff climb a half-mile past wind-sculpted whitebark pines to the top of Relay Peak, 5.3 miles from the trailhead, where a cairn and an old wooden tripod mark the summit. ▶4 At 10,338 feet, Relay Peak is the highest point on the entire circuit of the TRT. The stunning vista includes a good portion of Lake Tahoe basin, Tahoe Meadows and Incline Lake below, a piece of Washoe Lake through the gash of Ophir Creek canyon, backdropped by a parade of distant ranges extending east into the Great Basin. The Sierra Buttes dominate the northern skyline, but on clear days you may be able to make out Lassen Peak beyond, and on the clearest of days, Mt. Shasta. Unfortunately, the view is not all good, as immediately to the northwest you'll see the results of the extensive Martis Fire of 2001, which was sparked by an illegal campfire started by careless campers.

Great Views

Away from Relay Peak, you head down the crest of the ridge for 0.5 mile, before a series of switchbacks leads down the southern flanks of the peak on a protracted descent toward a significant saddle, losing 800 vertical feet in the process. Along the way, you have excellent views of the Donner Summit region, the seldom-traveled terrain of the West Fork Gray Creek, and, in the northwest, the trio of reservoirs on the Truckee River system and the distant plain of Sierra Valley.

More switchbacks lead to easier hiking as you approach the rocky flanks of Slab Cliffs. Nestled in the small basin below you, at the head of a branch of Third Creek, is Ginny Lake, a pleasant-looking body of water only 0.25 mile from the trail, but virtually inaccessible without a steep, off-trail descent. Continuing, you pass through scattered conifers as you traverse across the rock outcroppings of Slab Cliffs, with more fine views as your nearly constant companion. Away from Slab Cliffs, a lone switchback drops you into the next saddle along the ridge crest.

≈ **Lake**

A series of short switchbacks leads you down from the saddle to an unmarked junction with an unmaintained section of the old Western States Trail, where faint tread heads east to the private property around Incline Lake. Just downslope, a spring near a pocket of willows provides a reliable water source for most of the summer. Remaining on the TRT, you traverse the hillside, with exquisite

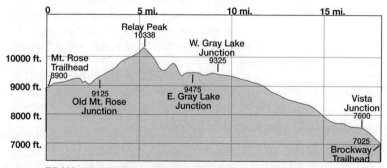

TRAIL 13 **TRT: Tahoe Meadows to Highway 267 Elevation Profile**

views of Lake Tahoe, and in 0.25 mile come directly above aptly named Mud Lake. Without a natural inlet or outlet, the brown pond of Mud Lake stagnates in its basin, progressively shrinking over the course of the summer, and in drought years disappearing altogether. Another 0.25 mile of gently graded trail brings you to yet another saddle along the crest, where nearby you'll find a junction with the old Western States Trail to Gray Lake, 7.5 miles from the Mt. Rose Highway (see side trip). ►5

▲ **Summit**

From the first junction to Gray Lake, the TRT skirts the east side of Rose Knob Peak, where excellent Tahoe views abound. You continue to traverse around the south side of the peak, through scattered hemlocks and across talus-covered slopes, before dropping to a saddle directly west of the peak, where a sprinkling of whitebark pines greets you. Heading away from the saddle, you traverse the ridgecrest over to the junction with the western branch of the old Western States Trail to Gray Lake, 8.9 miles from the highway. ►6

The traverse continues across mostly open slopes, where proclaiming the excellent views becomes almost redundant. Lake Tahoe glistens under typically sunny Sierra skies, while Incline Village, the Diamond Peak Ski Area, and the Mt. Rose Highway all lie at your feet. You skirt the slopes below Rose Knob—if even grander views are desired, you can make the 300-ft. climb to the top—and continue the traverse across hillsides carpeted, through mid-summer, with mule ears. Passing below unnamed Peak 9499 and 9271-foot Mt. Baldy, you reach the Mt. Rose Wilderness boundary amid scattered pines and then make a mild descent to an unceremonious crossing of the unsigned Nevada-California border.

A short zigzagging descent follows the long, open traverse, leading you down to a rock knob, from where you have another good lake view. A few

Side Trip to Gray Lake

OPTIONS

Unless you're in a hurry, the half-mile descent to Gray Lake is a worthwhile endeavor, especially if you need a campsite. Leave the TRT and descend away from the ridge on a section of the old Western States Trail, initially through whitebark pines and mountain hemlocks. In the midst of the descent you cross a small, flower-filled meadow and then continue to drop through a thicker forest of lodgepole pine. After hopping across the thin ribbon of a seasonal stream, you reach the floor of the small basin and meadow-rimmed Gray Lake.

Gray Lake is a kidney-bean-shaped, shallow body of water surrounded by verdant meadows. In the natural evolution of lakes and meadows, the lake is destined eventually to become a part of Gray Meadow, as it's only a matter of time before silt and debris fill the basin. On a human timetable, however, many years are left to enjoy this delightful lake. The sparkling, spring-fed water of the inlet flows down from above the lake along a rocky channel softened by rich, green moss and brilliant wildflowers. At the head of the canyon the gray, volcanic rock of Rose Knob Peak forms a stark, contrasting background to the vibrant meadows. Over the years, numerous avalanches have swept down the side of Rose Knob Peak, delivering an ample supply of timber to the slopes at the base of the peak.

The area around Gray Lake is devoid of any established campsites, due to lack of use, although an increase in campers is sure to follow the recent completion of the TRT. Firewood is plentiful for the time being. Swimming appears dubious, but anglers may find the fishing good.

To return to the TRT, you have the option of retracing your steps or ascending the moderately graded trail southwest from the lake to a connection with the TRT west of Rose Knob Peak, 1.2 miles from the first junction.

switchbacks drop you past some rock cliffs to a 0.75-mile descending traverse of a northwest-trending ridge, from where you are allowed occasional vistas of the Lake and the mountainous terrain of the North Tahoe area. A scattered, mixed forest along the ridge begins to thicken toward the end of the

OPTIONS

Side Trip to Martis Peak

For a bird's-eye view from the lookout on Martis Peak, continue on the jeep road for 0.2 mile to a junction with the paved Martis Peak Road (FS16N02B). Turn right and head uphill, following the paved road for 0.7 mile to the lookout, perched on a small flat, 0.1 mile northwest of the true summit. Along with the restored lookout, you'll find a picnic table and an outhouse. Thanks to the paved road, you may also find tourists. At one time, Martis Peak was the only staffed fire lookout in the Tahoe Basin.

traverse, where the trail leaves the ridge to make a moderate descent to a saddle. From the saddle, a half-mile of easy trail through open areas of rock alternating with stands of forest brings you to a jeep road. ▶7 The TRT follows the course of the jeep road for about 0.4 mile before single-track trail resumes. At this point one can make a side trip to Martis Peak (see sidebar).

Leave the jeep road and descend on the single-track trail, quickly leaving the forest, to break out into a sloping meadow carpeted with mule ears. A short way beyond the meadow, you curve around the south ridge of Martis Peak and come to a rocky viewpoint. Once again, the TRT hiker is blessed with a superb vista of the Lake Tahoe basin. You see not only almost the entire lake, but the major summits surrounding the lake as well.

Great Views

Tearing yourself away from the beautiful view, you descend moderately back into scattered-to-light red-fir forest, interrupted on occasion by yet another clearing filled with mule ears, and farther on by a patch of head-high tobacco brush. At 2.25 miles from the Brockway Summit trailhead, you hop over a thin ribbon of water trickling down the hillside, where wildflowers, grasses and clumps of willow add a splash of vegetation that contrasts vividly with the otherwise dry surroundings. Beyond the thin rivulet, milder trail takes you through selectively logged forest. You then descend more moderately, to the crossing of well-graded gravel FS Road 16N33, just 150 yards southeast of the junction with paved Martis Peak Road. After crossing the road, just over a half-mile of easy hiking brings you to a junction with a spur trail to the top of Peak 7755. ▶8

A mildly graded 0.3-mile ascent takes you through trees and shrubs, including chinquapin, tobacco brush and huckleberry oak, up to a pile of rocks at the top of a hill. After the spectacular vistas previously encountered, this view seems fairly pedestrian. However, one last look at the lake may be warranted before you descend the last viewless mile of trail to the trailhead.

From the junction, 1.2 miles of hiking remain, as you follow the TRT on a moderate descent through a selectively logged forest of mainly white firs, with a few Jeffrey pines. As you near the Brockway Summit trailhead, a trio of switchbacks leads you down the hillside above California 267, past the TRT signboard, and out FS Road 56 to the highway. ▶9

🚶 MILESTONES

▶1 0.0 Start at Tahoe Meadows trailhead

▶2 2.5 Turn left at junction of old Mt. Rose Trail

▶3 3.25 Turn right at junction of Relay Ridge service road

▶4 5.3 Summit of Relay Peak

▶5 7.5 East Gray Lake junction

▶6 8.9 West Gray Lake junction

▶7 13.3 Jeep road

▶8 16.8 Viewpoint junction

▶9 18.0 End at Brockway trailhead

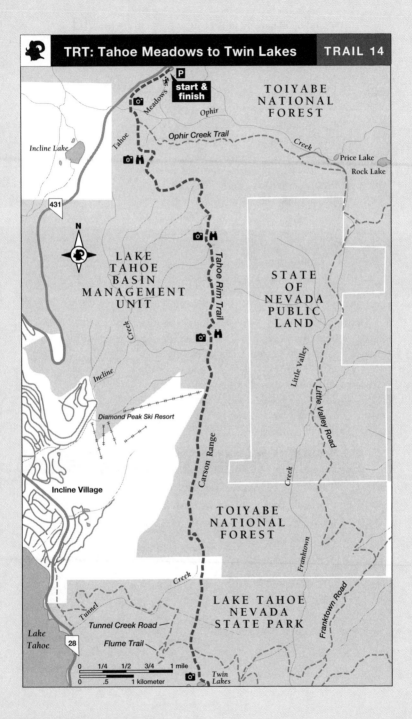

TRT: Tahoe Meadows to Twin Lakes

TRAIL 14

TOIYABE NATIONAL FOREST

P start & finish

Meadows

Ophir

Ophir Creek Trail

Creek

Price Lake

Rock Lake

Incline Lake

Tahoe

431

N

LAKE TAHOE BASIN MANAGEMENT UNIT

STATE OF NEVADA PUBLIC LAND

Tahoe Rim Trail

Creek

Incline

Little Valley

Little Valley Road

Diamond Peak Ski Resort

Carson Range

Incline Village

TOIYABE NATIONAL FOREST

Creek

Franktown

Creek

Franktown Road

LAKE TAHOE NEVADA STATE PARK

Tunnel

Tunnel Creek Road

Flume Trail

Creek

Lake Tahoe

28

0   1/4   1/2   3/4   1 mile

0   .5   1 kilometer

Twin Lakes

Tahoe Rim Trail: Tahoe Meadows to Twin Lakes

Much of this section of the Tahoe Rim Trail closely follows the crest of the Carson Range, affording travelers excellent views of the Lake Tahoe Basin to the west and the Great Basin to the east. Aside from a moderate climb from Tahoe Meadows, most of the trail follows an easy grade to Twin Lakes, a pair of shallow ponds that shrink considerably over the course of the average summer. Even considering the pleasantly graded trail, the 19-mile round-trip distance makes this suitable only for hikers in good condition. Lesser mortals can pick a shorter turn-around point and still be more than satisfied with the superb vistas. Although the largest part of this trail passes across sandy soil ill suited for wildflowers, the initial segment across Tahoe Meadows is an amateur botanists delight.

Best Time

This section of the Tahoe Rim Trail affords hikers excellent views of the Lake Tahoe Basin to the west and the Carson Valley to the east from Mid-July through October. Mid-summer is the best time to view the flowers in Tahoe Meadows.

Finding the Trail

From Reno, take Highway 395 to the Mt. Rose Highway (State Route 431) and travel west to the Mt. Rose Summit (8911 feet) and continue 0.7 mile to the Tahoe Rim trailhead parking lot on the south side of the highway, where you'll find restrooms and

TRAIL USE
Hike, Run, Bike, Horse
LENGTH
19.0 miles, 10 hours
VERTICAL FEET
±3525'
DIFFICULTY
– 1 2 3 **4** 5 +
TRAIL TYPE
Out & Back
SURFACE TYPE
Dirt

FEATURES
Dogs Allowed
Mountain
Wildflowers
Birds
Great Views
Photo Opportunity
Camping

FACILITIES
Restrooms
Picnic Tables
Water

running water. From Incline Village, the parking area is about 7.3 miles east of the 28/431 junction.

Logistics

Mountain Biking

Mountain biking is allowed on this section of the Tahoe Rim Trail from Tahoe Meadows to Tunnel Creek Road, but only on even days of the month. Hikers may want to limit their trips to the odd days, as the TRT itself and the connecting Tunnel Creek Road are very popular with the two-wheeled crowd.

Backpackers attempting the 23-mile segment of the TRT from Tahoe Meadows to Spooner Summit should be forewarned that water is at a premium along the entire route and that camping is limited to two designated sites inside Lake Tahoe Nevada State Park, Marlette Peak Campground, 13 miles south of the trailhead, and North Canyon Campground, 1.3 miles west of the TRT.

Trail Description

Wildflowers

▶1 Leave the TRT parking area and parallel the Mt. Rose Highway as you head southwest along the fringe of verdant Tahoe Meadows, stepping across several seeps along the way. Approaching a stand of lodgepole pines near the far end of the meadows, the trail veers south across the wildflower-carpeted meadowlands to a short, wood bridge over gurgling Ophir Creek. Depending on the season, you may see the blooms of buttercup, penstemon, marsh marigold, shooting star, and elephant head among the many species of wildflower that live near the creek. Remaining on the trail to avoid damaging the sensitive flora, you continue across the meadows and into the pines, soon meeting a use-trail to the Mt. Rose Highway. A short distance farther, veer right (south) at a signed Y-junction with the Ophir Creek Trail, 0.8 mile from the trailhead. ▶2

Tahoe Meadows

From the junction you follow the TRT on a moderate climb of a forested hillside where, near the crest, you get a partial view of Lake Tahoe. Step across an old dirt road and begin a traverse of the sparsely forested slopes above the Incline Creek watershed, arcing southeast and then east around peak 8996. Scattered western white pines allow periodic views across the lake of the peaks and ridges lining the Sierra crest and of additional Tahoe landmarks around the near shore. Where the sandy trail turns south again, approximately 3 miles from the trailhead, you encounter a pair of tiny rivulets, nascent tributaries of Incline Creek. ►3 These rivulets, lined with willows, wildflowers, and young aspens, may provide the only water source along the TRT between Ophir Creek and Twin Lakes, although late in the season both the rivulets and the lakes may be dry.

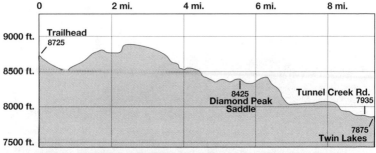

TRAIL 14 TRT: Tahoe Meadows to Twin Lakes Elevation Profile

Great Views

Continue traversing along the west side of the ridge, below the north-south apex of the Carson Range through sparse forest, which now includes some mountain hemlocks. Following a pair of switchbacks, you follow descending trail to a prominent saddle north of Peak 8777. Just beyond the saddle, the trail crosses to the east side of the ridge and you have your first views of Washoe Lake, Carson Valley, and the Virginia Range.

Follow the narrow ridgecrest, with alternating views to the east and west. Near the 5-mile mark you encounter an excellent viewpoint just off the trail, where flat-topped granite boulders provide a fine perch for enjoying the Tahoe view. Away from the vista point, the trail follows the east side of the ridge into a thicker forest of western white pines and red firs. Several signs and the top of a ski lift herald your arrival at another saddle, this one above the Diamond Peak Ski Resort between Peaks 8538 and 8510, 5.7 miles from the trailhead. ▶4

Leaving the saddle behind, the trail follows the west side of the ridge through scattered Jeffrey pines. In between the pines you have more excellent views of Lake Tahoe, as well as ski runs on Diamond Peak, Incline Village below, and the long ridge between Mt. Baldy and Relay Peak to the north. About 1 mile from the saddle, the trail once again crosses to the east side of the ridge and proceeds through fir forest. A little over a mile farther, you begin a moderate descent, with good views to the east. Eventually the path returns to the west side of the ridge, offering a few more lake views before entering a thick forest of red and white firs. You follow a mildly undulating trail through the trees to a well-signed junction at Tunnel Creek Road, 9.2 miles from the trailhead. ▶5

Cross the road and continue along the mildly graded TRT through a scattered forest of western white pines, red and white firs, and lodgepole pines, with an understory of pinemat manzanita. At 0.3 mile from the road, you encounter the eastern Twin Lake, in a broad, shallow bowl that is rimmed by forested hills. ▶6

🚶 MILESTONES

▶1	0.0	Start at trailhead
▶2	0.8	Veer right at Ophir Creek Trail junction
▶3	3±	Crossings of Incline Creek
▶4	5.7	Diamond Peak Saddle
▶5	9.2	Junction of Tunnel Creek Road
▶6	9.5	Twin Lakes

West Tahoe

West Tahoe

S andwiched between the mega-ski resorts of north Tahoe and the casinos and commercialism of south Tahoe, the west side of the lake seems relaxed and sedate. More than the other sides of the lake, the backcountry above the west shore is about walking through dense forests and strolling along peaceful streams, although the area is not entirely devoid of high summits with excellent vistas. You'll find plenty of history here as well, as a couple of state parks provide glimpses into the past.

Highway 89 provides the principal access to the west side of Lake Tahoe, with no other paved highways crossing the mountains between Tahoe City and South Lake Tahoe.

The Lake Tahoe Basin Management Unit oversees the national forests on the west side of the lake. Two state parks, Sugar Pine Point and D.L. Bliss, administer lakeshore units involving trails described in this chapter.

Maps and Permits

Permits are not required for either dayhikes or backpacks. Entry fees are collected for state parks.

Forest Service maps covering west Tahoe are available at the Taylor Creek Visitor Center or the ranger station in Truckee. USGS maps pertaining to the trips described in this chapter are listed in the Appendix.

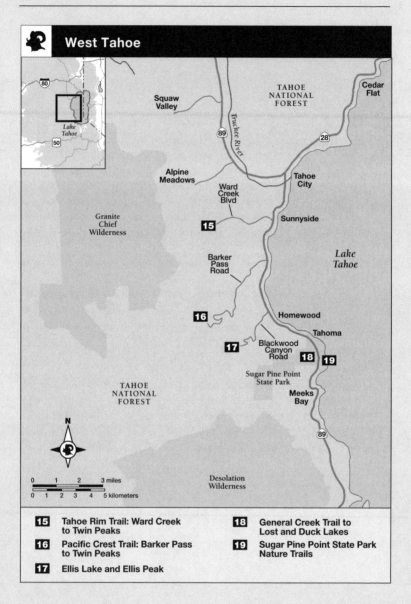

West Tahoe

Squaw Valley

TAHOE NATIONAL FOREST

Cedar Flat

80

Lake Tahoe

50

89

Truckee River

28

Alpine Meadows

Ward Creek Blvd

Tahoe City

Granite Chief Wilderness

15

Sunnyside

Lake Tahoe

Barker Pass Road

16

Homewood

Tahoma

17

Blackwood Canyon Road

18 **19**

Sugar Pine Point State Park

TAHOE NATIONAL FOREST

Meeks Bay

N

89

0   1   2   3 miles
0 1 2 3 4 5 kilometers

Desolation Wilderness

15	Tahoe Rim Trail: Ward Creek to Twin Peaks	**18**	General Creek Trail to Lost and Duck Lakes
16	Pacific Crest Trail: Barker Pass to Twin Peaks	**19**	Sugar Pine Point State Park Nature Trails
17	Ellis Lake and Ellis Peak		

West Lake Trails

TRAIL	Difficulty	Length	Type	USES & ACCESS	TERRAIN	FLORA & FAUNA	OTHER
15	3	11.6	↗	🚶 🏃 🚴 🐎 🐕	🏞️ ⛰️ △ 🏞️ ▮ ✳️		🔭 📷
16	4	11.2	↗	🚶 🏃 🚴 🐕	⛰️ △ ≋ ✳️ 🐦		🔭 📷
17	4	8.6	↗	🚶 🏃 🚴 🐕	⛰️ △ ≋		🔭 📷 △ 🙍
18	3	13.0	↗	🚶 🏃 🚴 🐎 👫 🏞️ ⛰️ 🏞️ ≋		🍃 🔭	△ 🙍
19	1	1.7	↻	🚶 ♿ 👫 ≋ ✳️ 🦌 🍃 🔭			

USE & ACCESS
- 🚶 Hiking
- 🏃 Trail Running
- 🚴 Mountain Biking
- 🐎 Horses
- 👫 Child Friendly
- 🐕 Dogs Allowed
- ♿ Handicap Access
- Permit Required
- P Parking Fee

TERRAIN
- 🏞️ Canyon
- ⛰️ Mountain
- △ Summit

WATER
- 🏞️ Stream
- ▮ Waterfall
- ≋ Lake/Shore

FLORA & FAUNA
- Autumn Colors
- ✳️ Wildflowers
- Birds
- 🦌 Wildlife

DIFFICULTY
- 1 2 3 4 5 +
less   more

OTHER
- 🔭 Cool & Shady
- 🔭 Great Views
- 📷 Photo Opportunity
- Secluded
- Historic
- Geologic Interest
- Moonlight Hiking
- Steep
- △ Camping

West Tahoe

TRAIL 18

Hike, Run, Bike, Horse
13.0 miles, Out & Back
Difficulty: 1 2 **3** 4 5

TRAIL 19

Hike
0.25 to 1.7 miles
Out & Back or Loop
Difficulty: **1** 2 3 4 5

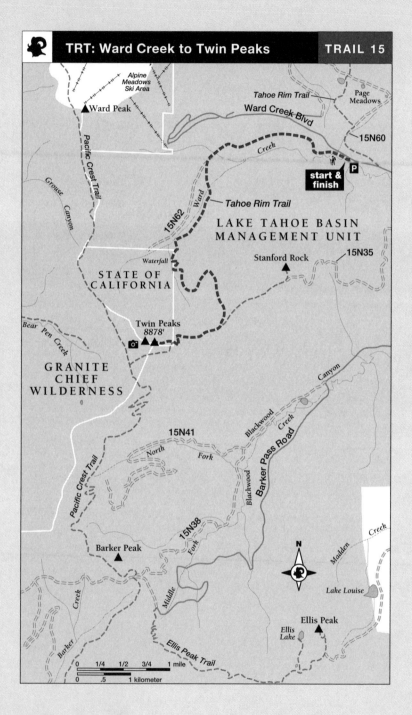

Alpine
Meadows
Ski Area

Tahoe Rim Trail

Page
Meadows

▲ Ward Peak

Ward Creek Blvd

15N60

Pacific Crest Trail

Creek

start &
finish

Grouse

Canyon

15N62

Ward

Tahoe Rim Trail

LAKE TAHOE BASIN
MANAGEMENT UNIT

Waterfall

Stanford Rock ▲

15N35

STATE OF
CALIFORNIA

Bear Pen Creek

Twin Peaks
8878'

📷 ▲ ▲

GRANITE
CHIEF
WILDERNESS

Canyon

15N41

Blackwood Creek

Barker Pass Road

North

Fork

Blackwood

Pacific Crest Trail

15N38

Fork

Barker Peak ▲

Middle

N

Madden

Creek

Lake Louise

Creek

Barker

Ellis Peak ▲

Ellis
Lake

Ellis Peak Trail

0   1/4   1/2   3/4   1 mile
0   .5   1 kilometer

Tahoe Rim Trail: Ward Creek to Twin Peaks

This trip combines of one of the best wildflower displays with one of the best summit views found anywhere in the Tahoe Basin. Despite such natural beauty, the trail is not as heavily used as one would expect. Most of the route follows the well-built Tahoe Rim Trail, but the last quarter-mile to the summit of east Twin Peak is a steep off-trail climb requiring a bit of scrambling.

Best Time

The spectacular wildflower display along Ward Creek peaks during July and early August, but the excellent view from the summit of Twin Peaks is fine anytime between mid-July and late October.

Finding the Trail

From Highway 89 near the community of Sunnyside, turn west onto Ward Creek Blvd. and proceed along paved road for 2 miles to a small turnout on the left-hand shoulder, where the trail is marked by a small TRT signboard and a 6 x 6 post.

Option

It is possible to arrange for a shuttle and combine this trip with Trip 17 to create a point-to-point excursion.

Trail Description

▶1 From the turnout, walk around a closed gate and follow a gently graded road through a mixed forest

TRAIL USE
Hike, Run, Bike, Horse
LENGTH
11.6 miles, 6 hours
VERTICAL FEET
±2400'
DIFFICULTY
– 1 2 **3** 4 5 +
TRAIL TYPE
Out & Back
SURFACE TYPE
Dirt

FEATURES
Dogs Allowed
Canyon
Mountain
Summit
Stream
Waterfall
Wildflowers
Great Views
Photo Opportunity

FACILITIES
None

of firs and pines, just to the left of bubbling, meadow-lined Ward Creek. Plenty of shrubs grow beside the road, including bitterbrush, currant, manzanita, and pinemat manzanita, interspersed with verdant grasses and a wide variety of wildflowers.

After 0.5 mile the road bends slightly away from the creek and proceeds along the valley floor, offering filtered views of the peaks and ridges along the canyon rim.

Wildflowers

You enter a verdant garden of wildflowers near the crossing of a tributary stream, 1.75 miles from Ward Creek Blvd., and continue another 0.5 mile through lush meadowlands to boulder hop across the main channel of Ward Creek. Beyond the crossing, head upstream, climbing mildly alongside the dancing creek amid more lush gardens. The profusion of wildflowers you're apt to see along Ward Canyon include aster, columbine, daisy, lupine, paintbrush, elephant head, corn lily, arnica, and Mariposa lily. At its height, this is one of the best wildflower displays in the Tahoe Basin. Continuing up the canyon, you encounter a thicker, mixed forest of lodgepole pines, western white pines, red firs, Jeffrey pines, and aspens, interspersed with pockets of lush foliage.

Waterfall

Eventually the trail bends away from the main channel of Ward Creek and follows a steeper route

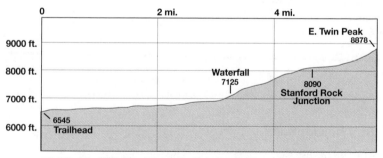

TRAIL 15   TRT: Ward Creek to Twin Peaks Elevation Profile

up the canyon of a side stream. Soon the sound of tumbling water heralds your approach to a 30-foot-high waterfall, 3.3 miles from the trailhead. Although the stream and fall fail to appear on the USGS map, the fall is known to locals as McLoud Falls. ▶2 Continue a switchbacking climb across flower-filled slopes and pockets of light forest, with improving views of the surrounding topography. At 4.8 miles from the trailhead, you reach the crest of the ridge and encounter a signed three-way junction with a path to your left, which heads toward the summit of Stanford Rock. ▶3 Peak baggers wishing to add Stanford Rock to their list of accomplishments can opt to follow this 0.9-mile one-way route to the top.

Turn right (west) at the junction and follow a rising trail along the ridge through western white pines and mountain hemlocks, with pinemat manzanita as the principal groundcover. Soon a steeper, switchbacking climb leads past a rock knob to an unmarked Y-junction at 5.5 miles. ▶4 (The TRT veers left and continues on a 0.5-mile traverse below Twin Peaks to a junction with the Pacific Crest Trail).

Veer right at the junction and climb steeply up the east ridge of Twin Peaks, where you'll be treated to stunning views across wildflower-covered slopes of Lake Tahoe, the summits of Desolation Wilderness, and all the surrounding canyons. Continue the steep ascent of the ridge and scramble over rocks to the east summit of Twin Peaks and an awe-inspiring 360° view. ▶5

> Be sure to pack along a map of the Tahoe area to help you identify all the landmarks visible from the vantage point of Twin Peaks.

▲ **Summit**

🚶	**MILESTONES**

▶1	0.0	Start at trailhead
▶2	3.3	McLoud Falls
▶3	4.8	Turn right (east) at Stanford Rock junction
▶4	5.5	Veer right at unmarked junction with use trail to summit
▶5	5.8	Summit of east Twin Peak

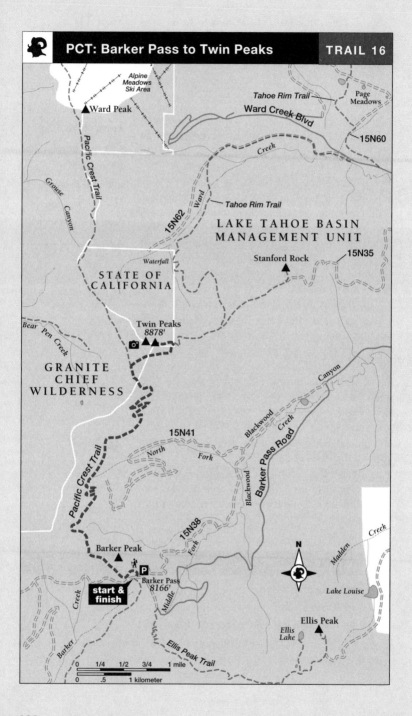

Alpine
Meadows
Ski Area

▲ Ward Peak

Tahoe Rim Trail

Page
Meadows

Ward Creek Blvd

15N60

Creek

Grouse

Canyon

Pacific Crest Trail

15N62

Ward

Tahoe Rim Trail

LAKE TAHOE BASIN
MANAGEMENT UNIT

Stanford Rock ▲

15N35

Waterfall

STATE OF
CALIFORNIA

Bear Pen Creek

Twin Peaks
8878'

📷 ▲ ▲

GRANITE
CHIEF
WILDERNESS

Canyon

Blackwood Creek

Pacific Crest Trail

15N41

North

Fork

Barker Pass Road

Blackwood

15N38

Fork

Barker Peak

▲

Madden Creek

N

🧭

Barker Pass
8166'

**start &
finish**

P

🚶

Lake Louise

Middle

Creek

Ellis Peak

Ellis
Lake

▲

Barker

Creek

Ellis Peak Trail

Middle

0   1/4   1/2   3/4   1 mile

0   .5   1 kilometer

Pacific Crest Trail: Barker Pass to Twin Peaks

Follow a segment of the Pacific Crest and Tahoe Rim trails to the east summit of Twin Peaks, from where hikers experience a fine view of Lake Tahoe and the surrounding terrain. From an open ridge along the Sierra crest, just before the PCT/TRT junction, you'll have additional views into the heart of Granite Chief Wilderness and the peaks of the more distant Desolation Wilderness.

Best Time

At this elevation the trail usually is snow free from mid-July to mid-October.

Finding the Trail

Near the community of Tahoe Pines, approximately 4.3 miles south of Tahoe City, turn west from Highway 89 onto Barker Pass Road (the junction is marked by signs for Sno-Park and Kaspian Campground). Follow paved road up Blackwood Canyon for 2.3 miles and bend left at a junction with FS Road 15N38, which continues straight ahead to an OHV staging area. Head across a bridge over Blackwood Creek and start the long climb toward the pass on the left side of the canyon. At 4.7 miles from the creek, reach the end of paved road near the rough dirt parking area for the Ellis Peak trailhead on the left. Continue on the well-graded dirt road another 0.4 mile to Barker Pass and the signed Pacific Crest Trail parking area on the right.

TRAIL USE
Hike, Run, Bike

LENGTH
11.2 miles, 8-12 hours

VERTICAL FEET
±1300'

DIFFICULTY
– 1 2 3 **4** 5 +

TRAIL TYPE
Out & Back

SURFACE TYPE
Dirt, Paved

FEATURES
Dogs Allowed
Mountains
Summit
Lake
Wildflowers
Birds
Great Views
Photo Opportunity

FACILITIES
None

Trail Description

 Summit

►1 Follow the wide, well-graded, and heavily-used PCT/TRT through light forest around the slopes of Barker Peak, to an open hillside carpeted with scattered shrubs and mule ears, with a fine view to the north of a pair of unnamed volcanic knobs along the Sierra crest. You continue in and out of light forest, crossing over an old road about a mile from the trailhead. A short distance beyond the road, a path branches away from the trail and quickly leads to the edge of the ridge, from where you have a good view of Blackwood Canyon. On rising trail you head northeast to a 4 x 4 post below the easternmost volcanic knob, 1.7 miles from the trailhead, where a short path followed by an easy scramble leads to a partial lake view atop the knob.

Away from the knob, you drop off the ridge and follow a switchbacking 1.7-mile descent across the head of the canyon of the North Fork Blackwood Creek, through mountain hemlocks, western white pines, and red firs, crossing numerous lushly-lined streams and seeps along the way.

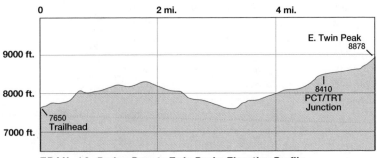

TRAIL 16 Barker Pass to Twin Peaks Elevation Profile

After bottoming out, you begin a switchbacking, mile-long climb through alternating sections of light forest and shrub-covered slopes toward a rocky sub-ridge above. Approaching the crest, follow the trail around the nose of the ridge and suddenly encounter a dramatic view of your ultimate goal, Twin Peaks. Continue climbing toward the Sierra crest, crossing the signed boundary of Granite Chief Wilderness on the way. From the exposed ridge you have a fine view down into the canyon of Bear Pen Creek. Reach the PCT/TRT junction at 4.8 miles from the trailhead. ▶2

Turn right to follow the TRT across the south slope below Twin Peaks. After 0.5 mile you encounter an unsigned junction with a use-trail to the top of the eastern peak. ▶3 Veer left at the junction and climb steeply up the east ridge of Twin Peaks, where you'll be treated to stunning views across wildflower-covered slopes of Lake Tahoe, the summits of Desolation Wilderness, and the surrounding canyons. Continue the steep ascent of the ridge and scramble over rocks to the east summit of Twin Peaks and an awe-inspiring 360° view. ▶4

Be sure to pack along a map of the Tahoe area to help you identify all the landmarks visible from the vantage point of Twin Peaks.

Great Views

🚶	**MILESTONES**	
▶1	0.0	Start at trailhead
▶2	4.8	Turn right (east) at PCT/TRT junction
▶3	5.3	Veer left at unmarked junction
▶4	5.6	Summit of Twin Peaks

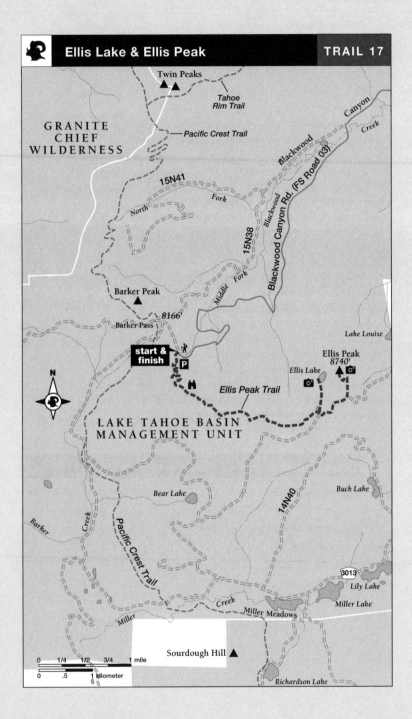

GRANITE
CHIEF
WILDERNESS

Twin Peaks

Tahoe
Rim Trail

Pacific Crest Trail

Canyon

Creek

Blackwood

Blackwood Canyon Rd. (FS Road 03)

15N41

North

Fork

15N38

Middle Fork

Barker Peak

8166'

Barker Pass

Lake Louise

start &
finish

P

Ellis Peak
8740'

Ellis Lake

Ellis Peak Trail

LAKE TAHOE BASIN
MANAGEMENT UNIT

N

Bear Lake

Buck Lake

14N40

Barker

Creek

Pacific Crest Trail

3013

Lily Lake

Miller Lake

Creek

Miller Meadows

Miller

0   1/4   1/2   3/4   1 mile

0   .5   1 kilometer

Sourdough Hill

Richardson Lake

Ellis Lake and Ellis Peak

Ellis Lake and Ellis Peak occupy a ridgetop that lies between Blackwood and McKinney canyons. Blackwood Canyon contains a paved road, while a major OHV track runs through McKinney Canyon. In contrast, Ellis Lake and Peak are an island backcountry sanctuary. Although the first 0.7 miles of trail are as steep as any in the Tahoe Basin, and motorcycles are unfortunately allowed, few routes will take you in such a short distance to both a scenic lake and a 360° mountaintop vista.

Best Time

Once the snow leaves the trail in mid-July, trail users can usually enjoy the vistas from the summit or the shores of the lake until the end of October.

Finding the Trail

Near the community of Tahoe Pines, approximately 4.3 miles south of Tahoe City, turn west from Highway 89 onto Barker Pass Road (the junction is marked by signs for Sno-Park and Kaspian Campground). Follow paved road up Blackwood Canyon for 2.3 miles and bend left at a junction with FS Road 15N38, which continues straight ahead to an OHV staging area. Head across a bridge over Blackwood Creek and start the long climb toward the pass on the left side of the canyon. At 4.7 miles from the creek and 0.4 mile before Barker Pass, reach the end of paved road and, on the left, find the rough dirt parking area for the Ellis Peak trailhead.

TRAIL USE
Hike, Run, Bike
LENGTH
8.6 miles, 5 hours
VERTICAL FEET
+1475'/-425'
DIFFICULTY
− 1 2 3 **4** 5 +
TRAIL TYPE
Out & Back
SURFACE TYPE
Dirt

FEATURES
Dogs Allowed
Mountain
Summit
Lake
Great Views
Photo Opportunity
Camping
Steep

FACILITIES
None

Ellis Lake

Trail Description

►1 In a take-no-prisoners fashion, the Ellis Peak Trail starts climbing steeply right from the start, as you follow stiff, winding trail up the red-fir and lodgepole-pine-forested hillside. If you survive the first 0.7-mile, the grade becomes less sadistic at the crest of an open ridge, where good views of Desolation Wilderness, Twin Peaks, and Blackwood Canyon will cheer you while you attempt to catch your breath.

Steep

Leaving the switchbacks and the forest behind, you make a less intimidating ascent along the crest of the ridge through very widely scattered, wind beaten pines and a mixture of shrubs, including bitterbrush, sagebrush, and tobacco brush. In mid-summer, mule ears and lupines add splashes of color to the desert-like slopes. Ascend the ridge for 0.5 mile, before leaving the ridge and the views behind on a 0.75-mile descent through a forest of firs, lodgepole pines, and mountain hemlocks, reaching a small meadow in a broad saddle near the 2-mile mark.

A gently graded section of old road leads away from the saddle and across slopes that were selectively logged at some time in the past. Just before the road becomes steeper, you reach an unmarked junction with a faint path, on your left. Make the short and steep climb up the road to a signed junction, 2.7 miles from the trailhead. ▶2

To reach Ellis Lake, turn left (north) at the junction and follow the road on a mild descent through the trees. After 0.4 mile you reach the southwest shore of the forest-rimmed lake, which is nicely backdropped by the rugged cliffs of Ellis Peak. ▶3 A few passable campsites can be found scattered around the lake.

▲ **Camping**

To reach Ellis Peak, follow the single-track trail that climbs steeply up the hillside from the junction. ▶4 After 0.3 mile, the trail merges with the road again (the right-hand road at the junction) and you continue climbing toward the summit, which has recently come into view. The road rises steeply toward the base of the summit rocks, but watch carefully for a cairn marking a section of faint single-track trail that ascends the right-hand side of the peak to the far end of the ridge at the summit of Ellis Peak. ▶5 From the summit you have a commanding view of Lake Tahoe to the east and the peaks of Desolation Wilderness to the southwest. Straight down the steep cliffs on the west face of the peak is shimmering Ellis Lake, and across the deep cleft of Blackwood Canyon is Twin Peaks.

🚶 **MILESTONES**

▶1   0.0   Start at trailhead
▶2   2.7   Turn left (north) at junction for Ellis Lake
▶3   3.1   Ellis Lake
▶4   3.5   Return to junction and turn left (northeast) for Ellis Peak
▶5   4.3   Summit of Ellis Peak

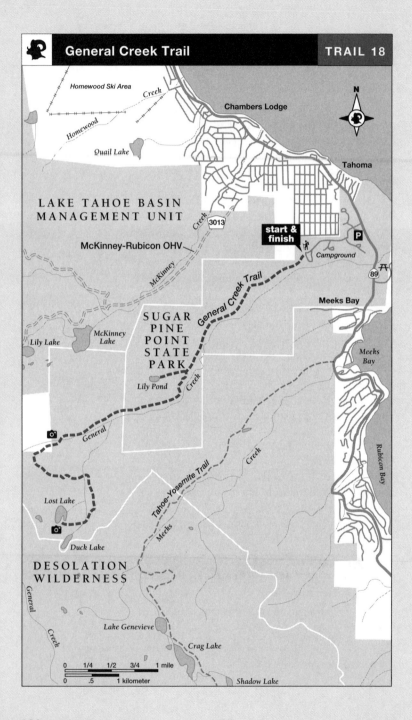

General Creek Trail

TRAIL 18

N

Homewood Ski Area

Creek

Chambers Lodge

Homewood

Quail Lake

Tahoma

LAKE TAHOE BASIN
MANAGEMENT UNIT

Creek

3013

McKinney-Rubicon OHV

**start &
finish**

P

Campground

89

McKinney

General Creek Trail

Meeks Bay

SUGAR
PINE
POINT
STATE
PARK

McKinney
Lake

Meeks
Bay

Lily Lake

Lily Pond

Creek

General

Tahoe-Yosemite Trail

Creek

Rubicon Bay

Lost Lake

Meeks

DESOLATION
WILDERNESS

Duck Lake

General

Creek

Lake Genevieve

Crag Lake

0   1/4   1/2   3/4   1 mile
0   .5   1 kilometer

Shadow Lake

General Creek Trail to Lost and Duck Lakes

These two quiet lakes are far enough off the beaten path to insure a peaceful visit for those in search of some serenity. The first 2.75 miles follow a cool and shady course up the wide, forested valley of General Creek, gaining only 200 feet of elevation along the way to the Lily Pond junction. A short climb beyond the junction to Lily Pond leads to a good turnaround point for groups with young children, or anyone else looking for a relaxing stroll. Past the junction, the General Creek Trail climbs more steeply before reaching the lakes, which provide refreshing swimming opportunities.

Best Time

The trip along General Creek can be done as early as June in average years, but you'll have to wait until mid-July for the lakes trail to be snow free. Mid-October is generally the best time to view the vivid autumn colors along the creek, before the first snowfall blankets the area in November.

Finding the Trail

Drive Highway 89 to the west entrance into Sugar Pine Point State Park, approximately 9 miles south of Tahoe City and 18 miles north of the junction of Highways 50 and 89 in South Lake Tahoe. Following signs for General Creek Campground, head past the entrance station (fee required), and continue to the day-use parking lot.

TRAIL USE
Hike, Run, Bike, Horse
LENGTH
13.0 miles, 7 hours
VERTICAL FEET
±1600'
DIFFICULTY
– 1 2 **3** 4 5 +
TRAIL TYPE
Out & Back
SURFACE TYPE
Dirt

FEATURES
Child Friendly
Canyon
Mountain
Stream
Lakes
Cool & Shady
Great Views
Camping
Secluded

FACILITIES
Visitor Center
Restrooms
Picnic Tables
Water
Phone

131

Lost Lake

Trail Description

▶1 From the day-use parking area, follow paved paths to the end of the campground and the start of the North Fire Road near campsite No. 150. Head southwest on the wide dirt track of the old road on a gentle grade amid shady, mixed forest composed of red and white firs, Jeffrey pines, incense cedars, and — the park's namesake trees — sugar pines. Eventually you find yourself on a single-track trail that makes a virtually imperceptible climb up the broad floor of the canyon, a good distance away from the placid, meandering creek and bordering meadowlands. Continue the gentle stroll through the serenity of a dense forest. Beyond a bridge over a diminutive side stream, you reach a junction marked by a 4 x 4 post, 2.75 miles from the parking lot, where the right-hand path follows a short climb to Lily Pond (no bikes). ▶2 Although not the most scenic body of water on this trip, shallow Lily Pond will provide amateur botanists with a few interesting plant species, including pond lilies and bulrushes.

To continue to Lost and Duck lakes, veer left at the Lily Pond junction and continue upstream along the General Creek Trail, through dense forest and lush trailside plants. Eventually the gentle terrain comes to an end where the canyon walls narrow and the grade increases, forcing the trail away from the valley floor on a moderate climb across the right-hand side of the gorge. The steady climb is briefly interrupted at a 4 x 4 post, where, following signage for Lost Lake, you turn left and drop to a crossing of General Creek, at 4.4 miles from the trailhead. ▶3 Short cascades drop into lovely pools along this section of the creek, providing a fine opportunity for a rest stop, lunch break, or perhaps a refreshing dip.

Beyond the creek crossing, make a 0.3-mile climb over granite slabs and around granite humps and boulders to a T-junction marked with a 6 x 6 post. ▶4 Following signed directions for Lost Lake, you turn left and proceed on the wide track of an old dirt road on a short, steep climb to the crest of a minor ridge. A forested descent from the ridge offers a brief respite from the laborious ascent, beneath the shade of lodgepole pines and firs. All too soon you start climbing again on rocky road. After awhile, a thick tangle of alders, grasses, and wildflowers heralds your arrival at a crossing of the creek draining Lost and Duck lakes, 5.5 miles from the trailhead. Continue climbing for another 0.6 mile to a second crossing of the creek. Here the road bends west and follows a gentle 0.4-mile course to a peninsula at the south shore of forest-rimmed Lost Lake. ▶5 Although no defined path exists, Duck Lake is an easy 250-yard trek south from Lost Lake.

Lily Pond provides a good destination for those interested in a short, easy hike.

▶◀ **Stream**

MILESTONES

▶1	0.0	Start at trailhead
▶2	2.75	Veer left at Lily Pond junction
▶3	4.4	Turn left and cross General Creek
▶4	4.7	Turn left at junction
▶5	6.5	Lost Lake

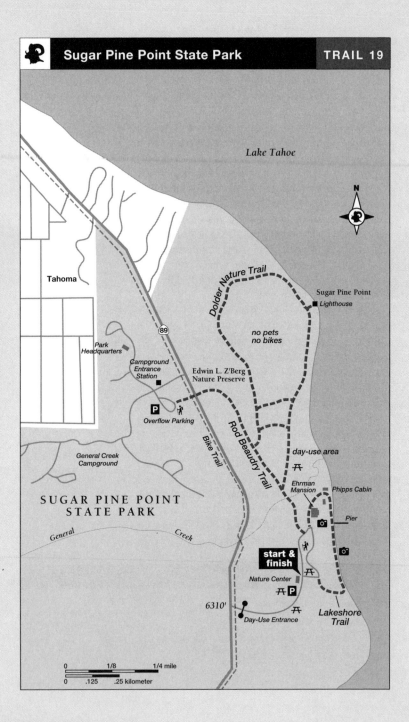

Lake Tahoe

N

Dolder Nature Trail

Sugar Pine Point
■ Lighthouse

no pets
no bikes

Tahoma

89

Park
Headquarters

Campground
Entrance
Station

Edwin L. Z'Berg
Nature Preserve

P

Overflow Parking

General Creek
Campground

Bike Trail

Rod Beaudry Trail

day-use area

Ehrman
Mansion

Phipps Cabin

Pier

SUGAR PINE POINT
STATE PARK

General   Creek

start &
finish

Nature Center

P

6310'

Day-Use Entrance

Lakeshore
Trail

0   1/8   1/4 mile
0   .125   .25 kilometer

Sugar Pine Point State Park Nature Trails

Sugar Pine Point State Park has a trio of easy nature trails that are sure to please the most discriminating sightseer. History abounds on the quarter-mile Lakefront Interpretive Trail, including the opportunity to tour one of Tahoe's splendid architectural wonders, the Hellman-Erhman Mansion. The Rod Beaudry Trail provides a connection between the mansion grounds and the General Creek Campground through the Edwin L. Zberg Natural Preserve. The 1.7-mile loop along the Dolder Nature Trail offers a serene stroll past a sandy beach with beautiful lake views to the Sugar Pine Point Lighthouse, and a return through quiet forest to the day-use parking area. Be sure to pack a lunch to enjoy at any of the several excellent picnic spots sprinkled around the park.

Best Time

Expect to find conditions good from May to November on these short lakeshore trails. Tours of the Hellman-Erhman Mansion are conducted twice daily from July to Labor Day.

Finding the Trail

Drive Highway 89 to the east entrance into Sugar Pine Point State Park, approximately 10 miles south

TRAIL USE
Hike
LENGTH*
VERTICAL FEET*
DIFFICULTY*
*See table below
TRAIL TYPE
Out & Back, Loop
SURFACE TYPE
Paved, Dirt

FEATURES
Child Friendly
Handicap Accessible
Shore
Wildflowers
Wildlife
Cool & Shady
Great Views

FACILITIES
Restrooms
Picnic Tables
Water
Visitor Center

🚶 DESTINATIONS	LENGTH	VERTICAL FEET	DIFFICULTY
Lakefront Interpretive Tr.	0.25 mile, 15 minutes	negligible	– **1** 2 3 4 5 +
Ron Beadry Trail	1.0 mile, 0.5 hour	negligible	– **1** 2 3 4 5 +
Dolder Nature Trail	1.7 miles, 1 hour	negligible	– **1** 2 3 4 5 +

of Tahoe City and 17 miles north of the junction of Highways 50 and 89 in South Lake Tahoe. Follow the short access road to the day-use parking lot (fee required) near the Nature Center and the Hellman-Erhman Mansion.

Trail Description

Lakefront Interpretive Trail: From the day-use parking lot, acquire a guide from the Nature Center (and tickets for the Mansion tour, if you are so inclined) and then wander down a dirt road toward the shoreline of Lake Tahoe to the start of the paved Lakefront Interpretive Trail. Begin your stroll near the South Boathouse and proceed northbound along the picturesque shore. You have excellent views across the sapphire-blue waters of the lake to a number of significant Tahoe landmarks, including several Carson Range peaks above the far shore. Picnic tables and park benches invite you to relax, linger and enjoy the scenery. Nearing the end of the quarter-mile trail, you pass below the expansive manicured lawn rising up to the striking Hellman-Ehrman Mansion, also known as Pine Lodge. The mansion was built in 1903 and was sold to California State Parks in 1965. The Lakefront Interpretive Trail ends near a cluster of buildings at the north end. From there you can retrace your steps to the parking lot, or follow the road behind the mansion and past the Nature Center to the day-use area.

Rod Beaudry Trail: From the day-use parking lot, follow paved road past the Nature Center and tennis courts to the beginning of the trail near the public restroom building. Turn left, leave the Mansion grounds and follow a paved path on a short descent to a wood bridge over lushly lined General Creek.

Shore

Hellman-Ehrman Mansion

Beyond the bridge you enter the Edwin L. Zberg Natural Preserve, named for a California legislator who championed many environmental protections for Lake Tahoe in the 1960s. Reach a Y-junction just beyond the bridge, where the dirt path of the Dolder Nature Trail veers left.

Continue on paved trail, passing through mixed forest typical of the west shore, including incense cedars, red and white firs, Jeffrey pine, and an occasional sugar pine. Soon a grassy clearing appears, which allows filtered glimpses of Lake Tahoe through the trees on the far side of the clearing. After a short while, you reach another junction with a dirt path that provides an alternate connection to the Dolder Nature Trail and, in the opposite direction, access to a small stretch of beach. Back into forest, a mildly rising climb leads to a crossing of

Ehrman boat dock

Highway 89 and the bike path just beyond the far shoulder. A short walk from there brings you to the day-use parking lot near General Creek Campground. Without arrangements for pickup, you'll have to retrace your steps to the day-use parking area near the Nature Center.

 Great Views

Dolder Nature Trail: ▶1 From the day-use parking lot, follow the Rod Beaudry Trail, described above, to the junction with the Dolder Nature Trail (bicycles and dogs are not permitted). ▶2

Head north on a dirt, single-track trail through light forest and verdant groundcover to a grassy clearing which, in summer, is sprinkled with lupine and penstemon. Veering toward the lakeshore, you cross a couple of connecting trails that provide access from the Rod Beaudry Trail to a section of sandy beach and a fine lake view. Back into forest, parallel the now rocky shoreline of Lake Tahoe until reaching a three-way junction, 0.6 mile from the day-use parking lot. ▶3 A short walk down the path toward the lake leads to the Sugar Pine Point Lighthouse, which in modern times is simply a blinking light atop a steel pole, mounted on a wood deck supported by four concrete pillars. Although less than noteworthy in appearance, the 6200-foot elevation makes this "lighthouse" the world's highest operational navigational light.

Back on the main trail, you continue the secluded forest stroll; eventually arcing away from the shoreline and following a mildly rising trail toward the trailhead. Ignore a couple of little-used paths from the General Creek Campground and proceed to a junction in a clearing. ▶4 A right turn will get you to the Rod Beaudry Trail, while a left turn connects to the beginning section of the Dolder Nature Trail. You can return to the day-use parking area via either trail. ▶5

🚶	**MILESTONES (DOLDER NATURE TRAIL)**

▶1	0.0	Start at day-use parking lot
▶2	0.15	Veer right at junction with Dolder Nature Trail
▶3	0.6	Junction with trail to lighthouse
▶4	1.5	Junction with return trails
▶5	1.7	Return to day-use parking lot

CHAPTER 3

South Tahoe

South Tahoe

The area around the south shore of Lake Tahoe contains some of the most picturesque and consequently most heavily used terrain around the lake. D.L. Bliss State Park and neighboring Emerald Bay State Park manage lakeshore tracts around Lake Tahoe that draw tourists and recreationists like a magnet to sandy beaches, picnic areas, campgrounds, and historical sites. Trails in these parks offer some of the best lakeshore views of Tahoe within the basin.

The 63,960-acre Desolation Wilderness, being blessed with an abundance of glacier-scoured lakes and granite peaks, is the most visited wilderness per square mile of any wilderness area in the entire country. The 105,165-acre Mokelumne Wilderness, south of Lake Tahoe, is a rugged landscape of volcanic peaks and lofty ridges that tower over deep canyons. The part of the wilderness that lies near Carson Pass is nearly as popular as Desolation.

Access to trailheads around the south shore of Lake Tahoe is straightforward via Highways 89 and 50, although summer traffic can be quite congested at times, especially in South Lake Tahoe. A mass transit system for Lake Tahoe has received considerable attention since President Clinton's Lake Tahoe Summit in the 1990s, but more work is needed in order for the system to be effective. Highway 88 services trailheads in and around the Mokelumne Wilderness.

Permits and Maps

The South Tahoe region is administered by a number of state and federal agencies. California State Parks oversees 6 miles of Lake Tahoe' shoreline and 1830 acres of surrounding lands in D.L. Bliss and Emerald Bay state parks. Free brochures with sketch maps are available from the parks, or for online viewing at the state parks website, **www.parks.ca.gov**. Trips 21-23 occur within these parks. Both parks charge a nominal entry fee.

The Lake Tahoe Basin Management Unit and the Eldorado National Forest manage trips 20, and 24-32, all which enter Desolation Wilderness at some point. Available by self-registration at most trailheads, free day-use permits are required for all dayhikes that enter the wilderness. In addition, parking at the Eagle Lake (Trip 24) and Pyramid Creek (Trip 32) trailheads is subject to a nominal fee.

Backpackers wishing to overnight within Desolation Wilderness have a rigorous set of hoops to jump through in order to secure a permit. Wilderness permits are required throughout the year, but an overnight quota is in effect from Memorial Day weekend through the end of September. Half the permits can be reserved ahead of time, beginning the third Thursday in April, either by phone: (530) 644-2349, by fax: (530) 295-5624, or by mail: 3070 Camino Heights Dr., Camino, CA 95709. A nonrefundable $5 fee per party is charged for each permit. Reserved permits can be picked up in person, mailed, or faxed. The other half of the permits can be picked up at participating ranger stations on a first-come, first served basis.

In addition to the $5 reservation charge, fees are also collected for overnight use of Desolation Wilderness. Per-person costs for one night in the backcountry are $5 and $10 for 2 or more nights, up to 14 nights total. The cost of a single permit is not to exceed $100 per party. Children 12 and under are free. All fees are payable by credit card check, or money order.

Trips 33-34 are within areas managed by the Eldorado National Forest. Currently, permits are not necessary for dayhikes into the Mokelumne Wilderness, but overnight visits do require a free wilderness permit. Within the Carson Pass Management Area, between Memorial Day and Labor Day weekends, a two-night limit is in effect for Round Top and Winnemucca lakes (three-night limit for Fourth of July Lake), and camping is limited to designated sites. Permits for these campsites are available on a first-come, first-served basis from the Carson Pass Information Station. Campfires are not permitted within the CPMA or along the Blue Hole Trail, but are allowed below 8,000 feet within the rest of the wilderness.

The USFS produces excellent waterproof plastic topographic maps of both Desolation Wilderness and Mokelumne Wilderness at a scale of 2 inches = 1 mile for $7.00 each. Maps are available from the Taylor Creek and Carson Pass visitor centers as well as from Forest Service headquarters and district ranger stations. The USGS 7.5-minute quadrangles specific to this area are listed in the Appendix.

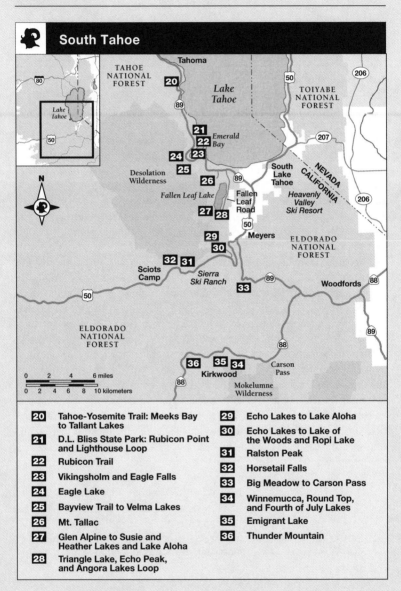

South Tahoe

20	Tahoe-Yosemite Trail: Meeks Bay to Tallant Lakes
21	D.L. Bliss State Park: Rubicon Point and Lighthouse Loop
22	Rubicon Trail
23	Vikingsholm and Eagle Falls
24	Eagle Lake
25	Bayview Trail to Velma Lakes
26	Mt. Tallac
27	Glen Alpine to Susie and Heather Lakes and Lake Aloha
28	Triangle Lake, Echo Peak, and Angora Lakes Loop
29	Echo Lakes to Lake Aloha
30	Echo Lakes to Lake of the Woods and Ropi Lake
31	Ralston Peak
32	Horsetail Falls
33	Big Meadow to Carson Pass
34	Winnemucca, Round Top, and Fourth of July Lakes
35	Emigrant Lake
36	Thunder Mountain

South Lake Trails

TRAIL	Difficulty	Length	Type	USES & ACCESS	TERRAIN	FLORA & FAUNA	OTHER
20	4	16.0	↗	Hiking, Trail Running, Horses, Dogs Allowed	Canyon, Mountain, Summit, Stream, Lake/Shore	Wildflowers	Photo Opportunity, Camping
21	1	2.0	↻	Hiking, Child Friendly	Lake/Shore		Great Views, Photo Opportunity
22	2	5.0	↘	Hiking, Child Friendly	Lake/Shore		Great Views, Photo Opportunity
23	2	2.5	↗	Hiking, Handicap Access, Child Friendly	Waterfall, Lake/Shore		Great Views, Photo Opportunity, Secluded, Historic
24	2	2.0	↗	Hiking, Trail Running, Dogs Allowed, Child Friendly	Canyon, Mountain, Stream, Waterfall, Lake/Shore		Photo Opportunity, Camping, Geologic Interest
25	4	10.5	↻	Hiking, Trail Running, Horses, Dogs Allowed	Canyon, Mountain, Stream, Lake/Shore	Wildflowers	Photo Opportunity, Camping
26	5	9.4	↗	Hiking, Trail Running, Dogs Allowed	Canyon, Summit, Stream, Mountain, Lake/Shore	Wildflowers	Great Views, Photo Opportunity
27	4	11.8	↗	Hiking, Trail Running, Horses, Dogs Allowed	Canyon, Mountain, Stream, Waterfall, Lake/Shore	Wildflowers	Great Views, Photo Opportunity, Camping
28	5	7.2	↻	Hiking	Canyon, Mountain, Summit, Lake/Shore	Wildflowers	Great Views, Photo Opportunity, Secluded, Steep
29	2-3	12.6	↗	Hiking, Trail Running, Horses, Dogs Allowed, Child Friendly	Mountain, Lake/Shore	Wildflowers	Photo Opportunity, Camping
30	3-4	13.0	↗	Hiking, Trail Running, Horses, Dogs Allowed	Mountain, Lake/Shore	Wildflowers, Birds	Camping
31	4	6.0	↗	Hiking, Trail Running, Dogs Allowed	Canyon, Mountain, Summit	Wildflowers, Birds	Great Views, Photo Opportunity, Steep, Secluded
32	3	3.0	↗	Hiking	Canyon, Mountain, Stream, Waterfall		Great Views, Photo Opportunity
33	3	10.4	↘	Hiking, Trail Running, Horses, Dogs Allowed	Canyon, Mountain, Stream, Lake/Shore	Wildflowers, Autumn Colors, Birds, Wildlife	Historic, Great Views, Photo Opportunity, Camping, Steep
34	3	4.8	↻	Hiking, Trail Running, Horses, Dogs Allowed	Canyon, Mountain, Stream, Lake/Shore	Wildflowers	Photo Opportunity, Camping, Historic
35	3	8.2	↗	Hiking, Trail Running, Horses, Dogs Allowed	Canyon, Mountain, Stream, Lake/Shore	Wildflowers	Photo Opportunity, Camping, Secluded
36	3	8.5	↗	Hiking, Trail Running, Mountain Biking, Horses, Dogs Allowed	Mountain, Summit	Wildlife	Great Views, Photo Opportunity

Legend

USE & ACCESS
- Hiking
- Trail Running
- Mountain Biking
- Horses
- Child Friendly
- Dogs Allowed
- Handicap Access
- Permit Required
- P Parking Fee

TERRAIN
- Canyon
- Mountain
- Summit

WATER
- Stream
- Waterfall
- Lake/Shore

FLORA & FAUNA
- Autumn Colors
- Wildflowers
- Birds
- Wildlife

OTHER
- Cool & Shady
- Great Views
- Photo Opportunity
- Secluded
- Historic
- Geologic Interest
- Moonlight Hiking
- Steep
- Camping

DIFFICULTY
- 1 2 3 4 5 +
less   more

South Tahoe

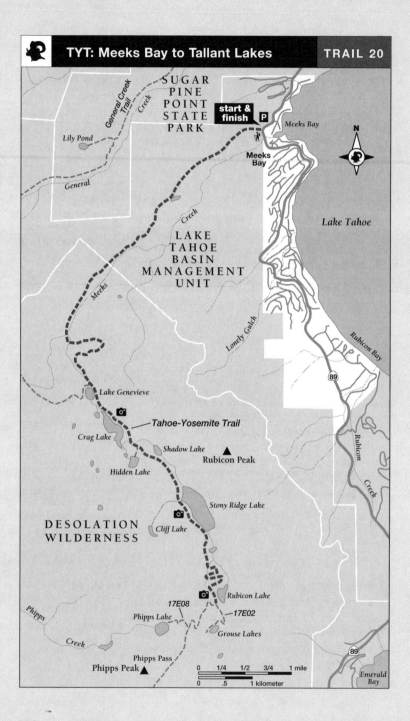

SUGAR
PINE
POINT
STATE
PARK

General Creek Trail

Creek

start &
finish P

Meeks Bay

Lily Pond

General

N

Creek

Meeks Bay

Lake Tahoe

LAKE
TAHOE
BASIN
MANAGEMENT
UNIT

Meeks

Lonely Gulch

Rubicon Bay

89

Rubicon

Lake Genevieve

Tahoe-Yosemite Trail

Crag Lake

Shadow Lake

Rubicon Peak

Rubicon

Creek

Hidden Lake

Stony Ridge Lake

DESOLATION
WILDERNESS

Cliff Lake

Phipps

17E08

Rubicon Lake

Phipps Lake

17E02

Creek

Grouse Lakes

89

Phipps Pass

Phipps Peak

| 0 | 1/4 | 1/2 | 3/4 | 1 mile |
| 0 | .5 | | 1 kilometer | |

Emerald
Bay

Tahoe-Yosemite Trail:
Meeks Bay to Tallant Lakes

Along the north section of the famed Tahoe-Yosemite Trail, hikers follow Meeks Creek from its placid terminus at Meeks Bay upstream into Desolation Wilderness along a raucous course to its headwaters below Phipps Pass. The upper canyon boasts a string of seven picturesque lakes, precious jewels known locally as the Tallant Lakes, offering excellent opportunities for fishing, swimming, camping, or simply relaxing. Backpackers and equestrians with extra time will find plenty of connecting trails providing several options for lengthier journeys into the heart of the backcountry.

Best Time

Snow covers this section of the TYT until mid-July. Wildflowers are generally at their peak from late July to mid-August, but so are the mosquitoes. September offers mild weather, fewer people, and fewer mosquitoes.

Finding the Trail

Follow Highway 89 to Meeks Bay and find the trailhead near a closed gate on the west side of the highway, 0.1 mile north of the entrance to the Meeks Bay Campground. The trailhead is approximately 16.5 miles north of the Highway 50-89 junction in South Lake Tahoe, and 11 miles south of Tahoe City.

TRAIL USE
Hike, Run, Horse
LENGTH
16.0 miles, 8 hours
VERTICAL FEET
±2200'
DIFFICULTY
− 1 2 3 **4** 5 +
TRAIL TYPE
Out & Back
SURFACE TYPE
Dirt

FEATURES
Dogs Allowed
Canyon
Mountain
Stream
Lakes
Wildflowers
Photo Opportunity
Camping

FACILITIES
None

Logistics

Overnight visitors must have a wilderness permit. The closest location to the trailhead to obtain one is the Taylor Creek Visitor Center.

Trail Description

▶1 Follow the gentle incline of an old dirt road across the north side of the broad, lush valley of Meeks Creek through a mixed forest of incense cedars, white firs, lodgepole pines, ponderosa pines, and sugar pines. After an easy 1.5 miles, the grade increases, as you forsake the old road at a well-marked junction and follow single-track trail past verdant foliage near a seeping spring to the signed wilderness boundary, at 2.5 miles.

Beyond the wilderness boundary, the trail roughly parallels the creek, which is within earshot but mostly out of sight. Through alternating groves of conifers and pocket meadows you continue up the canyon to a log and timber bridge across the creek at 3.3 miles.

A moderate climb follows an arcing path around a red-fir-forested side canyon filled with thimbleberry, fireweed, vine maple, and currant. Climbing out of this canyon, you circle around the nose of an open sub-ridge with a partial view of Lake Tahoe to rejoin Meeks Creek. A steady climb alongside the tumbling creek leads to a three-way junction marked by a 6 x 6 post, 4.6 miles from the trailhead. ▶2 The old Lake Genevieve Trail leading off to the right is a seldom-used lateral providing connections to the General Creek and Pacific Crest trails. Just beyond the junction is Lake Genevieve, a greenish, shallow lake rimmed by pines. A number of fair campsites are spread around the far shoreline, but more appealing sites with better scenery are just a short distance up the trail at Crag Lake.

 Camping

Granite slabs *along the Tahoe-Yosemite Trail*

Follow the TYT around the east shore of Lake Genevieve and make a short steady climb through western white pines, red firs, and Jeffrey pines to Crag Lake. ▶3 The lake has a splendid backdrop from the granitic slopes of 9054-foot Crag Peak to the south. Overnighters should look for good campsites above the northeast shore.

〰 Lake

Pass around the lengthy east shore of Crag Lake and ascend rocky trail to a boulder hop of Meeks Creek. Just past the creek, an unmarked use-trail travels southwest to Hidden Lake, a shallow, irregularly shaped pond near the base of Crag Peak. A steeper climb through thick forest ascends some morainal ridges above the west shore of meadow-rimmed Shadow Lake, whose shallow waters are sprinkled with lily pads. A moderate climb follows the course of Meeks Creek, tumbling and plunging its way down the rocky canyon. At 6.3 miles you reach the north shore of Stony Ridge Lake, the largest of the Tallant Lakes. ▶4 Except for the steep east shore, the lake is bordered by lodgepole pines.

⚠ **Camping**

A number of excellent campsites will lure overnighters.

Follow the TYT on a gentle grade around the west shore of Stony Ridge Lake, hopping over the outlet from isolated Cliff Lake along the way. Near the far end of the lake, a mildly rising ascent leads above the verdant meadow above the south shore and leads past a well-watered hillside carpeted with wildflowers. Eventually the trail resumes its climbing ways, switchbacking between the two upper tributaries of Meeks Creek, on the way to the last of the Tallant Lakes. At 8 miles from the trailhead, you reach the east shore of Rubicon Lake. ▶5 Rubicon is perhaps the prettiest of the lakes, rimmed by mountain hemlocks and lodgepole pines, which shelter a number of excellent campsites.

🚶 MILESTONES

▶1 0.0 Start at trailhead
▶2 4.6 Lake Genevieve junction
▶3 4.9 Crag Lake
▶4 6.3 Stony Ridge Lake
▶5 8.0 Rubicon Lake

Bathers *at one of the Tallant Lakes*

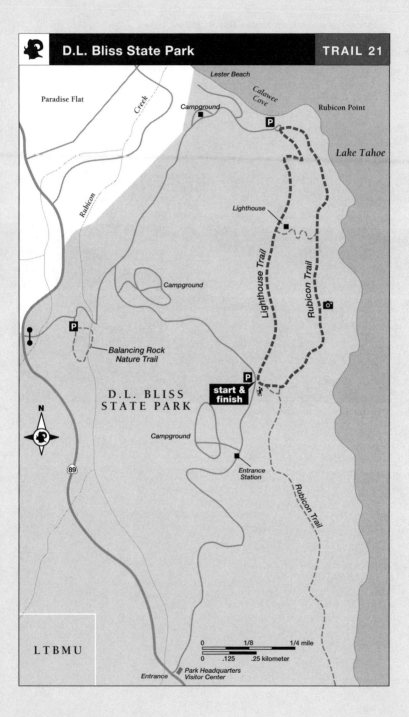

Paradise Flat

Creek

Lester Beach

Calawee Cove

Rubicon Point

Campground

Lake Tahoe

Rubicon

Lighthouse

Lighthouse Trail

Rubicon Trail

Campground

P

Balancing Rock
Nature Trail

D.L. BLISS
STATE PARK

P
start &
finish

N

89

Campground

Entrance
Station

Rubicon Trail

LTBMU

| 0 | 1/8 | 1/4 mile |
| 0 | .125 | .25 kilometer |

Entrance

Park Headquarters
Visitor Center

D.L. Bliss State Park: Rubicon Point and Lighthouse Loop

For good reasons, the Rubicon Trail is popular with hikers and tourists alike. Following above the lakeshore, travelers are treated to incredible lake views throughout the mile-long section of trail to Calawee Cove. By combining the Rubicon Trail with the Lighthouse Trail, you can follow a two-mile loop, complete with Tahoe views and a bit of history at the old Rubicon Point Lighthouse.

TRAIL USE
Hike
LENGTH
2 miles, 1 hour
VERTICAL FEET
±550'
DIFFICULTY
− **1** 2 3 4 5 +
TRAIL TYPE
Loop
SURFACE TYPE
Dirt

FEATURES
Child Friendly
Shore
Great Views
Photo Opportunity

FACILITIES
Restrooms
Picnic Tables
Water
Phone
Visitor Center

Best Time

D.L. Bliss State Park is generally open from mid-May through the end of September.

Finding the Trail

Drive Highway 89 to the entrance into D.L. Bliss State Park, approximately 11 miles north of the Highway 50-89 junction in South Lake Tahoe and 16 miles south of Tahoe City. Proceed on paved road to the campground entrance station (fee required) and continue to the small parking lot on the left-hand shoulder, 1.1 miles from the highway. Both the Rubicon and Lighthouse trails begin on the opposite side of the road from the parking area.

Trail Description

▶1 Follow signs for the Rubicon Trail, to the right of the Lighthouse Trail, which will be your return route. Walk on wide and gently graded old roadbed through mostly fir forest, soon encountering the end of the road at a loop. ▶2 Find the beginning of the

Rubicon Point Lighthouse

single-track Rubicon Trail on the far side of the loop and turn left, obeying signage for Calawee Cove.

Proceed on well-maintained trail, where through the trees you can see Lake Tahoe and the peaks above the far shore. Soon scattered Jeffrey pines and firs allow better lake views, which improve even more where you reach open, shrub-covered slopes of chinquapin, manzanita, and tobacco brush. The excellent lake views continue until you come to a junction with a lateral on the left, which climbs the hillside to the lighthouse.

Great Views

Past the lateral junction, you descend granite stairs to an unmarked path that travels a short distance to a vista point offering a superb Lake Tahoe view. Beyond the vista point, the main trail continues to the edge of a sheer cliff that you negotiate with the aid of a narrow boardwalk and chain fence.

This area can be a logjam on busy summer weekends, as tourists queue up to wait their turn at the single-file passage. Once the crux of the route is safely negotiated, easier trail leads to the parking lot at Rubicon Point-Calawee Cove, 1 mile from the trailhead. ▶3

To continue the loop, follow the Lighthouse Trail from the parking lot on a mild to moderate climb, across a forested hillside to a switchback. As you climb away from the switchback, you may notice evidence of a previous fire. Eventually the grade eases where the trail nears the top of the ridge. Proceed to a junction with short path that leads down granite steps to the edge of the hillside and the restored Rubicon Point Lighthouse. ▶4 If you're familiar with seacoast lighthouses, you may be surprised at the diminutive stature of this lighthouse, which is about the size of a port-a-potty. However, what the structure lacks in appearance is more than made up for by the stunning view you have here of Lake Tahoe. Renovation and stabilization of the Rubicon Point Lighthouse was completed in 2001.

Away from the lighthouse junction, you continue to ascend for a brief time before the trail leaves the boulder-studded ridge and follows a moderate descent through mixed forest back to the trailhead. ▶5

> Rubicon Point Lighthouse's claim to fame is its elevation — the highest lighthouse in the world on a navigable body of water.

🚶 MILESTONES

▶1   0.0   Start at trailhead
▶2   0.1   Turn left (north) at junction with Rubicon Trail
▶3   1.0   Parking lot at Calawee Cove/beginning of Lighthouse Trail
▶4   1.5   Junction with trail to Lighthouse
▶5   2.0   Return to trailhead

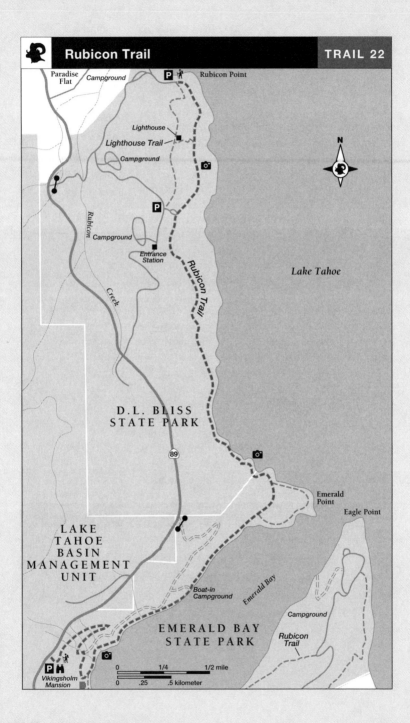

Rubicon Trail — TRAIL 22

Paradise Flat

Campground

Rubicon Point

Lighthouse

Lighthouse Trail

Campground

Rubicon

Campground

Entrance Station

Rubicon Trail

Lake Tahoe

Creek

D.L. BLISS STATE PARK

89

Emerald Point

Eagle Point

LAKE TAHOE BASIN MANAGEMENT UNIT

Boat-in Campground

Emerald Bay

Campground

Rubicon Trail

EMERALD BAY STATE PARK

Vikingsholm Mansion

0   1/4   1/2 mile

0   .25   .5 kilometer

Rubicon Trail

If lakeside views across the sapphire-blue waters of Lake Tahoe are what you're looking for, look no farther than the Rubicon Trail, which follows a 5-mile stretch of shoreline along Emerald Bay and the southwest shore of Tahoe, between Vikingsholm and Calawee Cove. Thanks to the beautiful scenery and the relatively easy route, the trail is popular with hikers and sightseers alike, especially on summer weekends. Plan on an early start to find a parking place and beat the crowds, although photographers will appreciate the lighting later in the day, when the sun is high or fading in the west.

Best Time

The Rubicon Trail stays close to the shoreline of Lake Tahoe, providing snow-free hiking from mid-may to November. If you're hiking on a weekend between Memorial Day and Labor Day, make sure you arrive early, as the Vikingsholm parking lot fills up fast.

Finding the Trail

START: Drive Highway 89 to the Vikingsholm parking lot above Emerald Bay on the west side of the highway, approximately 9 miles from the Highway 50-89 junction in South Lake Tahoe and 18 miles south of Tahoe City. The parking lot is 0.25 mile north of the Eagle Falls parking lot.

END: Drive Highway 89 to the entrance into D.L. Bliss State Park, approximately 11 miles north of the

TRAIL USE
Hike
LENGTH
5.0 miles, 2.5 hours
VERTICAL FEET
+375'/-700'
DIFFICULTY
− 1 **2** 3 4 5 +
TRAIL TYPE
Point to Point
SURFACE TYPE
Dirt

FEATURES
Child Friendly
Shore
Great Views
Photo Opportunity

FACILITIES
Restrooms
Picnic Tables
Water
Phone
Campground
Visitor Center

Highway 50-89 junction in South Lake Tahoe and 16 miles south of Tahoe City. Proceed on paved road past the campground entrance station (fee required) and past the small parking lot on the left-hand shoulder, 1 1 miles from the highway, where the Rubicon and Lighthouse trails begin on the opposite side of the road. Continue on paved road another 0.5 mile to a stop sign at a T-junction and turn right, reaching the large parking lot at the end of the road, near Calawee Cove, 2.4 miles from Highway 89.

Trail Description

Photo Opportunity

▶1 Find a paved road at the northwest end of the parking lot and descend steeply along this road, which once provided residents and guests access to the Vikingsholm mansion, below. Follow the road as it switchbacks 400 feet down the wall of the canyon above Emerald Bay, toward the mansion grounds at the bottom, where the Rubicon Trail begins near the lakeshore.

Head north from the beach area, passing outbuildings and picnic tables on the way to a number of bridges spanning small creeks and seeps that trickle down shady nooks filled with lush foliage. Proceed through mixed forest of incense cedars, Jeffrey pines, white firs, and sugar pines along the shoreline of Emerald Bay past Parson Rock, a hump

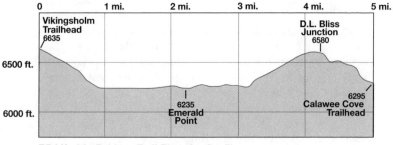

TRAIL 22 Rubicon Trail Elevation Profile

Rock outcrops *along the Rubicon Trail overlook Lake Tahoe*

of granite that provides shutterbugs with a superb
Tahoe view and swimmers with an excellent diving
spot. Past the last of the bridges, you pass through
Emerald Bay Boat-in Campground and continue
along the trail past tall willows toward Emerald
Point. At the start of this peninsula, 2.2 miles from
the parking lot, a lightly used path veers right to
follow the shoreline around Emerald Point, recon-
necting with the Rubicon Trail 0.2 mile farther. ▶2

The Rubicon Trail climbs over a low moraine to
the north junction with the Emerald Point Trail at a
picturesque cove. ▶3 Nearby, a small stretch of sandy
beach provides the last easily accessible piece of
lakeshore until the end of the trail, at Calawee Cove.
Climbing away from the cove, you reach a vista point
at a pile of large boulders that provide a vantage
point for a grand view of the lake. Follow a short,
zigzagging climb and continue above the lakeshore
before a short descent leads to a thimbleberry-lined
stream spilling across the path. Farther on, after a
pair of switchbacks, the trail veers away from the picturesque lake views to enter dense forest.

For the next mile, you make a steady climb
through the trees to the trail's high point and then
follow a short decline to a signed junction with the
old road from D.L. Bliss State Park, 4.2 miles from
the parking lot. ▶4 If time is of the essence, pickup
could be arranged 0.1 mile away, at the Rubicon-
Lighthouse trailhead (see Trip 21), rather than at
Calawee Cove.

If you're not in a hurry, Emerald Point provides an excellent view of Emerald Bay and the surrounding terrain, including Maggies Peaks.

≋ Shore

From the junction, continue descending on well-maintained trail, enjoying filtered views through the trees of Lake Tahoe and the peaks above the far shore. Soon, scattered Jeffrey pines and firs allow better lake views, which improve even more where you reach open shrub-covered slopes of chinquapin, manzanita, and tobacco brush. The excellent lake views continue to a junction with a lateral on the left, which climbs the hillside to the Rubicon Point Lighthouse (see Trip 21).

Great Views

Past the lateral to the lighthouse, you descend granite stairs to an unmarked path, which travels a short distance to a vista point offering a superb Lake Tahoe view. Beyond the vista point, the main trail continues to the edge of a sheer cliff that you negotiate with the aid of a narrow boardwalk and chain fence. This area can be logjam on busy summer weekends, as tourists queue up to wait their turn at the single file passage. Once the crux of the route is safely negotiated, easier trail leads to the parking lot near Rubicon Point at Calawee Cove. ▶5

🚶	**MILESTONES**

- ▶1 0.0 Start at Vikingsholm parking lot
- ▶2 2.2 South junction of Emerald Point Trail
- ▶3 2.3 North junction of Emerald Point Trail
- ▶4 4.2 Continue straight ahead at junction with trail to D.L. Bliss State Park
- ▶5 5.0 Reach Calawee Cove parking lot

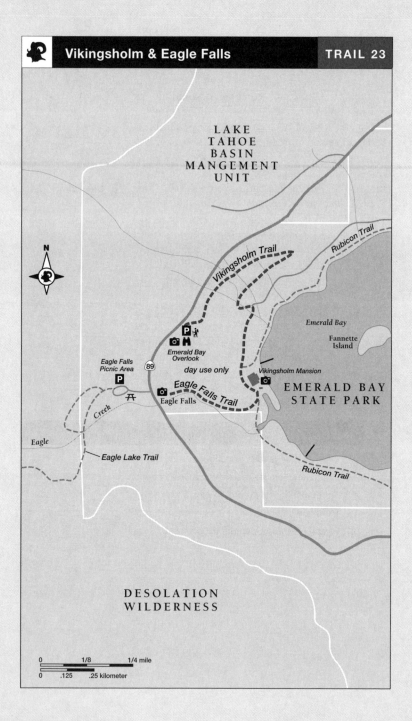

LAKE
TAHOE
BASIN
MANGEMENT
UNIT

Vikingsholm Trail

Rubicon Trail

N

Emerald Bay

Fannette
Island

Emerald Bay
Overlook

day use only

Eagle Falls
Picnic Area

89

Vikingsholm Mansion

EMERALD BAY
STATE PARK

Eagle Falls Trail

Eagle Falls

Creek

Eagle

Eagle Lake Trail

Rubicon Trail

DESOLATION
WILDERNESS

0   1/8   1/4 mile
0   .125   .25 kilometer

Vikingsholm and Eagle Falls

Purchased by the state of California in 1953, designated a National Natural Landmark in 1969, and designated an underwater state park in 1994, Emerald Bay is Lake Tahoe's crown jewel. Along with a plethora of spectacular views, visitors to Emerald Bay State Park who come by boat or descend the 1.25-mile trail will find many diversions, including sandy beaches for sunbathing, excellent picnic spots, a vibrant waterfall, and the architectural wonder of Vikingsholm mansion.

Best Time

The view of Lake Tahoe across Emerald Bay is spectacular any time of year, but snow-free trails beckon hikers and sightseers from May to November. Eagle Falls provides the height of drama during peak flows when the creek is swollen with snowmelt from the mountains above, usually throughout the month of June. A tour of Vikingsholm Castle (mid-June through September) is an absolute must for any visitor to Emerald Bay State Park. If your hike is planned for a weekend between Memorial Day and Labor Day, make sure you arrive early, as the Vikingsholm parking lot fills up quickly.

Finding the Trail

Drive Highway 89 to the Vikingsholm parking lot above Emerald Bay on the west side of the highway, approximately 9 miles from the Highway 50-89 junction in South Lake Tahoe and 18 miles south of

TRAIL USE
Hike
LENGTH
2.5 miles, 1.5 hours
VERTICAL FEET
±730'
DIFFICULTY
– 1 **2** 3 4 5 +
TRAIL TYPE
Out & Back
SURFACE TYPE
Paved, Dirt

FEATURES
Child Friendly
Handicap Accessible
Waterfall
Lake
Cool & Shady
Great Views
Photo Opportunity
Historic

FACILITIES
Restrooms
Picnic Tables
Water
Phone
Visitor Center
Campground

Tahoe City. The parking lot is 0.25 mile north of the Eagle Falls parking lot.

Logistics

You can camp on both shores of Emerald Bay, but the Vikingsholm area, including Eagle Falls, is only open from 6 AM to 9 PM.

Trail Description

Before you head down to Vikingsholm, take in the view of Emerald Bay and Lake Tahoe from the nearby overlook. The vista is a Tahoe classic, and you will definitely want your camera if either the Tahoe Queen or M.S. Dixie is visiting Emerald Bay. Tiny Fannette Island, near the west end of the bay, is the only island in Lake Tahoe.

▶1 After enjoying the view from the overlook, find a paved road at the northwest end of the parking lot and descend steeply along this road, which once provided residents and guests vehicular access to the Vikingsholm mansion, below. Follow the road as it switchbacks 400 feet down the wall of the canyon above Emerald Bay toward the shady mansion grounds at the bottom. By obeying all signs for Vikingsholm, you'll reach the front of the magnificent mansion, 0.9 mile from the parking lot. ▶2 To tour the mansion, walk a short distance south to the

Historic

Side Trips along Emerald Bay

Hikers with extra energy can extend their trip by following the Rubicon Trail north from Vikingsholm to Calawee Cove along the shoreline of Emerald Bay and Lake Tahoe as described in Trip 22 (shuttle required). A shorter alternative follows the south shore of Emerald Bay through the campgrounds to Eagle Point and back.

OPTIONS

Vikingsholm

Mrs. Lora Josephine Knight, of Santa Barbara, secured the property around Emerald Bay, including Fannette Island, in 1928 for a price of $250,000. With her nephew by marriage, Lennart Palme, a Swedish-born architect, Mrs. Knight set out to design and build a structure that would be one of the finest examples of Scandinavian architecture in the western hemisphere. At great expense, the 38-room mansion was completed in September of 1929 by employing 200 craftsmen utilizing old-world techniques, such as hand-hewing large timbers, making intricate carvings, and fabricating hinges and latches. Following Mrs. Knight's wishes, not a single large tree was disturbed in the construction of her magnificent residence. Most of the construction materials came from the Tahoe basin, including the granite stones in the foundation and walls. However, the furnishings inside Vikingsholm were either Scandinavian imports or meticulous reproductions of priceless treasures from Norwegian and Swedish museums. A handful of less spectacular outbuildings were also built, including the stone Tea House on Fannette Island. Servants would boat Mrs. Knight and her guests out to the island each summer day for afternoon tea. Mrs. Knight spent her summers at Vikingsholm, until her death in 1945. In 1953, the property was generously sold to the State of California for half its appraised value.

Visitor Center and purchase a ticket ($3). Guided tours are conducted every half hour between 10 AM and 4 PM.

Waterfall

To visit Eagle Falls, find the start of the signed trail near the Visitor Center. ▶3 Head west on single-track trail, paralleling lushly lined Eagle Creek through cool forest. Soon the grade increases and you climb shrub-covered slabs to a fenced viewing area near the base of the falls, 0.2 mile from the Visitor Center. ▶4

🚶 MILESTONES

▶1 0.0   Start at Vikingsholm parking lot
▶2 0.9   Vikingsholm Mansion
▶3 1.0   Visitor Center/Eagle Falls Trail
▶4 1.25 Eagle Falls

Eagle Lake *(Trail 24)*

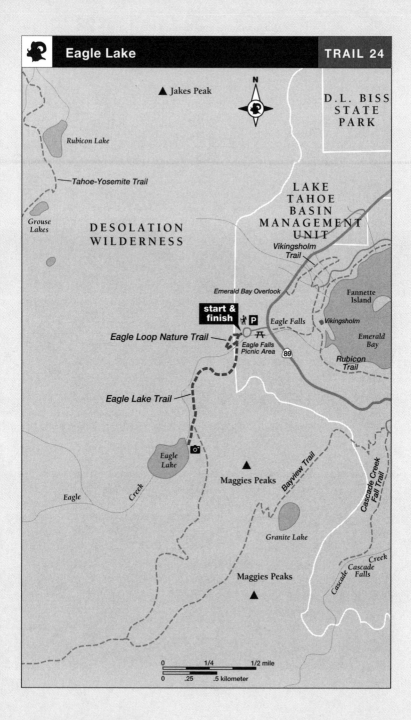

▲ Jakes Peak

N

D.L. BISS
STATE
PARK

Rubicon Lake

Tahoe-Yosemite Trail

LAKE
TAHOE
BASIN
MANAGEMENT
UNIT

Grouse
Lakes

DESOLATION
WILDERNESS

Vikingsholm
Trail

Emerald Bay Overlook

Fannette
Island

start &
finish

Eagle Falls

Vikingsholm

Eagle Loop Nature Trail

Emerald
Bay

Eagle Falls
Picnic Area

89

Rubicon
Trail

Eagle Lake Trail

Eagle
Lake

Maggies Peaks

Bayview Trail

Cascade Creek Fall Trail

Eagle

Creek

Granite Lake

Cascade Creek

Maggies Peaks

Cascade
Falls

Cascade

0   1/4   1/2 mile

0   .25   .5 kilometer

Eagle Lake

The short but steep one-mile climb to Eagle Lake along the Eagle Lake Trail is one of Tahoe's most popular hikes, and for good reason. Where else can one visit such a picturesque lake tucked into an alpine-like granite cirque with such little effort. The Forest Service has recently built a short nature trail close to the trailhead, providing hikers and sight-seers with an interesting and informative loop diversion.

Best Time

Even though the backcountry beyond Eagle Lake remains snowbound until mid-July, the 1-mile trail to the lake is typically open by late June and usually remains snow free until November. Parking at the Eagle Lake trailhead is at a premium all summer long, so arrive early if you expect to snag a parking space, especially on weekends.

Finding the Trail

Follow Highway 89 to Emerald Bay and locate the popular Eagle Falls trailhead, on the east side of the highway approximately 9 miles to the north of the Highway 50-89 junction and 19 miles south of Tahoe City. The trailhead is complete with picnic tables, barbecue pits, toilets, and running water. The Forest Service charges $3 per day for parking. Very limited free parking is available along the highway just outside of the trailhead parking area.

TRAIL USE
Hike, Run
LENGTH
2.0 miles, 1.5 hours
VERTICAL FEET
±450'
DIFFICULTY
− 1 **2** 3 4 5 +
TRAIL TYPE
Out & Back
SURFACE TYPE
Dirt

FEATURES
Dogs Allowed
Child Friendly
Canyon
Mountain
Stream
Waterfall
Lake
Photo Opportunity
Camping
Geologic Interest

FACILITIES
Restrooms
Picnic
Water

Logistics

Wilderness permits are required for both dayhikes and overnight backpacks. Dayhikers may self-register at the trailhead. Backpackers bound for the Velma Lakes and points beyond can obtain their permits from the Lake Tahoe Visitor Center, 5.5 miles south on Highway 89.

Trail Description

▶1 Climb away from the well-signed trailhead and follow wood-beam steps to a junction with the Eagle Loop Nature Trail, which is clearly marked by a 6 x 6 post. ▶2 Veer left at the junction and proceed through shrubs and scattered conifers, past a vertical cliff to the Eagle Creek Bridge, which is 0.2 mile from the trailhead. ▶3

From the bridge, follow granite steps across a field of blocky talus, soon crossing the signed Desolation Wilderness boundary. Past a patch of dense shrubs and lush trailside vegetation, you break out into the open across granite slabs, with grand views of Lake Tahoe and the towering cliffs rimming the canyon. Continue past scattered Jeffrey pines and junipers on a gentler grade, eventually encountering a denser forest of primarily lodgepole pines where the trail nears Eagle Creek. A short, stiff climb leads to a junction with the lateral to Eagle Lake, 0.8 mile from the trailhead. ▶4

Take the lateral on the right and climb across shrubby slopes to the northwest shore of Eagle Lake. ▶5 The scenic lake reposes serenely in an impressive granite cirque composed of steep cliffs. The shrub-

Geologic Interest

covered slopes surrounding the lake, dotted with Jeffrey pines and white firs, offer limited access to the abrupt shoreline, providing a challenge for both swimmers interested in a chilly dip and anglers plying the waters for the resident trout.

You can vary the route of your return slightly by following the Eagle Loop Nature Trail. Immediately after crossing the Eagle Creek Bridge, ►6 veer left at a junction with the Eagle Loop. ►7 Just past an informational sign about the first sighting of Lake Tahoe by John C. Fremont and Charles Pruess, you reach another junction. The left-hand trail climbs granite steps and slabs to a viewpoint of Emerald Bay and Lake Tahoe, complete with benches and informational signs. The right-hand trail descends open slopes past more signs, to the lower junction with the Eagle Falls Trail. ►8 From there, follow the main trail back to the trailhead.

🚶	**MILESTONES**

►1	0.0	Start at trailhead; veer left at Nature Trail lower junction
►2	0.2	Veer left at Nature Trail upper junction
►3	0.2	Eagle Creek Bridge
►4	0.8	Veer right at Eagle Lake lateral
►5	1.0	Eagle Lake
►6	1.8	Return to Eagle Creek Bridge
►7	1.8	Turn left at Nature Trail upper junction
►8	2.0	Veer right at Nature Trail lower junction; return to trailhead

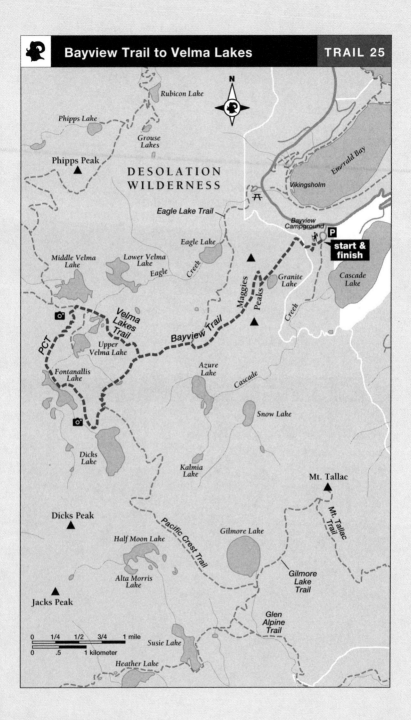

N

DESOLATION
WILDERNESS

Rubicon Lake

Phipps Lake

Grouse
Lakes

Phipps Peak ▲

Eagle Lake Trail

Eagle Lake

Middle Velma
Lake

Lower Velma
Lake

Eagle

Eagle   Creek

Velma
Lakes
Trail

Bayview Trail

PCT

Upper
Velma Lake

Fontanallis
Lake

Azure
Lake

Cascade

Snow Lake

Dicks
Lake

Kalmia
Lake

Dicks Peak ▲

Half Moon Lake

Pacific Crest Trail

Gilmore Lake

Alta Morris
Lake

Jacks Peak ▲

Susie Lake

Heather Lake

Emerald Bay

Vikingsholm

Bayview
Campground

start &
finish
P

Cascade
Lake

Maggies

Peaks

Granite
Lake

Creek

Mt. Tallac ▲

Mt. Tallac
Trail

Gilmore
Lake
Trail

Glen
Alpine
Trail

0   1/4   1/2   3/4   1 mile
0   .5   1 kilometer

Bayview Trail to Velma Lakes

This partial loop trip, consisting of 10.5 miles through the heart of the Desolation Wilderness, samples several cirque-bound lakes amid the characteristic granite terrain that makes the area so picturesque. Whether you're just out for the day or on an overnight backpack, the lakes provide great scenery, along with fine swimming and fishing.

Best Time

Desolation's backcountry usually frees itself from snow by mid-July. Wildflowers bloom from then until late August, when swimmers will find the water in the lakes the least chilly. The hiking season ends with the first major snowfall, which generally occurs in late October. On summer weekends, plan on arriving early to secure a parking space.

Finding the Trail

Drive Highway 89 to Emerald Bay and locate the Bayview Trailhead on the south side of the highway, approximately 7.5 miles from the Highway 50-89 junction and 19.5 miles south of Tahoe City.

Logistics

Wilderness permits are required for both dayhikes and overnight backpacks. Dayhikers may register themselves at the trailhead. Backpackers bound for the Velma Lakes and points beyond can obtain their permits from the Lake Tahoe Visitor Center, 4.5 miles south on Highway 89.

TRAIL USE
Hike, Run, Horse
LENGTH
10.5 miles, 5 hours
VERTICAL FEET
±2725'
DIFFICULTY
– 1 2 3 **4** 5 +
TRAIL TYPE
Loop
SURFACE TYPE
Dirt

FEATURES
Dogs Allowed
Canyon
Mountain
Stream
Lake
Wildflowers
Photo Opportunity
Camping

FACILITIES
Restrooms
Picnic Tables
Water

Trail Description

►1 Just past the trailhead, you reach a junction with the trail to Cascade Falls. Following a sign for Desolation Wilderness, turn right at the junction and make a stiff, switchbacking climb through mixed forest of primarily white fir with a chinquapin understory. Beyond the wilderness boundary you follow the crest of a ridge, where the forest parts enough to allow good views of Emerald Bay and Lake Tahoe. Leaving the ridge, the trail follows Granite Lake's alder-lined outlet on a gentler ascent through bracken ferns, thimbleberry, wildflowers, and a mixture of shrubs, including chinquapin, tobacco brush, greenleaf and pinemat manzanita.

As you progress up the trail, lodgepole pines and western white pines join the forest on the way to serene Granite Lake, 1.0 mile from the trailhead. ►2

Near the far end of Granite Lake, the trail begins a switchbacking climb across the south-facing slope below the twin summits of Maggies Peaks. After a 0.75-mile climb, you bid farewell to the lake basin and follow mildly graded trail along the backside of South Maggies Peak to a gentle descent along the forested southwest ridge. At 2.7 miles from the trailhead, you reach a saddle and a signed three-way junction with the Eagle Lake Trail. ►3

Veer left at the junction and follow sandy trail on a mildly undulating route through widely scattered mixed forest and around granite boulders and slabs. At 0.6 mile from the junction, you intersect the Velma Lakes Trail (17E34). ►4

Bear right and follow the Velma Lakes Trail on a downhill course through acres of granite slabs, boulders, rocks and widely scattered pines, which allow occasional glimpses of the unnamed pond directly north of Upper Velma Lake. Reaching the floor of the lakes basin, you walk along the north shore of the pond, ford the outlet, and come to a three-way

Velma Lakes *from Phipps Pass area*

junction marked with a 6 x 6 post, 4.1 miles from the trailhead. ▶5 Reach Upper Velma Lake via the trail to the left (south), which dead ends after a half-mile, near the inlet.

Continue straight ahead at the junction and make a short climb to intersect the Pacific Crest Trail, 4.25 miles from the trailhead. ▶6 A short walk northbound on the PCT leads to an unobstructed view of Middle Velma Lake.

Turn left at the junction and head south on the PCT on a moderate, winding climb above Upper Velma Lake. Where the rate of ascent eases, Dicks Pass and Fontanillis Lake pop into view and then you make a short drop to the crossing of the lake's outlet. Cross Fontanillis Lake's multi-hued rock

 Camping

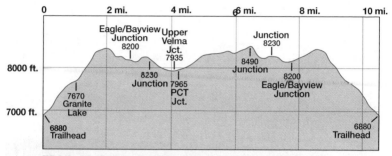

TRAIL 25 Bayview to Velma Lakes Elevation Profile

basin along the east shore of the lake, which lies in the shadow of towering Dicks Peak. Here, on the popular PCT, several campsites sheltered in groves of lodgepole pines and mountain hemlocks offer fine overnight accommodations for backpackers.

At the far end of the lake, a brief ascent across boulder-covered slopes leads to the top of a rise and the short lateral to Dicks Lake, where backpackers will find additional campsites. From the lateral, the PCT bends away from the cirque of Dicks Lake on a mild ascent to a junction with the Eagle Lake Trail, 6.4 miles from the trailhead. ▶7

A steep 0.3-mile descent from the PCT leads to milder trail, which traverses a pond-dotted basin. You reach the three-way junction of the Eagle Falls Lake and Velma Lakes trails at 7.2 miles, closing the loop section. ▶8 From there, retrace your steps 0.6 mile to the Bayview-Eagle Lake junction ▶9 and then 2.7 miles to the Bayview trailhead. ▶10

Upper Velma Lake

🚶 MILESTONES

▶1   0.0   Start at trailhead

▶2   1.0   Granite Lake

▶3   2.7   Turn left at Eagle Lake Trail junction

▶4   3.3   Turn right at Velma Lakes Trail junction

▶5   4.1   Go straight ahead at junction with trail to Upper Velma Lake

▶6   4.25 Turn left at Pacific Crest Trail junction

▶7   6.4   Turn left at Eagle Lake Trail junction

▶8   7.2   Turn right at Velma Lakes Trail junction

▶9   7.8   Turn right at Eagle Lake-Bayview junction

▶10   10.5 Return to trailhead

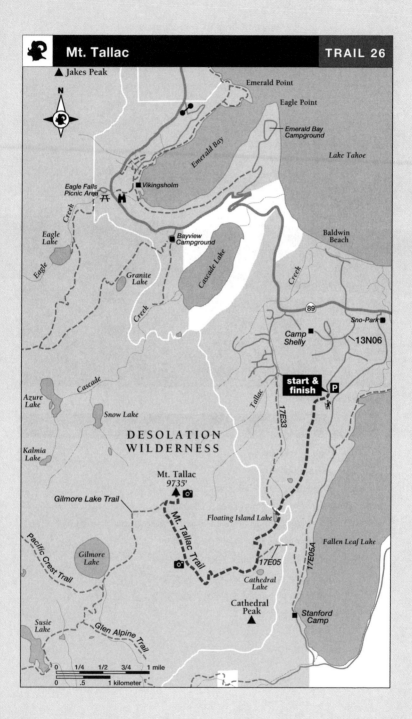

▲ Jakes Peak

N

Emerald Point

Eagle Point

Emerald Bay

Emerald Bay Campground

Lake Tahoe

Eagle Falls Picnic Area

■ *Vikingsholm*

Baldwin Beach

Eagle Lake

■ *Bayview Campground*

Cascade Lake

Granite Lake

Creek

Eagle

Creek

89

Sno-Park ■

Camp Shelly

13N06

Cascade

start & finish P

Azure Lake

Snow Lake

17E33

Tallac

DESOLATION
WILDERNESS

Kalmia Lake

Mt. Tallac
9735'

▲

Gilmore Lake Trail

Floating Island Lake

Mt. Tallac Trail

Fallen Leaf Lake

Pacific Crest Trail

Gilmore Lake

17E05

17E05A

Cathedral Lake

Susie Lake

Glen Alpine Trail

Cathedral
Peak
▲

■ *Stanford Camp*

0   1/4   1/2   3/4   1 mile

0   .5   1 kilometer

Mt. Tallac

Mt. Tallac is regarded by many as the quintessential Tahoe peak. The dark, metamorphic hulk looms over the south end of the lake in dominant fashion, casting a long shadow over the surrounding terrain. *Tallac* is a Native American word meaning "Great Mountain," an appropriate moniker for this stately peak. Not only is the mountain imposing when viewed from various points around the basin, the vista from the summit is equally stunning. Prospective peak baggers don't need specialized mountaineering skills in order to reach the incredible view, as a maintained trail can be followed all the way to the top of the peak.

Best Time

At 9735 feet, Mt. Tallac holds onto its winter mantle well into mid-summer—don't expect snow-free trails until after mid-July. At this altitude, high winds and winter weather usually signal an end to the hiking season on Mt. Tallac during early to mid-October.

Finding the Trail

Drive Highway 89 to Forest Service Road 13N06, which is opposite the road to the Lake Tahoe Visitor Center. Turn south on 13N06, obeying a sign reading TALLAC TRAILHEAD, and follow paved road for 0.3 mile to an intersection. Turn left and proceed 0.2 mile to a junction with a road on the left to Camp Concord. Continue straight ahead at the junction, reaching the trailhead parking area at 1.0 mile from the highway.

TRAIL USE
Hike, Run
LENGTH
9.4 miles, 6 hours
VERTICAL FEET
±3400'
DIFFICULTY
– 1 2 3 4 **5** +
TRAIL TYPE
Out & Back
SURFACE TYPE
Dirt

FEATURES
Dogs Allowed
Canyon
Mountain
Summit
Stream
Lakes
Wildflowers
Great Views
Photo Opportunity

FACILITIES
None

Logistics

Since part of the Mt. Tallac Trail lies within Desolation Wilderness, you will need a permit for both dayhikes and backpacks. Dayhikers may self-register at the trailhead, but backpackers will need to get their permits from the Lake Tahoe Visitor Center.

Trail Description

▶1 From the trailhead, follow an old gravel roadbed on a mild climb through scattered Jeffrey pines and white firs. Beyond some backcountry signs the grade increases, the forest thickens, and on single-track trail you gain the crest of a morainal ridge. As you climb steadily along the ridge, Fallen Leaf Lake springs dramatically into view across a hillside carpeted with huckleberry oak and greenleaf manzanita. As fine as these views are, even better ones await farther up the trail. About 1.25 miles from the trailhead, the trail forsakes the ridge crest, drops briefly into a gully, and then on a steep ascent comes alongside the outlet from Floating Island Lake. Eventually, the grade eases and you reach the northeast shore of the serene, forest-rimmed lake, soon after crossing the Desolation Wilderness boundary, 1.7 miles from the trailhead. ▶2

Five-acre Floating Island Lake was named in the late 1800s for a 20-foot diameter, grass-and shrub-covered natural island that at one time sported thriving conifers. Since that time several more grassy mats have sloughed off from the lakeshore and floated about the lake, although at the time of research, the surface was devoid of floating islands. The quiet lake is bordered by dense, mostly red-fir forest.

Mild trail follows the shoreline past the lake and leads to a winding climb over rocky terrain and through thinning trees before it enters back into

Wildflowers and talus *along Mt. Tallac Trail*

dense forest and thick shrubs, alongside Floating Island Lake's inlet. Soon you break out of the trees and climb across an open slope carpeted with sagebrush, serviceberry, currant, and wildflowers, which allow fine views of Mt. Tallac.

❀ **Wildflowers**

Back into the trees, the trail drops to a crossing of Cathedral Creek, lined with a luxuriant swath of vegetation, and then climbs to a junction with Trail 17E05. ▶3 This trail provides a steep, exposed, 1-mile connection to Trail 17E05A, above the southwest shore of Fallen Leaf Lake. By following this trail to the north, you'll reach a tiny parking area in the Fallen Leaf Tract of summer homes. By heading south, you'll encounter Stanford Camp, the private university's extension campus, where there is absolutely no public parking and, therefore, no shortcut to Tallac's summit.

Continue climbing from the junction and soon reach Cathedral Lake, 2.5 miles from the trailhead. ▶4 The diminutive lake sits in a steep rock basin surrounded by talus and sheltered by a few clumps of pines. Although reasonably attractive, the lake fails to inspire much reverential awe, having received its name from the nearby cliff on Tallac's southeast ridge.

Beyond Cathedral Lake the trail leaves the dense forest behind and attacks the hillside with a vengeance. On steep, rocky trail you climb across shrub-covered slopes with increasingly fine views of Lake Tahoe and the peaks rimming the southeast shore. A small brook adorned with wildflowers, including monkey flower, fireweed, larkspur, forget-me-not, and thimbleberry, provides the last reliable water for the remainder of the ascent. Long-legged switchbacks lead across slopes covered with tobacco brush, sagebrush, and bitterbrush, to the crest of Mt. Tallac's southeast ridge.

 Great Views

Now heading northwest, you follow the ridge through wildflowers, shrubs, and groves of stunted conifers, including western white pines, mountain hemlocks, whitebark pines, and lodgepole pines. Improving views to the west of the Crystal Range peaks and the canyons of Desolation Wilderness are quite impressive. The steep ascent eventually leads to a marked junction at 4.4 miles with the trail to to Gilmore Lake. ▶5

 Summit

Veer to the right at the junction and continue the ascent over rocky slopes through diminishing pines around the south side of Mt. Tallac. As you regain the southeast ridge, Lake Tahoe springs back into view and you follow the ridge the last 150 vertical feet to the summit. ▶6 At a mere 3.5 miles from the lakeshore, the top of Mt. Tallac offers one of the Tahoe Basin's finest vistas.

🚶 MILESTONES

▶1   0.0   Start at trailhead
▶2   1.7   Floating Island Lake
▶3   2.4   Proceed straight ahead at Trail 17E05 junction
▶4   2.5   Cathedral Lake
▶5   4.4   Veer right (east) at Gilmore Lake trail junction
▶6   4.7   Summit of Mt. Tallac

Gilmore Lake and Pyramid Peak *from Mt. Tallac*

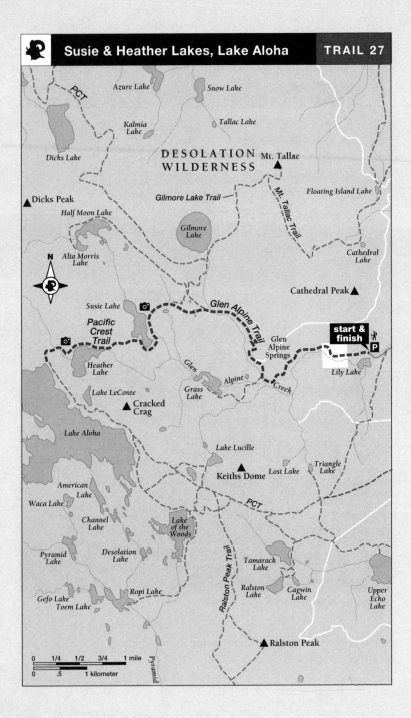

Glen Alpine to Susie and Heather Lakes and Lake Aloha

This trip provides a fine example of the classic Desolation Wilderness experience. An easy section of trail takes visitors to the historical setting of Glen Alpine Springs, before a moderate climb leads to three picturesque lakes in the shadow of Jacks Peak. John Muir's endorsement of the area reads, "The Glen Alpine Springs tourist resort seems to me one of the delightful places in all the famous Tahoe region. From no other valley, as far as I know, may excursions be made in a single day to so many peaks, wild gardens, glacier lakes, glacier meadows and alpine groves, cascades, etc." Don't anticipate huge doses of solitude, as this area is deservedly popular with hikers and backpackers alike.

TRAIL USE
Hike, Run, Horse
LENGTH
11.8 miles, 7 hours
VERTICAL FEET
±2125'
DIFFICULTY
– 1 2 3 **4** 5 +
TRAIL TYPE
Out & Back
SURFACE TYPE
Dirt

FEATURES
Dogs Allowed
Canyon
Mountain
Stream
Waterfall
Lakes
Wildflowers
Photo Opportunity

FACILITIES
Restrooms
Picnic Tables
Camping

Best Time

The short hike to Glen Alpine Springs can be done as early as the beginning of June, but the trail to the lakes is usually snow covered until mid-July. Patches of snow may remain over the trail in the upper cirque basins even longer.

Finding the Trail

Follow Highway 89 to Fallen Leaf Road, approximately 3 miles northwest of the Y-junction with U.S. 50 in South Lake Tahoe. Turn south and follow Fallen Leaf Road for 4.6 miles to the far end of Fallen Leaf Lake and a signed junction for Glen Alpine. Turn left at the junction and proceed on a very narrow paved road for 0.5 mile to the trailhead parking area, just past a bridge over Glen Alpine Creek.

Logistics

Backpackers will need a wilderness permit from the Lake Tahoe Visitor Center. Dayhikers can register themselves at the trailhead.

Trail Description

▶1 Begin hiking on a closed gravel road past private cabins and alongside lush riparian vegetation on the left, which obscures views of neighboring Lily Lake. The hillside to the right is covered with a mixed forest of junipers, Jeffrey pines, incense cedars, lodgepole pines, firs, and aspens. Continue along the road past Lily Lake to a scenic waterfall on Glen Alpine Creek and proceed to Glen Alpine Springs, 1.0 mile from the trailhead. ▶2

 Waterfall

Dirt road continues beyond Glen Alpine Springs for a short distance, until single-track trail climbs through mixed forest, followed by open, shrub-covered terrain with good views of the surrounding peaks and ridges. You enter the signed Desolation Wilderness and soon encounter a junction with the Grass Lake Trail, 1.6 miles from the trailhead. ▶3

Turn right (north) and follow an extended, switchback climb over open granite slopes up the canyon of Gilmore Lake's outlet. Back under forest cover, you hop across an alder-lined rivulet, continue climbing to a ford of the outlet, and soon encounter a junction at 3.0 miles. ▶4

Veer left at the junction and follow Trail 17E32 toward Susie Lake. A short climb continues through the trees and leads to a westward traverse past a quartet of shallow ponds covered with lily pads. Beyond the ponds the path descends to a junction with the Pacific Crest Trail near a wildflower-covered meadow, 3.5 miles from the trailhead. ▶5

Wildflowers

Turn left and follow the PCT past two more ponds and over a ridge to an overlook of rockbound

Glen Alpine Springs

HISTORY

While searching for stray cattle in 1863, Nathan Gilmore discovered the mineral springs that his wife would name Glen Alpine Springs, after a verse in a romantic poem by Sir Walter Scott. Gilmore built a wagon road to the springs from Fallen Leaf Lake, bottled and sold the carbonated water, and developed a first-class resort, which attracted several noteworthy figures over the years. A summer camp was established in 1878 and a post office in 1904, both of which were later relocated to Fallen Leaf Lake. Several structures remain from the bygone days, including the resort's social hall, a steel, red-wood, stone, and glass edifice designed by Bernard Maybeck, the noted architect who also designed the San Francisco Palace of Fine Arts. Nowadays, Glen Alpine Springs is under the care of a non-profit corporation, in conjunction with the Forest Service, with a mission of preserving, restoring and interpreting the site's resources. The old social hall houses an interpretive center, and guided tours and docents are available from mid-June to mid-September. Glen Alpine Springs also sponsors special events throughout the summer. For more information, call (530) 573-2405.

Susie Lake. A mild descent leads to a ford of the outlet near the southeast shore, a potentially difficult crossing in early season. Named either for Nathan Gilmore's oldest daughter or for the matriarch of the Washoe Indian squaws, Susie Lake is an enchanting lake cradled into the sort of rocky bowl that characterizes the heart of Desolation Wilderness. ►6 The metamorphic hulk of Jacks Peak provides a fine backdrop to the long, irregularly shaped lake, which is bordered by clumps of heather.

Great Views

To continue to Heather Lake, follow the trail around the south shore of Susie Lake and make a steady climb toward the V-shaped notch of the outlet. Climb over the low, barren ridge to drop into Heather Lake's basin well above the shore, and continue toward the far end of the lake. ►7

A rocky trail climbs to a nice view of a waterfall and across Heather Lake's inlet. Continue the ascent past a placid tarn and to the crest of a ridge between the basins of Heather Lake and Lake Aloha. Here you have a marvelous view of the jagged Crystal Range, beyond the island-dotted surface of sizeable Lake Aloha. Dropping off the crest, you reach a junction with the Rubicon Trail at the northeast corner of Lake Aloha. ▶8 The lake is most attractive in mid-summer, before the level of the lake drops to the point where it becomes a series of interconnected ponds.

≋ **Lake**

🚶	**MILESTONES**

- ▶1   0.0   Start at trailhead
- ▶2   1.0   Glen Alpine Springs
- ▶3   1.6   Turn right (north) at Grass Lake Trail junction
- ▶4   3.0   Veer left at junction
- ▶5   3.5   Turn left at junction of Pacific Crest Trail
- ▶6   4.1   Susie Lake
- ▶7   5.0   Heather Lake
- ▶8   5.9   Lake Aloha

Lake Aloha

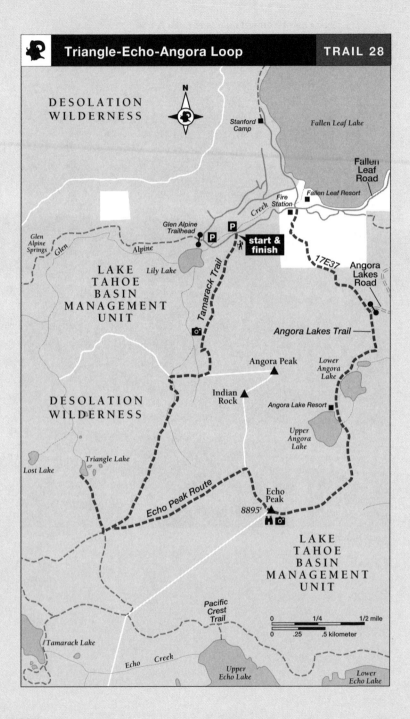

DESOLATION
WILDERNESS

Stanford Camp

Fallen Leaf Lake

Fallen Leaf Road

Creek

Fire Station

Fallen Leaf Resort

Glen Alpine Trailhead

P

P

start & finish

17E37

Angora Lakes Road

Glen Alpine Springs

Glen

Alpine

LAKE
TAHOE
BASIN
MANAGEMENT
UNIT

Lily Lake

Tamarack Trail

Angora Lakes Trail

DESOLATION
WILDERNESS

Angora Peak ▲

Lower Angora Lake

Indian Rock ▲

Angora Lake Resort

Upper Angora Lake

Triangle Lake

Lost Lake

Echo Peak Route

Echo Peak

8895'

LAKE
TAHOE
BASIN
MANAGEMENT
UNIT

Pacific Crest Trail

0	1/4	1/2 mile

0	.25	.5 kilometer

Tamarack Lake

Echo   Creek

Upper Echo Lake

Lower Echo Lake

Triangle Lake, Echo Peak, and Angora Lakes Loop

Hikers searching for a more challenging adventure will find this loop trip right up their alley. Just locating the trailhead can be a daunting task for first timers. From there, an unmaintained, primitive trail follows a stiff ascent up the canyon of the south fork of Glen Alpine Creek before gentler terrain leads to Triangle Lake and the summit of Echo Peak. The steep, off-trail descent from Echo Peak to Angora Lakes is the crux of the route, but a refreshing dip in the upper lake followed by a glass of world-famous, fresh-squeezed lemonade at Angora Lakes Resort are worthy rewards. An easy hike along roads and trail completes the return to the trailhead. The views throughout the trip of Lake Tahoe and the surrounding terrain are alone worth the trip.

Best Time

The end of July to the middle of September provide the best conditions for the climb and descent of Echo Peak. Earlier in the season, some of the crossings of Glen Alpine Creek can be treacherous.

Finding the Trail

Finding the start of the trail may be the most difficult part of the trip. Follow Highway 89 to Fallen Leaf Road, approximately 3 miles northwest of the Y-junction with U.S. 50 in South Lake Tahoe. Turn south and follow Fallen Leaf Road for 4.6 miles, to the far end of Fallen Leaf Lake and a signed junction for Glen Alpine. Turn left at the junction and proceed on a very narrow paved road for one-third mile

TRAIL USE
Hike
LENGTH
7.2 miles, 5 hours
VERTICAL FEET
±2750'
DIFFICULTY
– 1 2 3 4 **5** +
TRAIL TYPE
Loop
SURFACE TYPE
Dirt

FEATURES
Canyon
Mountain
Summit
Lake
Wildflowers
Cool & Shady
Good Views
Photo Opportunity
Steep

FACILITIES
None

to the unidentified start of the Tamarack Trail. Without a defined parking area or any signs marking the trailhead, a discernible path is almost impossible to spot from your car. The best plan may be to first park your vehicle in one of the few spaces that exist along the road, and then walk along the road until you see the defined track of the trail on the south side. If parking spots are not available along the road, you will have to park your car at the Glen Alpine trailhead at the end of the road.

Trail Description

►1 A short section of primitive trail leads away from the road through open terrain to a 6 x 6 post and a sign that would be much more helpful if it were next to the road. After walking through a small grove of Jeffrey pines, junipers, white firs, and lodgepole pines, you emerge into an open area of shrubs with nice views of the surrounding terrain, including Angora Peak and Indian Rock, high above. Soon back into forest, you start a steep climb on rocky tread through dense foliage. Aspen, thimbleberry, bracken fern, spirea, vine maple, alder, willow, currant, and tobacco brush crowd the trail, along with a colorful display of wildflowers, which includes columbine, leopard lily, lady slipper, and monk's hood. Eventually the jungle-like vegetation is left behind, as the stiff ascent continues across shrub-covered and boulder- dotted slopes with very scattered conifers, which allow improving views of Lake Tahoe, Fallen Leaf Lake, and the nearby topography. As you continue the climb up the canyon, you make several crossings of the thin, lushly lined stream, as mountain hemlocks and western white pines join the scattered forest.

Eventually the stiff climb abates as you reach the top of the canyon and follow gently graded trail through scattered timber and drier vegetation of

 Wildflowers

grasses, sedges, sagebrush, and assorted wildflowers, mainly lupines. At 2.2 miles, you pass an unmarked trail on the left, angling sharply away from the main trail, which will soon be your route to Echo Peak. ▶**2** Continue on the main trail about 100 yards farther, to the signed, four-way junction with a lateral to Triangle Lake on the right. ▶**3**

To visit **Triangle Lake**, head north on a mild descent through mixed forest and past small, flower-filled meadows. After a quarter mile the descent becomes steeper, eventually leading across a boggy meadow to the south shore of secluded Triangle Lake. ▶**4** The serene lake is sandwiched between low rock hummocks and surrounded by scattered conifers.

Retrace your steps 0.3 mile to the four-way junction ▶**3** and then 100 yards to the unmarked junction of the route to Echo Peak. ▶**2** Head northeast (right) on a mild-to-moderate climb through a mixed forest of lodgepole pines, western white pines, mountain hemlocks, whitebark pines, and white firs. After 0.8 mile you emerge from the forest and reach the low point of a ridge crest between Indian Rock and Echo Peak. From the brink of the ridge, you gaze straight down a nearly vertical cliff to shimmering Angora Lakes, 1300 feet below. Turn right and follow a ducked route along the crest, toward the granite blocks that form the summit of Echo Peak, where you'll enjoy a marvelous 360°

 Summit

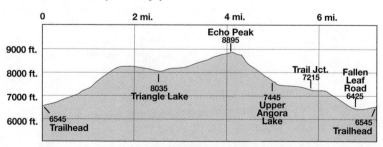

TRAIL 28 Triangle Lake, Echo Peak & Angora Lakes Elevation Profile

Great Views

view. ▶5 Some of the more notable Tahoe landmarks visible from the summit are Mt. Tallac, the Crystal Range, and the peaks near Carson Pass.

After reveling in the summit view, follow a well-defined path along the southeast ridge of Echo Peak for a short distance and then descend steeply down the northeast ridge toward the east side of Upper Angora Lake. Several descent routes seem to come and go, but the general route is easy to determine. Around 7775 feet, you reach a small flat southeast of the lake, where your knees will enjoy the temporary reprieve from the steep descent. Away from the flat, descend a steep hillside, cross a talus field, and reach the east shore of the upper lake. ▶6

On a typical summer day you're apt to have plenty of company here, as the family-run Angora Lakes Resort manages a large sandy beach, boat rentals, a snack shop, and eight housekeeping cabins, all of which make Upper Angora Lake a popular destination for swimmers, sunbathers, boaters and sightseers. Both lakes are stocked with trout, attracting many anglers as well. High, granite ledges above the south shore lure adventurous divers, but exercise caution—there have been a number of fatal accidents involving divers at the upper lake. On a brighter note, the fresh-squeezed lemonade from the snack shop is reportedly excellent.

Lake

From the upper lake, follow the wide road above the west shore of Lower Angora Lake, which, despite the presence of several summer cabins along the far shore, is much more serene than the upper lake. Remain on the road for a quarter-mile past the lower lake to the parking lot and continue to the far end, where the trail to Fallen Leaf Lake begins. ▶7

Although the trail is unmarked at the start, a 6 x 6 signpost a short distance down the path provides assurance that you're on the right route.

Leaving the hustle and bustle of Angora Lakes, a slightly rising trail amid white firs and lodgepole pines leads to a short and steep climb to the crest of a ridge, where through the trees you have filtered views of Fallen Leaf Lake and Mt. Tallac. A long angling descent incorporating a few switchbacks cuts across the hillside above the south shore of Fallen Leaf Lake. Farther down the slope, you encounter pockets of dense, head high foliage alternating with open areas that provide excellent views across the lake. A final series of short switchbacks takes you back into the trees and down to Fallen Leaf Road near the fire station and a chapel. ▶8 From there walk the road to Glen Alpine 0.3 mile, back to the start of the Tamarack Trail. ▶9

🚶	MILESTONES	
▶1	0.0	Start at trailhead
▶2	2.2	Continue straight ahead at use trail to Echo Peak
▶3	2.2	Turn right (north) at Triangle Lake junction
▶4	2.6	Triangle Lake
▶3	3.0	Backtrack to Triangle Lake junction
▶2	3.0	Backtrack to start of use trail to Echo Peak
▶5	4.1	Summit of Echo Peak
▶6	5.0	Upper Angora Lake
▶7	5.7	Start of trail to Fallen Leaf Lake
▶8	6.7	Fallen Leaf Road
▶9	7.2	Return to trailhead

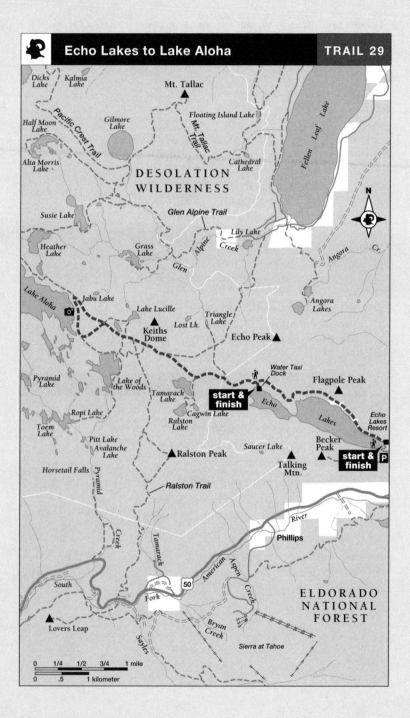

Dicks Lake

Kalmia Lake

Mt. Tallac

Half Moon Lake

Pacific Crest Trail

Gilmore Lake

Floating Island Lake

Mt. Tallac Trail

Cathedral Lake

Fallen Leaf Lake

Alta Morris Lake

DESOLATION WILDERNESS

Susie Lake

Glen Alpine Trail

Lily Lake

Alpine Creek

Angora Cr.

Heather Lake

Grass Lake

Glen

Angora

Lake Aloha

Jabu Lake

Lake Lucille

Lost Lk.

Triangle Lake

Angora Lakes

Keiths Dome

Echo Peak

Pyramid Lake

Lake of the Woods

Tamarack Lake

Water Taxi Dock

Flagpole Peak

start & finish

Echo

Echo Lakes

Echo Lakes Resort

Ropi Lake

Cagwin Lake

Ralston Lake

Toem Lake

Pitt Lake

Avalanche Lake

Saucer Lake

Becker Peak

start & finish

P

Horsetail Falls

Pyramid

▲Ralston Peak

Talking Mtn.

Ralston Trail

River

Creek

Phillips

South

Tamarack

50

American

Aspen

Creek

ELDORADO NATIONAL FOREST

Fork

Lovers Leap

Soyles

Bryan Creek

Sierra at Tahoe

N

0   1/4   1/2   3/4   1 mile
0   .5   1 kilometer

Echo Lakes to Lake Aloha

This section of the famed Pacific Crest Trail is perhaps the most popular route into the heart of Desolation Wilderness. The relatively high elevation start coupled with the ability to shave off 2.5 miles of hiking by taking the water taxi across the lakes make this a highly desirable entry point for backcountry enthusiasts. With a bounty of scenic lakes and plenty of dramatic mountain scenery so easily accessible, the area's popularity is no mystery. While backpackers contend for a limited number of wilderness permits, hikers are free to roam the backcountry within a day's journey at will—just don't expect to be alone.

TRAIL USE
Hike, Run, Horse
LENGTH*
VERTICAL FEET*
DIFFICULTY*
*See table below
TRAIL TYPE
Out & Back
SURFACE TYPE
Dirt

FEATURES
Dogs Allowed
Child Friendly
Mountain
Lakes
Wildflowers
Photo Opportunity
Camping

FACILITIES
Restrooms

Best Time

Hikers will typically find snow-free trails from mid-July to mid-October. The water taxi runs from July 4th to Labor Day weekend, with limited service after that, usually through September.

Finding the Trail

From U.S. 50, about 1.25 miles west of Echo Summit and 1.8 miles east of Sierra at Tahoe Ski Resort, following a sign for Berkeley Camp and Echo Lakes, turn east onto Johnson Pass Road and travel 0.5 mile and then turn left at Echo Lakes Road.

⚐ DESTINATIONS	LENGTH	VERTICAL FEET	DIFFICULTY
With water taxi	7.6 miles, 4 hours	+3425'	– 1 **2** 3 4 5 +
Without water taxi	12.6 miles, 7 hours	+1725'	– 1 2 **3** 4 5 +

Continue up this road for 0.9 mile to the large trail-head parking area above, the south shore of Lower Echo Lake.

Logistics

The Echo Lake Chalet offers water taxi service from the resort's dock at the south end of Lower Echo Lake to the public dock at the far end of Upper Echo Lake, reducing the hiking distance by 2.5 miles. The normal season runs from July 4th through Labor Day weekend, although service usually extends through September, depending on weather conditions and lake levels. At the time of research, the fee was $7 one-way with a 2-person minimum. A direct phone line from the upper dock to the Chalet can be used to arrange for pickup. When the channel to the upper lake is no longer navigable, usually by mid-September, passengers are dropped at the end of the lower lake for a $5 fee with a 4-person minimum. Call (530) 659-7207 (8 AM-6 PM, summer only) for more information.

Trail Description

Without water taxi service, you'll have to walk the extra 2.5 miles around the north shore of Echo Lakes and add that distance to the following mileages. ▶1 From the water taxi pier, climb to the junction with the Pacific Crest Trail. ▶2 Turn left (west) and proceed on rocky tread across open slopes on a westbound course, away from the lakes. Near the Desolation Wilderness boundary, 0.7 mile from the pier, you meet a junction with a lightly used trail to Triangle Lake. ▶3 Another 0.4 mile of hiking leads to a junction with a lateral to Tamarack, Ralston, and Cagwin lakes. ▶4 These three pictur-esque lakes are worth a visit if you have the extra time and energy.

 Lakes

Echo Lakes

Beyond the junction, the PCT follows a moderate climb to a diminutive rivulet coursing through a ravine and then continues the ascent via a pair of switchbacks to an open bench and a junction with the Tamarack Trail, 1.1 miles from the pier. ▶5

Gently ascending trail brings you along the northern fringe of the broad expanse of grass-covered Haypress Meadows, where early- to mid-summer wildflowers put on a fine floral display. Near the far end of the meadows, at 2.0 miles, is the junction with Trail 17E40 to Lake of the Woods (see Trip 30). ▶6

❀ Wildflowers

After a quarter mile stroll from the Lake of the Woods junction, you pass the lightly used Ralston Peak Trail near the high point of the journey and continue toward Lake Aloha. Reach another junction (after a mere 0.1 mile) with east end of Trail 17E09 to Lake Margery and Lake Lucille on the right. ►7 The 0.7-mile trail makes a fine diversion for a slight variation on the return trip. Proceed along the gently graded PCT to the Lake Aloha Trail, at 2.75 miles from the pier. ►8

Leave the PCT and turn left onto the Lake Aloha Trail heading southwest toward the sprawling lake. After 0.4 mile, pass a lateral heading southeast to Lake of the Woods. ►9 A short distance later encounter an unmarked path on the left that leads to Lake Aloha's dam, where swimming can be quite pleasant when the water level is accommodating. Continuing north on the main trail will take you along the east shore of Lake Aloha to a reunion with the PCT at 3.8 miles. ►10 Turn right (southeast) and follow the PCT back to the pier at Upper Echo Lake and call for the water taxi. ►11 Without taxi service, you'll have to hike the 2.5 miles back to the parking lot at Lower Echo Lake.

🚶	MILESTONES		
►1	0.0	(2.5)	Start at Upper Echo Lake pier
►2	0.1	(2.6)	Turn left (west) at PCT junction
►3	0.7	(3.2)	Continue straight ahead at Triangle Lake junction
►4	1.1	(3.6)	Continue straight ahead at Tamarack Lake junction
►5	2.0	(4.5)	Continue straight ahead at Lake of the Woods junction
►6	2.25	(4.75)	Continue straight ahead at Ralston Peak junction
►7	2.35	(4.85)	Continue straight ahead at Lake Margery junction
►8	2.75	(5.25)	Turn left (southwest) onto Lake Aloha Trail
►9	3.2	(5.7)	Veer right at lateral to Lake of the Woods
►10	3.8	(6.3)	Turn right (southeast) at PCT junction
►11	7.6	(10.1)	Return to Upper Echo Lake pier

Lake Aloha

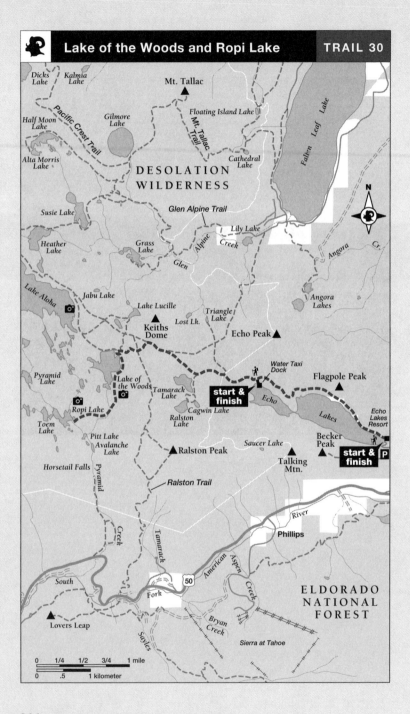

Dicks
Lake

Kalmia
Lake

Mt. Tallac

Floating Island Lake

Fallen Leaf Lake

Pacific Crest Trail

Half Moon
Lake

Gilmore
Lake

Mt. Tallac Trail

Alta Morris
Lake

Cathedral
Lake

**DESOLATION
WILDERNESS**

Susie Lake

Glen Alpine Trail

Lily Lake

N

Heather
Lake

Grass
Lake

Alpine

Creek

Angora

Cr.

Glen

Lake Aloha

Jabu Lake

Lake Lucille

Triangle
Lake

Angora
Lakes

Pyramid
Lake

Keiths
Dome

Lost Lk.

Echo Peak

Water Taxi
Dock

Lake of
the Woods

Tamarack
Lake

**start &
finish**

Echo

Flagpole Peak

Ropi Lake

Cagwin Lake

Lakes

Echo Lakes
Resort

Toem
Lake

Ralston
Lake

Becker
Peak

**start &
finish**

P

Pitt Lake
Avalanche
Lake

Ralston Peak

Saucer Lake

Horsetail Falls

Talking
Mtn.

Pyramid

Ralston Trail

Creek

River

Tamarack

Phillips

**ELDORADO
NATIONAL
FOREST**

50

American

Aspen

Creek

South

Fork

Lovers Leap

Bryan
Creek

Sayles

Sierra at Tahoe

0 1/4 1/2 3/4 1 mile

0 .5 1 kilometer

Echo Lakes to Lake of the Woods and Ropi Lake

Lake of the Woods, with numerous coves, islands, and campsites, is a popular destination accessible by maintained trail. The rest of Desolation Valley beyond Lake of the Woods is one of the most picturesque corners of Desolation Wilderness. Beneath the rugged east face of majestic Pyramid Peak, the granite, glacier scoured basin holds a plethora of lakes and ponds, most of which are not accessible by developed and maintained trail. Hikers and backpackers with rudimentary cross-country skills have a fantastic playground for exploration of the nooks and crannies of this alpine-like basin.

Best Time

Hikers will typically find snow-free trails from mid-July to mid-October. The water taxi runs from July 4th to Labor Day weekend, with limited service after that, usually through September.

Finding the Trail

From U.S.50, about 1.25 miles west of Echo Summit and 1.8 miles east of Sierra at Tahoe Ski Resort, following a sign for Berkeley Camp and Echo Lakes, turn east onto Johnson Pass Road and travel 0.5 mile and then turn left at Echo Lakes Road. Continue up this road for 0.9 mile to the large

TRAIL USE
Hike, Run, Horse
LENGTH*
VERTICAL FEET*
DIFFICULTY*
*See table below
TRAIL TYPE
Out & Back
SURFACE TYPE
Dirt

FEATURES
Dogs Allowed
Mountain
Lakes
Wildflowers
Birds
Photo Opportunity
Camping

FACILITIES
Restrooms

🚶 DESTINATIONS	LENGTH	VERTICAL FEET	DIFFICULTY
With water taxi	8.0 miles, 4 hours	±1190'	– 1 2 **3** 4 5 +
Without water taxi	13.0 miles, 7 hours	±2090'	– 1 2 3 **4** 5 +

trailhead parking area above the south shore of Lower Echo Lake.

Logistics

The Echo Lake Chalet offers water taxi service from the resort's dock at the south end of Lower Echo Lake to the public dock at the far end of Upper Echo Lake, reducing the hiking distance by over two miles. The normal season runs from July 4th through Labor Day weekend, although service usually extends through September depending on weather conditions and lake levels. At the time of research, the fee $7 one-way with a two-person minimum. A direct phone line from the upper dock to the Chalet can be used to arrange for for pickup. When the channel to the upper lake is no longer navigable, usually by mid-September, passengers are dropped at the end of the lower lake for a $5 fee with a four-person minimum. Call (530) 659-7207 (8 AM-6 PM, summer only) for more information.

Trail Description

Without water taxi service, you'll have to walk the extra 2.5 miles around the north shore of Echo Lakes and add that distance to the following mileages. ►1 From the pier, climb to the junction with the Pacific Crest Trail ►2 Turn left (west) and proceed on rocky tread across open slopes on a westbound course away from the lakes. Near the Desolation Wilderness boundary, 0.7 mile from the pier, you meet a junction with a lightly used trail to Triangle Lake. ►3 Another 0.4 mile of hiking leads to another junction, this one with a lateral to Tamarack, Ralston, and Cagwin lakes. ►4 These three picturesque lakes are worth a visit if you have the extra time and energy.

 Lake

Ropi Lake

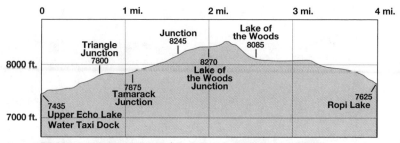

TRAIL 30   Lake of the Woods & Ropi Lake Elevation Profile

Beyond the junction, the PCT follows a moderate climb to a diminutive rivulet coursing through a ravine and then continues the ascent via a pair of switchbacks to an open bench and a junction with the Tamarack Trail, 1.1 miles from the pier. ▶5

Gently ascending trail brings you along the northern fringe of the broad expanse of grassy Haypress Meadows, where early- to midsummer wildflowers put on a fine floral display. Near the far end of the meadows, at 2.0 miles, is the junction with Trail 17E40 to Lake of the Woods. ▶6

Leave the PCT and head southwest skirting the edge of Haypress Meadows and climbing to the crest of a low ridge, where you cross the Ralston Peak Trail. ▶7 From the ridge, follow a moderately steep switchbacking descent to a junction near the north-east shore of Lake of the Woods, 2.6 miles from the Echo Lake pier. ▶8

To reach Ropi Lake head south along the east shore of Lake of the Woods and make a brief climb over the lip of the basin. On descending trail, you head down the canyon of the outlet to a crossing of the stream, at 3.5 miles. Follow the trail as it bends west and descends around a knob to the east shore of Ropi Lake. ▶9 From there, the trailless backcountry is your oyster, but make sure you pack a good topographic map and the requisite cross-country skills.

🚶	**MILESTONES**		
▶1	0.0	(2.5)	Start at Upper Echo Lake pier
▶2	0.1	(2.6)	Turn left (west) at PCT junction
▶3	0.7	(3.2)	Continue straight ahead at Triangle Lake junction
▶4	1.1	(3.6)	Continue straight ahead at Tamarack Lake junction
▶5	1.7	(4.2)	Continue straight ahead at Tamarack Trail junction
▶6	2.0	(4.5)	Turn left (southwest) at Lake of the Woods junction
▶7	2.25	(4.75)	Continue straight ahead at Ralston Peak junction
▶8	2.6	(5.1)	Lake of the Woods
▶9	4.0	(6.5)	Ropi Lake

17E11

DESOLATION
WILDERNESS

8690'

Cagwin
Lake

Ralston Lake

Pitt Lake

Avalanche Lake

Horsetail Falls

Lower Horsetail Falls

Ralston Peak
9235'

9168'

N

Cup Lake

Ralston Trail

Pyramid

Pyramid Creek Trail

Creek

Twin
Bridges

Tamarack

Creek

ELDORADO
NATIONAL
FOREST

Pinecrest
Camp

start &
finish

Sayles Flat P

Chapel of
Our Lady of
the Sierra

50

River

American

South

Camp
Sacramento

Fork

Sayles

Pony
Express
Trail

Bryan

Lovers Leap Trail

Creek

Sierra At Tahoe
ski area

Creek

0   1/4   1/2 mile

0   .25   .5 kilometer

Ralston Peak

Although the climb is steady and stiff, where else in the Tahoe Basin can you achieve such a grand view with only a 3-mile hike? Most hikers favor the route to Ralston Peak from Echo Lakes, which is a mile longer via the water taxi (3.5 miles longer without) but requires 800 fewer feet of elevation gain. This being the case, you may not have to share the serenity of the route described below with too many other hikers.

Best Time

Snow is off the peak by mid-to-late July, when wildflowers are at their peak. By the middle or end of October Ralston Peak has usually seen the first snowfall of the season.

Finding the Trail

Drive U.S. 50 to Sayles Flat and turn north onto a gravel and dirt road opposite the entrance into Camp Sacramento (about 5.75 miles west of Echo Summit and 1.25 miles east of Twin Bridges). Follow this road past the Chapel of Our Lady of the Sierra to the small parking area, 250 yards from the highway. If parking is not available at the trailhead, park along the broad shoulder of the highway at Sayles Flat.

Trail Description

►1 The Ralston Peak Trail starts climbing right off the bat through the cool shade of a dense fir forest, where an occasional chinquapin shrub steals

TRAIL USE
Hike, Run
LENGTH
6.0 miles, 5 hours
VERTICAL FEET
±2875'
DIFFICULTY
– 1 2 3 **4** 5 +
TRAIL TYPE
Out & Back
SURFACE TYPE
Dirt

FEATURES
Dogs Allowed
Canyon
Mountain
Summit
Wildflowers
Birds
Great Views
Photo Opportunity
Steep
Secluded

FACILITIES
None

Desolation Valley *from Ralston Peak*

enough sunlight to eke out an existence. The trail snakes up the hillside on a steady climb toward the huge moraine that forms the east lip of Pyramid Creek canyon, flirting with the possibility of a view into the deep gorge but failing to deliver until you've logged the first mile. At that point, a short use-trail wanders to the brink of the canyon, where a fine vista unfolds.

Soon the trail makes a very brief descent to follow alongside a lushly lined stretch of Tamarack Creek, where alders, ferns, and scattered wildflowers interrupt the otherwise dry surroundings. All too soon the trail forsakes the creek and returns to a winding ascent of the morainal ridge, as a lighter forest allows chinquapin, manzanita, and huckleberry oak to flourish. Near the 1.5-mile mark, you uneventfully cross the unsigned boundary into Desolation Wilderness and follow a switchbacking climb into more open forest, where shrubs and boulders dot the slope. Views of the surrounding terrain improve with the gain in elevation, and you get glimpses of Pyramid Peak, Lovers Leap, and the ski runs of Sierra at Tahoe ski resort. After stepping over a boggy stretch of trail wet from a tiny seep spilling across the path, you continue the ascent across dry, meadow-like slopes, carpeted with lupines, asters, and mule ears, to an unsigned junction, 2.25 miles from the trailhead. ▶2

Leave the Ralston Peak Trail and follow the faint track of a ducked path that steeply climbs the southwest ridge of Ralston Peak through scattered western white pines and red firs. Higher up the slope, you pass a colorful, spring-fed patch of grasses and wildflowers before a final climb over fractured rocks leads to the summit. ▶3 A splendid view of Desolation Wilderness is at your feet. More distant views include a part of Lake Tahoe and the Freel Peak area.

△ **Summit**

🚶 **MILESTONES**

▶1 0.0 Start at trailhead
▶2 2.25 Turn right (northeast) at use trail junction
▶3 3.0 Summit of Ralston Peak

Frata Lake

Osma
Lake

Ropi
Lake

17E11

Ralston
Peak

Pitt Lake

Avalanche Lake

DESOLATION WILDERNESS

Horsetail Falls

Ralston Trail

Lower Horsetail Falls

Pyramid

Pyramid Creek Trail

Creek

ELDORADO
NATIONAL
FOREST

Rocky

Tamarack

Creek

start &
finish

Twin Bridges

Pinecrest
Camp

Canyon

South

50

Sayles
Flat

Creek

River

Fork

American
Camp
Sacramento

Pony Express Trail

Lovers Leap Trail

| 0 | 1/4 | 1/2 mile |
| 0 | .25 | .5 kilometer |

Horsetail Falls

Tumbling down the head of the deep, ice-sculpted granite cleft of Pyramid Creek canyon, the thin ribbon of Horsetail Falls is dramatically scenic at any time of year, but especially spectacular during the height of snowmelt. Located a mere 1.5 miles from a major highway linking the Sacramento Valley with Lake Tahoe, conditions are ripe for this area to become very popular with both recreationists and sightseers alike. Parking improvements and construction of a short loop trail have made the area even more attractive.

Best Time

Horsetail Falls is most magnificent during the height of snowmelt, usually mid-June to mid-July. However, several deaths have occurred here over the years, and extreme caution should be exercised, especially when the rocks along Pyramid Creek are slick from spray. Families should keep a constant watch over young children.

Finding the Trail

Drive U.S. 50 to Twin Bridges, approximately 6.75 miles west of Echo Summit, and park in the well-marked Pyramid Creek parking lot ($3 day-use fee). The trailhead area is complete with flush toilets and running water.

TRAIL USE
Hike
LENGTH
3.0 miles, 1.5 hours
VERTICAL FEET
±675'
DIFFICULTY
– 1 2 **3** 4 5 +
TRAIL TYPE
Out & Back
SURFACE TYPE
Dirt

FEATURES
Canyon
Mountain
Stream
Waterfall
Great Views
Photo Opportunity

FACILITIES
Restrooms
Picnic Tables
Water

Logistics

Wilderness permits are required for overnight use. Overnight wilderness permit holders do not have to pay an additional day-use parking fee.

Trail Description

▶1 From the parking lot, follow single-track trail through oaks, incense cedars, white firs, and Jeffrey pines, with an understory of chinquapin, huckleberry oak, and manzanita, to a trail junction near an area of large, sloping granite slabs. ▶2 Turn right (east), obeying a sign marked PYRAMID CREEK LOOP, CASCADE VISTA. Follow hiker emblem signs attached to widely spaced conifers, as you hike over granite slabs alongside the twisting and turning course of Pyramid Creek, which tumbles over steps and swirls through cataracts. Continue climbing up the canyon, with occasional views of Horsetail Falls, following a route that alternates rock slabs with sections of dirt trail, progressing in and out of scattered forest. You veer away from the creek slightly and reach a junction, 0.75 mile from the trailhead. ▶3

To continue toward the falls, turn right (northwest) at the junction and hike over more slabs and sandy sections of trail to the signed Desolation Wilderness boundary and a dayhikers trail register just beyond. Proceed up the canyon a fair distance, away from the roaring creek through sparse stands of junipers and pines and patches of shrubs. Nearing the falls, the canyon narrows and the terrain becomes much steeper, forcing the rocky trail closer to the creek. Eventually, defined tread falters altogether as granite slabs and boulders bar the way. A short climb leads to a pool near the base of the lower falls, which should be the turnaround point for most parties, especially in early season when the water-polished bedrock above is wet and slippery. ▶4

Waterfall

Horsetail Falls

Although a well-known cross-country route continues up the canyon toward Desolation Valley, only skilled off-trail enthusiasts should contemplate this route.

You can streamline your return to the trailhead by following the Pyramid Creek Trail past the junctions with the Pyramid Creek Loop ►5, ►6 directly back to the parking lot. ►7

🚶 MILESTONES

►1	0.0	Start at trailhead
►2	0.25	Turn right (east) at lower Pyramid Creek Loop junction
►3	0.75	Turn right (northwest) at junction with Pyramid Creek Trail
►4	1.5	Base of lower Horsetail Falls
►5	2.25	Continue straight ahead at upper Pyramid Creek Loop junction
►6	2.75	Continue straight ahead at lower Pyramid Creek Loop junction
►7	3.0	Return to trailhead

Historic cabins *along the Upper Truckee River in Meiss Meadow (Trail 33)*

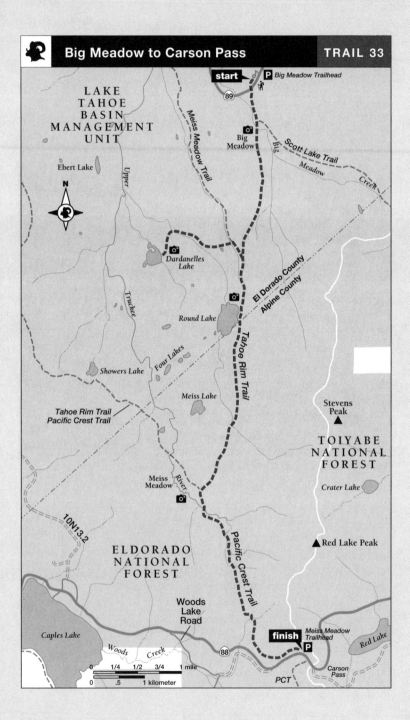

Big Meadow to Carson Pass — TRAIL 33

start — Big Meadow Trailhead

89

LAKE
TAHOE
BASIN
MANAGEMENT
UNIT

Big
Meadow

Scott Lake Trail

Meiss Meadow Trail

Big Meadow Creek

Ebert Lake

Upper

N

Dardanelles
Lake

Truckee

Round Lake

El Dorado County
Alpine County

Tahoe Rim Trail

Four Lakes

Showers Lake

Meiss Lake

Stevens
Peak

TOIYABE
NATIONAL
FOREST

Tahoe Rim Trail
Pacific Crest Trail

Crater Lake

Meiss
Meadow

River

Red Lake Peak

Pacific Crest Trail

10N13.2

ELDORADO
NATIONAL
FOREST

Woods
Lake
Road

finish — Meiss Meadow
Trailhead

Caples Lake

Woods Creek

88

Red Lake

Carson
Pass

PCT

0   1/4   1/2   3/4   1 mile
0   .5   1 kilometer

Big Meadow to Carson Pass

With arrangements for a shuttle, a nearly 8-mile trip travels through the heart of the proposed 31,100-acre Meiss Meadow Wilderness. Following sections of the Tahoe Rim and Pacific Crest trails, recreationists can travel from Highway 89 to Highway 88, visiting Big Meadows, Round Lake, and Meiss Meadows along the way. A 1.3-mile side trip to scenic Dardanelles Lake provides a fine diversion.

Best Time

Snow melts around the first of July and the wildflower season starts shortly thereafter, lasting until around mid-August. Autumn can be a fine time to hike this trail, as aspens and meadow grasses turn golden and the number of trail users drops considerably.

Finding the Trail

The drive between the trailheads is roughly 16 miles. START: Drive on Highway 89 to the well-signed Tahoe Rim Trail parking lot, 6 miles from the Highway 88 junction in Hope Valley, and 5 miles from the Highway 50 junction near Myers.

END: Follow Highway 88 to the Meiss Meadow trail-head parking lot, 0.2 mile west of Carson Pass.

Trail Description

▶1 Leave the parking area and follow the single-track Tahoe Rim Trail a short distance south to a crossing of Highway 89. Once across the highway,

---

TRAIL USE
Hike, Run, Horse
LENGTH
10.4 miles, 6 hours
VERTICAL FEET
+2075'/-1000'
DIFFICULTY
− 1 2 **3** 4 5 +
TRAIL TYPE
Point to Point
SURFACE TYPE
Dirt

FEATURES
Dogs Allowed
Canyon
Mountain
Stream
Lakes
Wildflowers
Autumn Colors
Birds
Wildlife
Photo Opportunity
Secluded
Camping
Historic

FACILITIES
Restrooms

---

start a winding, moderate climb through a forest of Jeffrey pines, lodgepole pines and red firs. At a switchback you have a fine view of the aspen-lined, rocky channel of Big Meadow Creek, which is alive with snowmelt in early July and golden color in autumn. Following more switchbacks, the grade eases just before reaching a three-way junction, 0.5 mile from the trailhead, where a trail to Scott Lake branches left. ►2

❋ Wildflowers

Veer right at the junction and quickly leave the trees behind, as you emerge into the grassy, flower-covered clearing of Big Meadow. Follow the trail through the meadow to a wood-plank bridge that spans the gurgling creek and proceed to the far edge, where a lightly forested ascent resumes. Sagebrush, currant, and drought-tolerant wildflowers, principally mule ears, line the path. Farther up the trail, wood-beam reinforced steps ameliorate the steeper sections of trail, alongside a diminishing tributary of Big Meadow Creek, a sprightly watercourse lined with luxuriant foliage. Continue climbing to a densely forested saddle, and then follow a switchbacking descent into the next canyon, through which flows an Upper Truckee River tributary. Reach the floor of the canyon and a three-way junction marked by an 8 x 8 post, where you meet the Meiss Meadow Trail, 2.2 miles from the trailhead. (See Side Trip to Dardanelles Lake). ►3

≋ Lakes

From the Meiss Meadow Trail junction, the route of the TRT follows a steady climb through dense forest. After 0.6 mile, you reach the lip of Round Lake's basin above the northeast shore and also an informal junction. ►6 From the junction a use-trail wraps around the lake's west shore, which is lined with rock outcrops and scattered forest, and then follows a cross-country route to Meiss Lake. The TRT skirts the east shore of Round Lake through thick forest, away from the lush meadows and thick willows that border the inlet at the south end.

OPTIONS

Side Trip to Dardanelles Lake

From the Meiss Meadow Trail junction, head northwest for 0.2 mile to another three-way junction. ▶4 Turn left (west), make a very brief descent to a boulder hop of the Upper Truckee River tributary, and soon encounter a ford of a wider stretch of the stream. Early in the season, you may need to search for logs upstream in order to make the second crossing without getting your feet wet. Away from the streams, stroll across a bench holding a small meadow and seasonal ponds. Descend off the bench, through dense forest of western white pines, red firs, and lodgepole pines, and follow an alder- and willow-lined stream down a canyon. The grade eases as you pass through meadow-like vegetation of grasses, wildflowers, and willows to the boulder hop of Round Lake's outlet. A short climb amid boulders and granite slabs leads to the west shore of Dardanelles Lake, 1.3 miles from the Tahoe Rim Trail. ▶5

Far enough off the thoroughfare of the TRT, you may be able to enjoy the relative seclusion of this lake. The lakeshore is shaded by light forest and dotted with boulders and slabs, and the picturesque cliffs of the Dardanelles loom above the south shore.

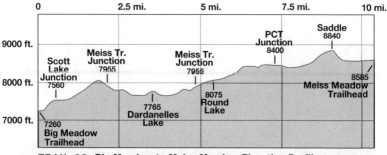

TRAIL 33 **Big Meadow to Meiss Meadow Elevation Profile**

Beyond the lake the TRT resumes its climbing ways, soon reaching an extensive, sloping meadow carpeted with willows, wildflowers, and other lush foliage, which is well watered by a thin, rock-lined rivulet spilling across the trail. Away from the meadow, you reenter forest cover and hop across a pair of trickling rivulets. Eventually the grade eases to a mellow stroll as you break out into an open forest sprinkled with stands of aspen and swaths of drier groundcover, which includes sagebrush, currant, grasses, and drought-tolerant wildflowers. A part of the extensive network of Meiss Meadow appears through scattered lodgepole pines to the right of the trail, with Meiss Lake lying just one-third mile to the west. Leaving the meadow behind, you hop across Round Lake's inlet and proceed to the crossing of a creek coursing through a rocky channel, 0.4 mile farther on. Here, open terrain allows views of the rugged slopes leading up to 10,059-foot Stevens Peak. Continue on gently

Red Lake Peak

OPTIONS

Peak baggers with extra time and energy could accept the challenge of climbing Red Lake Peak from the saddle, 1.2 miles northwest of the Meiss Meadow trailhead. ▶8 A bit of history: John C. Fremont and Charles Pruess reached the summit on Valentines Day in 1844, and made the first sighting of Lake Tahoe by Europeans.

graded trail through lodgepole pines to the heart of
Meiss Meadow and a well-signed junction with the
Pacific Crest Trail, 7.7 miles from the trailhead. ▶7

Near the junction, an old cabin hearkens back to
the days, not so long ago, when cattle were allowed
to graze the lush grasses of picturesque and pastoral
Meiss Meadow. Fortunately, the cows are gone, the
trampling of the meadows is over, the cow pies have
decomposed, and the trails have been left to the
bipeds. Heading south on the PCT from the junction, stroll across the pleasant meadowlands to a
crossing of the Upper Truckee River and follow it
upstream to a second crossing. Soon afterward, the
terrain gets steeper and you start a moderate climb
of a narrowing gorge to a saddle at the head of the
canyon just beyond a seasonal pond, 9.2 miles from
the trailhead. ▶8 From here, enjoy a fine view to the
south of the jagged peaks of the Carson Pass area.

Leaving the saddle, you make a steep 0.3-mile
descent across a stream and into light forest, followed by an arcing traverse across the hillside above
Highway 88. At 10.4 miles, you reach the Meiss
Meadows trailhead. ▶9

🏠 **Historic**

🔭 **Great Views**

🚶	**MILESTONES**
▶1	0.0	Start at Big Meadow trailhead
▶2	0.5	Veer right at junction with Scott Lake Trail
▶3	2.2	Turn right (northwest) at Meiss Meadow Trail junction
▶4	2.4	Turn left (west) at Dardanelles Lake junction
▶5	3.5	Dardanelles Lake
▶4	4.6	Return to Dardanelles Lake junction, turn right (east)
▶3	4.8	Return to Meiss Meadow Trail junction, turn right (southeast)
▶6	5.4	Round Lake
▶7	7.7	Turn left (south) at PCT junction
▶8	9.2	Saddle
▶9	10.4	Reach Meiss Meadow trailhead

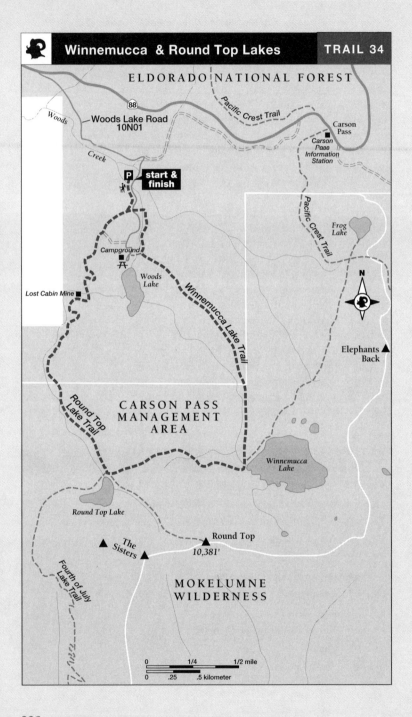

ELDORADO NATIONAL FOREST

88

Pacific Crest Trail

Woods

Woods Lake Road
10N01

Carson
Pass

Creek

Carson
Pass
Information
Station

P   start &
finish

Pacific Crest Trail

Frog
Lake

Campground

N

Woods
Lake

Winnemucca Lake Trail

Lost Cabin Mine

Elephants
Back

Round Top Lake Trail

CARSON PASS
MANAGEMENT
AREA

Winnemucca
Lake

Round Top Lake

Round Top
10,381'

The
Sisters

Fourth of July Lake Trail

MOKELUMNE
WILDERNESS

0   1/4   1/2 mile

0   .25   .5 kilometer

Winnemucca, Round Top, and Fourth of July Lakes

Two picturesque, near timberline lakes with a stunning backdrop from the craggy summits of The Sisters and Round Top are the chief attractions of this loop. The wildflower displays along the upper canyons of Woods Creek are quite colorful in season. Views of the Lost Canyon Mine add a touch of historical interest. Additional options for extending the journey include a 2.3-mile hike to Fourth of July Lake or a technically easy climb of Round Top.

Best Time

The Carson Pass region, with elevations over 8000 feet, tends to hold onto its mantle of snow well into the summer, especially after winters of heavy snowfall. Although mid-July may see trails open up in some years, late July is a better bet following an average winter. Wildflowers are at their peak from July to mid-August. Mild daytime temperatures usually continue until the end of September and, although cooler, autumn hiking can be quite pleasant until the first major storm, usually toward the end of October.

Finding the Trail

Finding the Trail: Follow California Highway 88 to the access road for Woods Lake, 1.7 miles west of Carson Pass. Follow the paved access road for 0.8 mile to a junction and turn right, driving another 0.1 mile to the Woods Lake trailhead parking lot (pit toilet).

TRAIL USE
Hike, Run, Horse
LENGTH
4.8 miles, 2-3 hours
VERTICAL FEET
±1200'
DIFFICULTY
− 1 2 **3** 4 5 +
TRAIL TYPE
Loop
SURFACE TYPE
Dirt

FEATURES
Dogs Allowed
Canyon
Mountain
Stream
Lakes
Wildflowers
Photo Opportunity
Camping
Historic

FACILITIES
Restrooms
Picnic Tables
Water
Campground

229

Winnemucca Lake

Logistics

Wilderness permit required for overnight use. Camping at Winnemucca, Round Top, and Fourth of July lakes is limited to designated sites only. Permits can be obtained at the information center at Carson Pass.

Trail Description

 Camping

▶1 From the parking lot, walk a short distance along the access road across a bridge to the start of the Round Top Lake Trail, No. 17E47. Proceed on dirt trail through a mixed forest of white firs, mountain hemlocks, and western white pines and soon come above the access road to Woods Lake Campground. Reaching a junction, you proceed to the right, following a sign for Round Top Lake. A short, moderate climb leads above the campground, where the single-track trail merges with an old road. Follow the road on a moderate, winding climb to the Lost Cabin Mine trailhead, 0.5 mile from the parking lot.

Back on single-track trail, climb amid scattered trees with a filtered view of Round Top to the southeast and Woods Lake below. After hopping across boulder- and willow-lined Woods Creek, you follow a switchbacking climb above the old structures of the Lost Cabin Mine. The mine was in operation until the early 1960s, producing copious quantities of gold, silver, copper, and lead.

🏠 **Historic**

Continue the ascent on a course roughly paralleling the west fork of Woods Creek. The grade eventually eases as you approach the wilderness boundary and the volcanic summits of The Sisters and Round Top spring into view. Farther upstream, the canyon widens and you pass through open, sub-alpine terrain carpeted with clumps of willow, patches of heather, and wildflowers.

Nearing Round Top Lake, a 4 x 4 post marks a Y-junction with a trail to Fourth of July Lake, 2 miles from the parking lot. ▶2 You could follow the 2.3-mile trail on an hour-long trip to the lake easily enough, but make sure you save plenty of energy for the 2300-foot climb back to the junction. Round Top Lake is a picturesque gem lined with stands of gnarled whitebark pines, dramatically backdropped by the dark, volcanic slopes of The Sisters and Round Top.

🐐 OPTIONS

Side Trip to Round Top

Ambitious adventurers with plenty of extra energy could accept the challenge of a summit bid on the 10,381-foot peak by following a boot-beaten path up the gully of the lake's inlet toward the saddle between east Sister and Round Top. Before reaching the saddle, the route veers into a distinct notch in a ridge and then follows the ridge towards a false summit. Many parties are content with reaching the false summit as their destination, as the true summit is not much higher and requires some exposed scrambling to reach. As expected, the view from either summit is quite extraordinary. Exercise caution and good judgment on a climb of Round Top, and be prepared for windy conditions and intense sunlight at this altitude.

From the Fourth of July junction, head east on a mildly rising climb over a granite ridge amid widely scattered, wind-battered whitebark pines and ground-hugging shrubs and grasses. From the crest of the ridge head down a gully on a moderate descent, cross the gully's stream and continue the descent through open terrain toward Winnemucca Lake. Nearing the lake, you cross the outlet on a flat-topped log and reach a 4 x 4 post at a three-way junction on the west shore, 2.9 miles from the trailhead. ▶3 Pockets of whitebark pine shelter designated campsites on the north shore of Winnemucca Lake, while dark cliffs rise up from the south shore, beneath the towering presence of Round Top. A mile to the northeast is the rounded hump of Elephants Back.

Great Views

From the junction, a 1.4-mile trail ascends the slope below Elephants Back to a connection near Frog Lake with the Pacific Crest Trail, which then heads up another mile to Carson Pass. Your route veers to the north and follows the course of the east branch of Woods Creek, through mostly open terrain covered with sagebrush, willows, and an assortment of seasonal wildflowers. Leave the Mokelumne Wilderness a half-mile from Winnemucca Lake and continue the steady descent into a light covering of mountain hemlocks. Nearing the trailhead, you pass a lateral to Woods Lake on the left, walk across a substantial wood bridge over the creek, cross the paved access road, and then return to the parking area. ▶4

MILESTONES

▶1	0.0	Start at trailhead
▶2	2.0	Round Top Lake/Proceed straight ahead at Fourth of July junction
▶3	2.9	Winnemucca Lake/Veer left at Carson Pass junction
▶4	4.8	Return to trailhead

Emigrant Lake *(Trail 35)*

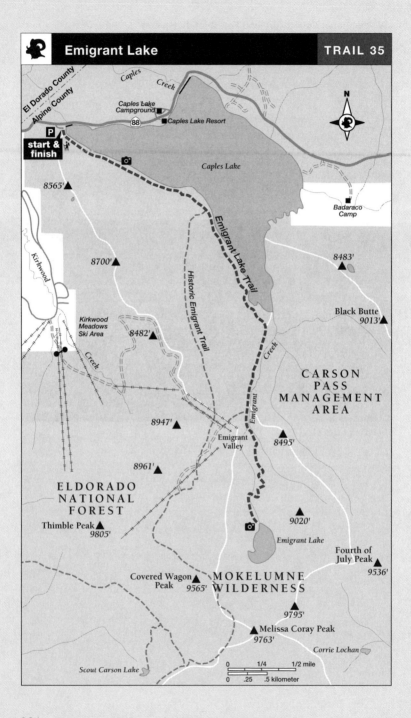

Emigrant Lake

TRAIL 35

Caples Creek

El Dorado County
Alpine County

Caples Lake
Campground

88

■ Caples Lake Resort

P

start & finish

📷

Caples Lake

Badaraco Camp ■

8565' ▲

8700' ▲

Kirkwood

8483' ▲

Black Butte
9013' ▲

Kirkwood
Meadows
Ski Area

8482' ▲

Historic Emigrant Trail

Emigrant Lake Trail

Creek

Emigrant Creek

CARSON
PASS
MANAGEMENT
AREA

8947' ▲

Emigrant
Valley

8495' ▲

8961' ▲

ELDORADO
NATIONAL
FOREST

Thimble Peak ▲
9805'

📷

9020' ▲

Emigrant Lake

Fourth of
July Peak ▲
9536'

Covered Wagon ▲
Peak   9565'

MOKELUMNE
WILDERNESS

9795' ▲

Melissa Coray Peak ▲
9763'

Corrie Lochan

Scout Carson Lake

0   1/4   1/2 mile
0   .25   .5 kilometer

N

Emigrant Lake

Two lakes, one large and one small, provide hikers with two distinctly different portraits of the Carson Pass environs. More than half the journey follows the shoreline of Caples Lake, a 600-acre, man-made reservoir, where scads of recreationists boat, swim, and fish. The 4-mile trail ends at Emigrant Lake, a diminutive, natural lake filling the basin of a steep cirque rimmed by 9500-foot-plus peaks.

Best Time

Dense forest cover along Emigrant Creek and the north-facing cirque containing Emigrant Lake provide cool conditions that inhibit any rapid melt of the previous winter's snowfall. Consequently, in average years you won't find a snow-free trail until mid-July. A brilliant floral display in the cirque will please wildflower enthusiasts from then until mid-August.

Finding the Trail

Drive Highway 88 to the west end of Caples Lake and the large parking area near the dam.

Logistics

Wilderness permit required for overnight visits.

Trail Description

▶1 From the parking lot, the trail makes a very brief climb to a nice view of Caples Lake and follows the

TRAIL USE
Hike, Run, Horse
LENGTH
8.2 miles, 5 hours
VERTICAL FEET
+800'/-25'
DIFFICULTY
− 1 2 **3** 4 5 +
TRAIL TYPE
Out & Back
SURFACE TYPE
Dirt

FEATURES
Dogs Allowed
Canyon
Mountain
Stream
Lakes
Wildflowers
Photo Opportunity
Cool & Shady
Camping

FACILITIES
Restrooms
Picnic Tables

shoreline of the reservoir and the edge of the Mokelumne Wilderness on a virtually level course for the first 2.3 miles of your journey. A mixed forest of lodgepole pines, white firs, western white pines, and mountain hemlocks rims the lake, but since the trail stays so close to the lakeshore you're guaranteed plenty of views across the lake of the surrounding cliffs, ridges, and peaks. Boaters on Caples Lake must observe a 5 mph speed limit, which tends to keep engine noise to a minimum and helps to maintain the tranquility of the hike.

Along the initial stretch of trail you're apt to pass several anglers plying the water in search of a trophy-sized trout. Enter a more open area strewn with boulders and reach a signed junction with the Historic Emigrant Trail, 1.3 miles from the trailhead. ▶2 This old route eventually climbs to the crest of the ridge above Emigrant Lake between Covered Wagon and Melissa Coray peaks.

Beyond the junction, follow the Emigrant Lake Trail back into the forest and continue the lakeshore stroll. Eventually the path moves farther away from

Caples Lake

HISTORY

Two small lakes known as Twin Lakes occupied this area before Pacific Gas and Electric dammed Caples Creek and created the Caples Lake reservoir. The lake and creek were named for James Caples, a physician, who in 1849 left Illinois with his family to join a wagon train bound for California. As a resident of California, Dr. Caples had stints as a miner and a merchant, before managing a 4000-acre ranch near Carson and Deer creeks.

the shoreline. Approaching Emigrant Creek, the trail veers south and begins a moderate climb up the forested canyon. Pass through a small meadow, where senecio and corn lily brighten the surroundings. Proceed upstream along the willow- and flower-lined creek to a signed T-junction, 3.0 miles from the trailhead, where a newly built section of trail heads west to Kirkwood Meadows. ▶3

About 0.1 mile beyond the junction the trail crosses Emigrant Creek and climbs more steeply upstream to a set of switchbacks. Beyond the switchbacks the grade eases and you stroll easily through thinning forest to the northeast shore of Emigrant Lake. ▶4

Cool & Shady

Nestled into a deep north-facing cirque of steep cliffs with vertical walls holding lingering snowfields, Emigrant Lake has a cool, alpine-like ambiance, punctuated by the chilly winds that sweep across the surface of the lake. While a few clumps of trees and pockets of willows dot the near shore, most of the shoreline is stark and exposed, which only augments the unprotected feeling of the surroundings. However, the austere beauty of the area is quite stunning and you won't be disappointed with the scenery.

MILESTONES

▶1 0.0 Start at trailhead
▶2 1.3 Continue straight ahead at Historic Emigrant Trail junction
▶3 3.0 Continue straight ahead at Kirkwood Meadows junction
▶4 4.1 Reach Emigrant Lake

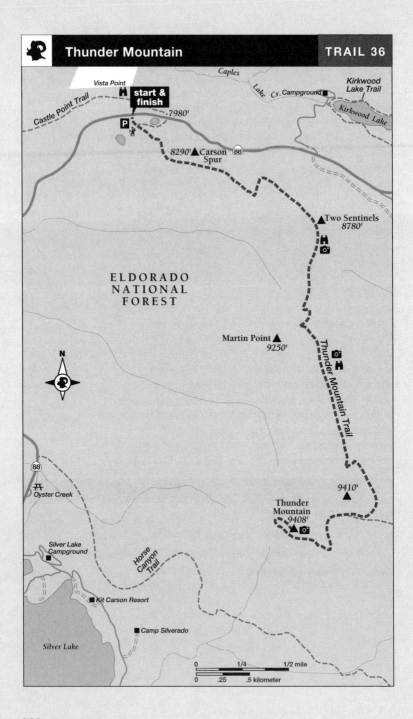

Thunder Mountain

Vista Point

Castle Point Trail

start & finish

7980'

Caples

Lake

Cr. Campground

Kirkwood Lake Trail

Kirkwood Lake

8290' ▲ Carson
Spur

88

▲ Two Sentinels
8780'

ELDORADO
NATIONAL
FOREST

Martin Point ▲
9250'

Thunder Mountain Trail

N

9410'
▲

Thunder
Mountain
9408'
▲

88

Oyster Creek

Silver Lake
Campground

Horse
Canyon
Trail

Kit Carson Resort

Camp Silverado

Silver Lake

| 0 | 1/4 | 1/2 mile |
| 0 | .25 | .5 kilometer |

Thunder Mountain

An incredible vista from a 9408-foot summit should sound intriguing, especially if the trail to that summit is only 2.75 miles long, has an elevation gain less than 1000 feet, and is accessible from a major highway. If that sounds too good to be true, think again, for such is the case with the Thunder Mountain Trail. Despite these positive attributes, the trail sees less use than you might imagine.

Best Time

The expansive view from the summit is good all the time, but getting there will be much easier once the trail becomes snow free, usually toward the end of July. Good conditions usually extend through summer and into fall, until the first storm of the season drops significant snowfall on the Sierra, usually by late October.

Finding the Trail

Follow Highway 88 to the roadside trailhead for the Thunder Mountain Loop near Carson Spur, 1.7 miles west of the Kirkwood Meadows junction.

Trail Description

►1 Pass through a cattle gate in a wire fence, where you'll see a couple of trail signs, one with an ominous warning about unexploded ordnance used during winter for avalanche control. Proceed through a mixed forest of red firs, lodgepole pines, and western white pines, soon encountering a T-junction with a

TRAIL USE
Hike, Run, Bike, Horse
LENGTH
8.5 miles, 5 hours
VERTICAL FEET
+950' -300'
DIFFICULTY
– 1 2 **3** 4 5 +
TRAIL TYPE
Out & Back
SURFACE TYPE
Dirt

FEATURES
Dogs Allowed
Mountain
Summit
Birds
Great Views
Photo Opportunity

FACILITIES
None

239

View from Thunder Mountain *east toward Silver Lake*

lightly used path that heads east to cross Highway 88 and then west to Castle Point. ▶2 Continue straight ahead on a moderate climb, breaking out of the trees as you climb across a sagebrush- and wildflower-covered hillside below Carson Spur, where the rocky crags of Two Sentinels comes into view. Briefly gain the crest at a saddle before a climb across the west side of the ridge leads into thickening forest. Following a pair of switchbacks, you traverse below the pinnacles of Two Sentinels to an open saddle, where the peaks of the Carson Pass area burst into view, along with Kirkwood Meadows and Caples Lake.

Head south along the ridge toward Martin Point, enjoying additional eastward views along the way. A couple of switchbacks lead to an upward traverse around the east side of Martin Point, revealing the impressive profile of Thunder Mountain's north face, where the dark volcanic rock, punctuated with clefts, gashes, pinnacles, and arêtes, creates a dramatic alpine scene. Continue the ascent along the ridgecrest toward Thunder Mountain. As you approach the northeast ridge of the peak, two more switchbacks lead to a mild traverse around the back of the ridge to a three-way junction, 3.5 miles from the trailhead. ▶3

Thunder Mountain's volcanic rock creates a dramatic alpine scene.

From the junction, veer to the right and follow an ascending, westward traverse through scattered lodgepole pines, western white pines, mountain hemlocks, and whitebark pines. The trees diminish as you reach the crest and then angle sharply to the east, following the ridge to the summit of Thunder Mountain. ▶4 An incredible view in all directions greets you at the top, from the mountains of northern Yosemite in the south to the peaks of Desolation Wilderness in the north. Nearby landmarks include Silver and Caples lakes and Round Top.

Great Views

🚶	**MILESTONES**

▶1   0.0   Start at trailhead
▶2   0.1   Proceed straight ahead at Castle Point junction
▶3   3.5   Turn right (southwest) at Thunder Mountain junction
▶4   4.25   Summit of Thunder Mountain

East Tahoe

East Tahoe

T he east side of the lake is perhaps the least developed area around Lake Tahoe. With such a distinction, the logical conclusion would be that this side of the lake would offer an abundance of backcountry trails. Ironically, until the relatively recent completion of the Tahoe Rim Trail, the area was considerably lacking in a developed and maintained trail system. Nowadays, with the building of the TRT and the closing of certain roadways in the backcountry of Lake Tahoe Nevada State Park to motorized travel, recreationists have plenty of opportunities to hike, bike, or ride in the mountainous terrain of east Tahoe.

Access to the forest lands is straightforward on two highways. The four-lane thoroughfare of Highway 50 climbs west to Spooner Summit from Carson City and then runs along the southeast shore of the lake before leaving the basin beyond South Lake Tahoe at Echo Summit. Nevada Highway 28, from a junction with Highway 50, takes motorists northbound along the east shore and into California.

Permits and Maps

The backcountry on the east side of the lake falls under the jurisdiction of three governing agencies, the Carson Ranger District of the Toiyabe National Forest, the Lake Tahoe Basin Management Unit of the federal government, and Lake Tahoe Nevada State Park. Without any designated wilderness areas, permits are not required for dayhikes or backpacks at this time. However, overnighters desiring to camp within the backcountry of Lake Tahoe Nevada State Park are restricted to designated campgrounds that require reservations. Contact (775) 831-0494 for reservations or more information. An entry fee is required for access into the state park.

Forest Service maps may be procured at ranger stations in Carson City and Truckee, or from the Taylor Creek Visitor Center. A full color map showing the multiplicity of routes in the backcountry of Lake Tahoe Nevada State Park is available at park headquarters near Spooner Lake, or from state park headquarters in Carson City. USGS 7.5 minute quadrangles for trips covered in this section are listed in the Appendix.

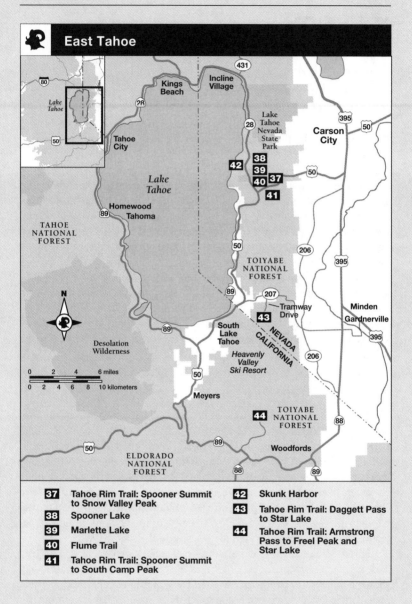

East Tahoe

37	Tahoe Rim Trail: Spooner Summit to Snow Valley Peak	**42** Skunk Harbor
38	Spooner Lake	**43** Tahoe Rim Trail: Daggett Pass to Star Lake
39	Marlette Lake	**44** Tahoe Rim Trail: Armstrong Pass to Freel Peak and Star Lake
40	Flume Trail	
41	Tahoe Rim Trail: Spooner Summit to South Camp Peak	

TRAIL FEATURE TABLE

East Lake Trails

TRAIL	Difficulty	Length	Type	USES & ACCESS	TERRAIN	FLORA & FAUNA	OTHER
37	4	12.4		Hiking, Trail Running, Horses, Dogs	Mountain, Summit	Autumn Colors, Birds	Great Views, Photo Opportunity, Cool & Shady, Secluded
38	1	1.8		Hiking, Trail Running, Handicap Access, Dogs, Child Friendly	Mountain, Lake/Shore	Autumn Colors, Wildflowers, Birds, Wildlife	Photo Opportunity, Historic
39	3	9.0		Hiking, Trail Running, Mountain Biking, Horses, Dogs	Canyon, Mountain, Waterfall, Lake/Shore	Autumn Colors, Wildflowers, Birds, Wildlife	Photo Opportunity
40	3	13.0		Mountain Biking	Canyon, Mountain, Lake/Shore	Autumn Colors	Great Views, Photo Opportunity
41	4	10.2		Hiking, Trail Running, Mountain Biking	Summit	Wildflowers	Photo Opportunity, Historic
42	3	3.2		Hiking, Trail Running, Mountain Biking, Child Friendly		Wildflowers	Great Views, Photo Opportunity
43	4	17.6		Hiking, Trail Running, Mountain Biking, Horses, Dogs	Mountain, Lake/Shore		Great Views, Photo Opportunity, Camping, Secluded
44	3	11.6		Hiking, Trail Running, Mountain Biking, Horses, Dogs	Mountain, Summit, Lake/Shore		Great Views, Photo Opportunity, Camping

Legend

USE & ACCESS
- Hiking
- Trail Running
- Mountain Biking
- Horses
- Child Friendly
- Dogs Allowed
- Handicap Access
- Permit Required
- P Parking Fee

TERRAIN
- Canyon
- Mountain
- Summit

WATER
- Stream
- Waterfall
- Lake/Shore

FLORA & FAUNA
- Autumn Colors
- Wildflowers
- Birds
- Wildlife

DIFFICULTY
- 1 2 3 4 5 +
less   more

OTHER
- Cool & Shady
- Great Views
- Photo Opportunity
- Secluded
- Historic
- Geologic Interest
- Moonlight Hiking
- Steep
- Camping

East Tahoe

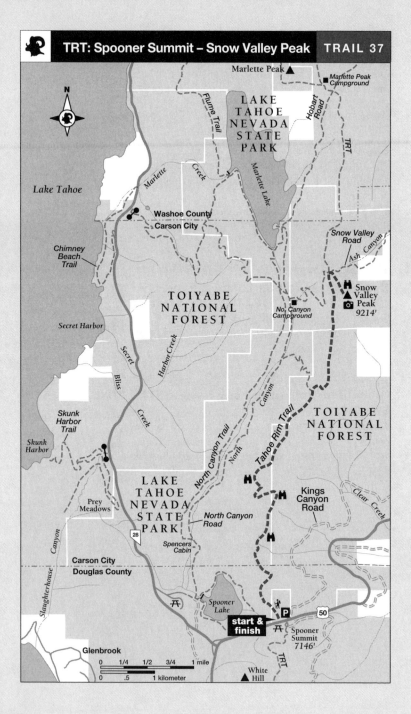

Marlette Peak ▲

■ Marlette Peak
Campground

**LAKE
TAHOE
NEVADA
STATE
PARK**

Flume Trail

Hobart Road

TRT

Marlette

Creek

Marlette Lake

Lake Tahoe

Washoe County
Carson City

Chimney
Beach
Trail

Snow Valley
Road

Ash Canyon

Snow
Valley
Peak
9214'

**TOIYABE
NATIONAL
FOREST**

No. Canyon
Campground

Secret Harbor

Harbor Creek

Secret Canyon

Skunk
Harbor
Trail

Bliss Creek

North Canyon Trail

North Canyon

Canyon

Tahoe Rim Trail

**TOIYABE
NATIONAL
FOREST**

Skunk
Harbor

Clear Creek

**LAKE
TAHOE
NEVADA
STATE
PARK**

Prey
Meadows

Kings
Canyon
Road

North Canyon
Road

28

Spencers
Cabin

Slaughterhouse Canyon

**Carson City
Douglas County**

Spooner
Lake

**start &
finish**

P

50

Spooner
Summit
7146'

TRT

Glenbrook

0   1/4   1/2   3/4   1 mile

0   .5   1 kilometer

White
Hill ▲

Tahoe Rim Trail: Spooner Summit to Snow Valley Peak

Views of Lake Tahoe from Snow Valley Peak are stunning. However, you'll have to journey through 4 miles of dense forest before the lake is revealed in all its glory. A trio of vista points within the first 2.25 miles offers limited views for those who prefer a shorter hike, but they fail to compare to the awesome grandeur at the trip's climax.

Best Time

Considering the shady forest that this section of the TRT passes through, one might get the impression that the previous winter's snowpack would hang around well into summer. However, since considerably less snow falls on the Carson Range than the Sierra crest to the west, this trail opens up sooner than might be expected. In most years hikers can anticipate snow-free hiking beginning in June. The downside is that by midsummer very little water, if any, will be available en route to Snow Valley Peak. The cooler clime of autumn makes for pleasant hiking, particularly when the aspens in North Canyon are ablaze with color.

Finding the Trail

Drive on Highway 50 to Spooner Summit, 0.75 mile east of the junction of SR 28. Parking is available in the well-signed TRT parking lot on the north side of the highway.

TRAIL USE
Hike, Run, Horse
LENGTH
12.4 miles, 7 hours
VERTICAL FEET
±2900'
DIFFICULTY
− 1 2 3 **4** 5 +
TRAIL TYPE
Out & Back
SURFACE TYPE
Dirt

FEATURES
Dogs Allowed
Mountain
Summit
Autumn Colors
Birds
Cool & Shady
Great Views
Photo Opportunity

FACILITIES
Restrooms
Picnic Tables

Trail Description

▶1 A short mild climb from the parking lot leads into light Jeffrey-pine-and-red-fir forest past a junction with a lateral to Spooner Lake. Beyond this junction, the grade of ascent becomes moderate and the forest cover increases. Sporadic gaps in the trees allow brief, partial glimpses of Spooner Lake below, but the majority of the first 4 miles of trail passes through thick forest. At 1.3 miles from the trailhead, a 4 x 4 post marks a short lateral leading to a vista point, which offers a view to the east of Highway 50 winding down Clear Creek canyon. ▶2

Continue the steady ascent, curving around minor hills and ridges. At 0.6 mile from the previous junction, you reach a second junction, marked by a 4 x 4 post, with a lateral to a viewpoint. The short path leads to a boulder-covered knoll and views of Carson Valley to the east and peaks in Desolation Wilderness above Lake Tahoe to the southwest. ▶3

Back on the TRT, proceed on a northbound course through moderate forest cover. After a while the trail veers west and you climb to the crest of a ridge, where, 2.3 miles from the trailhead, another 4 x 4 post signals a junction with another lateral to a viewpoint. Follow the lateral for a few hundred feet and then scramble over boulders to a hilltop view of Lake Tahoe. ▶4

From the junction, the TRT loosely follows the crest of the Carson Range for the next 1.75 miles, on a more gently graded ascent through mixed forest cover. At 4 miles from the trailhead, you encounter a junction with a 1.2-mile-long trail connecting with the North Canyon Road and Marlette Lake Trail, which is 700 vertical feet below. ▶5

Proceeding toward Snow Valley Peak, a mild climb leads away from the junction, passing through open terrain on the east side of the ridge, which allows views of Carson Valley and the Pine Nut Mountains. After a switchback, the trail shifts to the west side of the ridge, where Lake Tahoe and the surrounding peaks spring into view, an ample reward for the previous miles of viewless hiking. A few groves of conifers interrupt the views temporarily, but soon you break out into the open for good, following an angling ascent across a hillside carpeted with tobacco brush, sagebrush, and bitterbrush. The views of the Lake Tahoe basin are quite impressive. Rather than head directly toward the summit, the TRT climbs steadily toward a saddle directly northwest of the peak. In this saddle, 5.8 miles from the trailhead, you reach a junction with the old Snow Valley Peak jeep road. ▶6

Turn right, briefly follow the old road, and then turn right again onto an old track heading toward the summit of Snow Valley Peak. After a winding 0.4-mile climb, you reach the 9214-foot summit. ▶7 Despite the communication towers and accompanying equipment that occupy the summit, the views are stunning, although the broad topography of Snow Valley Peak requires that you move about to get the best views in all directions. Lake Tahoe is the preeminent gem, with Marlette Lake shimmering in the foreground below. Visible peaks are too numerous to list (be sure to pack along a map to help identify them). To the east are Carson City and Carson Valley, and to the northeast, Washoe Lake, Washoe Valley, and the Truckee Meadows.

⛰ **Summit**

🚶	**MILESTONES**
▶1	0.0 Start at trailhead
▶2	1.3 Lateral to first viewpoint
▶3	1.9 Lateral to second viewpoint
▶4	2.3 Lateral to third viewpoint
▶5	4.0 Continue straight ahead at junction
▶6	5.8 Turn right at Snow Valley Peak jeep road
▶7	6.2 Summit of Snow Valley Peak

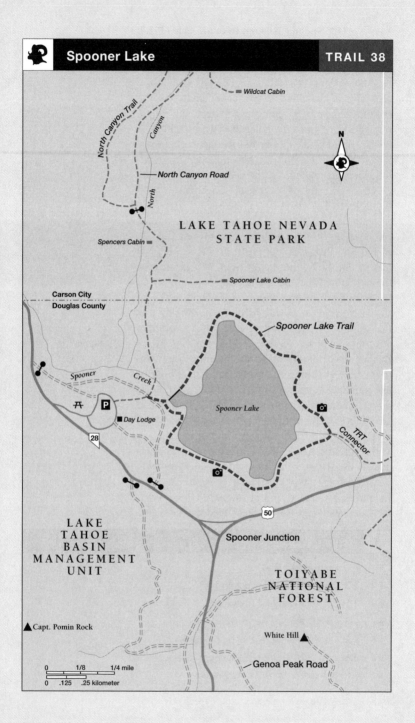

Wildcat Cabin

North Canyon Trail

Canyon

North Canyon Road

North

N

LAKE TAHOE NEVADA
STATE PARK

Spencers Cabin

Spooner Lake Cabin

Carson City
Douglas County

Spooner Lake Trail

Spooner   Creek

Spooner Lake

TRT
Connector

Day Lodge

28

Spooner Junction

LAKE
TAHOE
BASIN
MANAGEMENT
UNIT

TOIYABE
NATIONAL
FOREST

Capt. Pomin Rock

White Hill

Genoa Peak Road

0   1/8   1/4 mile

0   .125   .25 kilometer

Spooner Lake

Spooner Lake was created in the 1850s for use as a millpond when a timber company constructed a dam across Spooner Creek. The dam was rebuilt in 1929 for irrigation purposes. Nowadays, within Lake Tahoe Nevada State Park, recreation has replaced logging and irrigation as the principal activity around Spooner Lake, with hikers, naturalists, picnickers, and anglers flocking to the pleasant surroundings. A nearly level, 1.6 mile path encircles the lake, providing an easy hike complete with interpretive displays, park benches, and superb scenery. The trail passes through diverse plant communities, including Jeffrey pine forest, aspen groves, flower-filled meadows, and sagebrush scrub. The area is also home to a wide range of wildlife.

TRAIL USE
Hike, Run
LENGTH
1.8 miles, 1 hour
VERTICAL FEET
negligible
DIFFICULTY
– **1** 2 3 4 5 +
TRAIL TYPE
Loop
SURFACE TYPE
Dirt

FEATURES
Handicap Accessible
Dogs Allowed
Child Friendly
Mountain
Lake
Birds
Autumn Colors
Wildflowers
Wildlife
Photo Opportunity
Historic

FACILITIES
Restrooms
Picnic Tables
Water
Phone
Visitor Center

Best Time

The Spooner Lake section of Lake Tahoe Nevada State Park is open all year, with groomed cross-country ski trails replacing the mountain bike and hiking routes in the winter. The Spooner Lake trail should be snow free from May, when wildflowers begin their bloom, through October, when stands of aspen turn golden-yellow.

Finding the Trail

Drive on SR 28 to the entrance into the Spooner Lake section of Lake Tahoe Nevada State Park, 1 mile northwest of the junction with Highway 50. Follow the access road to the visitor center parking lot.

To avoid paying the $5 entrance fee, you could drive on Highway 50 to Spooner Summit, 0.75 mile east from the junction with Highway 28, and park on the north side of the road in the Tahoe Rim Trail parking lot. Follow the TRT north for approximately 50 yards to an informal junction. Turn left, leaving the TRT, and descend on a lateral, initially paralleling Highway 50. After 0.75 mile from the TRT trailhead, you reach a junction with the Spooner Lake Trail on the east side of the lake.

Logistics

Although mountain biking is perhaps the most popular form of recreation within the park, the Spooner Lake trail is open to pedestrians only. Pets must be leashed. Fishing is catch-and-release only, with mandatory use of barbless artificial lures. A $5 fee is charged for entry into the park.

Trail Description

 Historic

►1 A short walk from the parking lot leads to a signed, four-way junction. ►2 Following directions to Spooner Lake, you stroll past a signboard and begin a clockwise loop around the lake by passing over the dam. Interpretive signs placed around the loop provide opportunities to learn tidbits about the human and natural history of the area. Conveniently placed park benches provide ample opportunities to rest and enjoy the lake views. Circling the lake, you encounter a variety of vegetation: large clearings are filled with sagebrush, bitterbrush, and mule ears. Where the soil is able to hold onto more moisture, you'll see pockets of willows. Away from the lakeshore are thick stands of Jeffrey pine forest, interspersed with a smattering of white fir. Near the inlet, dense aspen groves shimmer with a splash of grayish green in summer and a blaze of yellow-gold in fall.

≋ **Lake**

On the southeast side of the lake, you reach a junction with the lateral on the left that climbs up to the Tahoe Rim trailhead near Spooner Summit. ▶3 Veer right here and proceed to a wood bridge across Spooner Creek. Beyond the bridge, the trail draws closer to the lakeshore and passes through a flower-filled meadow, which provides a fine habitat for several species of birds, including osprey, bald eagle, and killdeer. Continue around the lake to close the loop at the junction. ▶4 From there, follow the short trail back to the parking lot. ▶5

🚶 MILESTONES

▶1	0.0	Start at trailhead
▶2	0.1	Junction with North Canyon Road
▶3	1.2	Veer left at junction
▶4	1.7	Return to junction with North Canyon Road
▶5	1.8	Return to trailhead

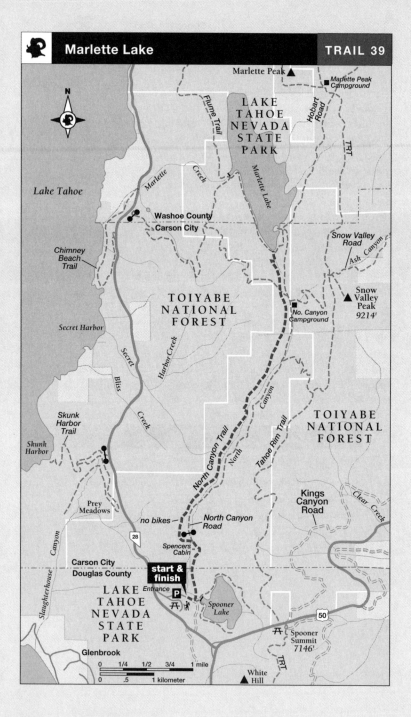

Marlette Peak ▲

■ Marlette Peak
Campground

N

LAKE
TAHOE
NEVADA
STATE
PARK

Flume Trail

Hobart Road

TRT

Marlette Creek

Marlette

Marlette Lake

Lake Tahoe

Washoe County
Carson City

Snow Valley
Road

Ash Canyon

Chimney
Beach
Trail

TOIYABE
NATIONAL
FOREST

▲ Snow
Valley
Peak
9214'

Secret Harbor

Harbor Creek

■ No. Canyon
Campground

Secret

Bliss

Skunk
Harbor
Trail

Creek

North Canyon Trail

North Canyon

Tahoe Rim Trail

TOIYABE
NATIONAL
FOREST

Skunk
Harbor

Kings
Canyon
Road

Clear Creek

Prey
Meadows

no bikes

North Canyon
Road

Canyon

28

Spencers
Cabin

Slaughterhouse

Carson City
Douglas County

**start &
finish**

Entrance

P

Spooner
Lake

50

LAKE
TAHOE
NEVADA
STATE
PARK

Spooner
Summit
7146'

Glenbrook

TRT

0   1/4   1/2   3/4   1 mile

0   .5   1 kilometer

▲ White
Hill

Marlette Lake

The trip to Marlette Lake along the North Canyon Road is very popular, especially with mountain bikers. Once the North Canyon Trail is completed, hikers and equestrians will be able to make most of the journey on single-track trail closed to bikes, leaving North Canyon Road to the exclusive use of mountain bikers. The 4.5-mile journey starts at one artificial lake, Spooner, and ends at another, Marlette. In between you stroll through mixed forest up North Canyon before a short descent leads to the scenic lakeshore. Hikers, bikers, and equestrians with extra time and energy have additional opportunities to reach fine Lake Tahoe views, colorful wildflower displays and extensive stands of aspens.

Best Time

The route to Marlette Lake is generally open for snow-free travel by June. Fall is an especially fine time for a visit, when the extensive aspen groves in North Canyon and along Marlette's west shore are ablaze in autumnal splendor.

Finding the Trail

Drive on Highway 28 to the entrance into the Spooner Lake section of Lake Tahoe Nevada State Park, 1 mile northwest of the junction with Highway 50. Follow the access road to the second parking lot, near the visitor center.

TRAIL USE
Hike, Run, Bike, Horse
LENGTH
9 miles, 5 hours
VERTICAL FEET
±1625'
DIFFICULTY
– 1 2 **3** 4 5 +
TRAIL TYPE
Out & Back
SURFACE TYPE
Dirt, Paved

FEATURES
Dogs Allowed
Canyon
Mountain
Stream
Lake
Autumn Colors
Wildflowers
Birds
Wildlife
Photo Opportunity

FACILITIES
Visitor Center
Restrooms
Picnic Tables
Water
Phone

Logistics

Mountain Biking

In an attempt to reduce the conflicts between hikers and mountain bikers on the ever-popular North Canyon Road, a hikers only, single-track trail was under construction in 2004 between Spencer's Cabin and Marlette Lake. Until the trail is completed, hikers, mountain bikers, and equestrians share the road. The trail was unfinished at the time of research—check with LTNSP about current conditions.

The bicycle route is a mile longer (total length 10 miles) than the hiking route in the milestones.

Trail Description

▶1 From the parking lot follow a wide path for 0.1 mile to a junction with North Canyon Road, just west of Spooner Lake's dam. ▶2 Head north on the road across Spooner Lake's outlet and proceed across an open area of sagebrush scrub before entering a mixed forest of lodgepole pines, white firs, and Jeffrey pines. Soon after entering the forest you pass a 0.25-mile lateral on the right to Spooner Lake Cabin, a hand-hewn Scandinavian style structure that sleeps four adults. The cabin is complete with cooking and heating stoves, kitchen supplies, and an odor-free composting toilet (check out the park's website at www.spoonerlake.com/ for reservations or more information). Not far past the lateral, you stroll by rustic Spencer's Cabin on the left, follow the road over the creek, and meet the junction with the new North Canyon Trail near a closed gate, 0.75 mile from the parking lot. ▶3

Stream

The plan for the new trail has it following the west bank of North Canyon Creek all the way from Spencer's Cabin to Marlette Lake. For the next 3 miles, you make a steady climb up North Canyon through mixed forest. Near the 2-mile mark, the trail crosses a tributary of Secret Harbor Creek, which diverts the majority of North Canyon Creek's

Marlette Lake

Marlette Lake was created in the summer of 1872 when D.L. Bliss and H.M. Yerington, co-owners of the Carson and Tahoe Lumber and Fluming Co., constructed a dirt-fill-and-stone dam across Marlette Creek. The lake was later named for Seneca Hunt Marlette, a New York native who obtained a civil-engineering degree, migrated west, and eventually served as the surveyor general for both California and Nevada. From the dam, water from Marlette Lake was diverted into a flume and traveled 4.75 miles north to Tunnel Creek Station, where it entered a 4500-foot tunnel descending southeast, carved out of the bedrock below the crest of the Carson Range. From there, the water dropped into a second flume, sinuously traveling to a terminus on a ridge near Lakeview. Here the water entered a pipe, and, after a nearly-2-mile descent, was propelled 5 miles uphill to another flume, which delivered Gold Hill's and Virginia City's water supply to a reservoir near the crest of the Virginia Range.

The design and construction of this water system was quite an engineering feat at the time, a testament not only to the engineers and builders, but to the incredible bonanza generated by the Comstock Lode as well. Although the mines were played out long ago, a more recent bonanza has swept the area. With the aid of volunteers, the Flume Trail was cleaned up and repaired, and nowadays is considered one of the premier mountain-bike trails in the nation.

stream flow away from Spooner Creek on a shortcut west to Lake Tahoe. At 3.2 miles from the parking lot, the North Canyon Campground lies directly east and should be accessed by a short lateral. ►4 Near the vicinity of the campground, a steep 1.2-mile trail provides a connection to the Tahoe Rim Trail.

Along the creek, stands of quaking aspen and pockets of meadow contrast nicely with the conifers. At 4 miles from the trailhead, in a saddle separating North Canyon from Marlette Lake's basin, you encounter an old, closed road on the right, which follows a steep westbound course down to Chimney Beach. ►5

From the high point a 0.5-mile descent leads to a road along the south shore of picturesque Marlette Lake. ►6 Nearby is a Nevada Division of Wildlife trout hatchery built in 1987 (fishing is not allowed in Marlette Lake). Since the lake is a domestic water source for Carson City, camping is not allowed, but swimming is permissible, and the temperature of the water can be quite refreshing on a hot summer day.

≈ **Lake**

OPTIONS

Exploring Beyond Marlette Lake

From where the trail meets the road at the south end of Marlette Lake, a left turn (northwest) leads to the dam and the beginning of the Flume Trail (see Trip 40, p. 265). A 0.3-mile stroll to the right (northeast) will take you to a junction near a restroom. From there, a 1-mile climb northeast past dense stands of aspen and luxuriant flower gardens leads to a wonderful view of Marlette Lake and Lake Tahoe from Marlette Overlook. By continuing on the road another 0.7 mile, you will intersect the Tahoe Rim Trail, which leads north toward Marlette Peak and Marlette Peak Campground, or south to the Spooner Lake trailhead.

Marlette Lake

| 🚶 | **MILESTONES (HIKING)** |

▶1   0.0   Start at trailhead

▶2   0.1   Head north on North Canyon Road

▶3   0.75 Turn left onto North Canyon Trail

▶4   3.2   North Canyon Campground lateral

▶5   4.0   Continue straight ahead at Chimney Beach junction

▶6   4.5   Reach south shore of Marlette Lake

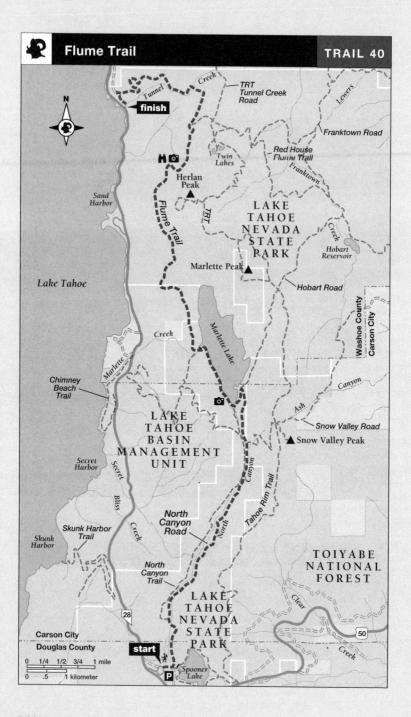

Flume Trail

The Flume Trail is one of the West's most renowned mountain bike trails, with great views of Lake Tahoe and an easy graded section of single-track trail combining for Tahoe's ultimate fat-tire excursion. While a stiff climb makes up the first 5 miles, once the incredible views begin the effort is quickly forgotten for the remainder of the downhill romp. All this grandeur does have one drawback—the trail can be quite crowded on sunny summer weekends.

Best Time

June through October.

Finding the Trail

START: Drive on Highway 28 to the entrance into the Spooner Lake section of Lake Tahoe Nevada State Park, 1 mile northwest of the junction with Highway 50. Follow the access road to the second parking lot near the visitor center.

END: Parking is nonexistent anywhere near where the Tunnel Creek Road meets Highway 28. Parking along the shoulder of the highway is not allowed in the immediate vicinity, and legal spaces farther along the highway are usually already occupied, especially on a summer weekend. Some groups park at the Ponderosa Ranch parking lot, but who knows if that's okay with the owners? Perhaps the best bet is to bite the bullet and pay the ten bucks for the Flume Trail Shuttle back to Spooner Lake. Visit the

TRAIL USE
Bike
LENGTH
13.0 miles, 4 hours
VERTICAL FEET
+1850'/-2625'
DIFFICULTY

– 1 2 **3** 4 5 +
TRAIL TYPE
Point to Point
SURFACE TYPE
Dirt

FEATURES
Canyon
Mountain
Lake
Autumn Colors
Great Views
Photo Opportunity

FACILITIES
Restrooms
Picnic Tables
Water
Phone
Visitor Center

web at www.theflumetrail.com, or call (775) 749-5349 for more information.

Logistics

Horses are not permitted on the Flume Trail, and while hikers *are* allowed, the author's recommendation is to leave this trail for mountain bikers.

Not only are mountain bikes available for rent, but reservations can be made for a pair of back-country cabins. Both the Spooner Lake Cabin and Wild Cat Cabin are hand hewn Scandinavian style structures that sleep two to four adults. The cabins are complete with cooking and heating stoves, kitchen supplies, and odor-free composting toilets. Check out the website at www.spoonerlake.com to make reservations or for more information.

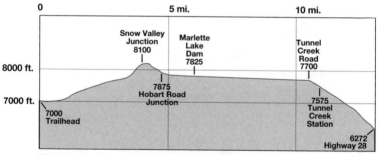

TRAIL 40 Flume Trail Elevation Profile

Trail Description

▶1 From the parking lot follow a wide path for 0.1 mile to a junction with North Canyon Road. ▶2 Head north on a gentle climb across an open area of sagebrush scrub into a mixed forest of lodgepole pines, white firs, and Jeffrey pines, where the grade of ascent increases. Continue a stiff climb through the rolling terrain of North Canyon, amid conifers and aspen groves. At 3.25 miles from the parking lot, a steeper 0.75-mile climb leads to the top of a

The Carson Range

The Flume Trail is in the Carson Range, a north-south-trending sub-range of the Sierra Nevada lying to the east of Lake Tahoe. Elevations range from 5000 feet near the eastern base to 10,881 feet at the summit of Freel Peak (in California). Such a wide elevation spectrum furthers the biological diversity: dry, sagebrush-covered slopes, common to much of the Great Basin, are present throughout the area, as expected, but so are lush streamside settings more reminiscent of canyons on the west side of the Sierra. Early summer offers hikers a wide array of wildflowers.

The Carson Range holds the most diverse collection of trees in Nevada. In the lower elevations pinyon pines and western junipers intermix with mountain mahoganies. From 5000 feet to 7500 feet is the Jeffrey-pine-white-fir zone, where you'll also find some ponderosa pine, sugar pine and incense cedar. From 7500 feet to 9000 feet is the red-fir zone, home to red fir, lodgepole, Jeffrey and western white pines, white firs, and mountain hemlocks. The upper forest zone, from 9300 feet to timberline, at 10,300 feet, features groves of whitebarks and some lodgepole pine and mountain hemlock.

The Carson Range is the backyard playground for residents of Reno-Sparks, Carson City and the Carson Valley towns of Minden and Gardnerville, as well as for visitors and residents of the communities around the east shore of Lake Tahoe. This proximity of urban centers means recreationists will be able to find everything necessary for hiking and backpacking trips into the Carson Range.

saddle and the high point of your journey, where roads branch off to Chimney Beach on the left and Snow Valley Peak on the right. ►3

With the last of the climbing behind, you head downhill toward a well-signed junction with Hobart Road, on the southeast side of scenic Marlette Lake. ►4 The lake provides an inviting swim if you're still hot from the climb. Turn left and follow the flat road around the south and west sides of the lake. During periods of high water you may have to carry your bike across some boulders and then across the outlet in order to reach the start of the Flume Trail proper, near the dam. ►5

Now on the Flume Trail, you ride pleasantly graded, single-track that makes a mild drop of 40 feet per mile. The trail is narrow and exposed in spots, and you may feel the need to walk your bike across some rockslides, but the stupendous views of Lake Tahoe along the way make the Flume Trail a world-famous ride. The mellow 4.5-mile ride along the Flume Trail ends where the trail merges with Tunnel Creek Road. ►6

Continue the northbound descent on the road for 0.4 mile to Tunnel Creek Station. ►7 From there, the steep, sandy road bends west and drops 1300 feet in 2 miles to Highway 28. ►8

🚶 MILESTONES

▶1 0.0 Start at trailhead

▶2 0.1 Head north on North Canyon Road

▶3 4.0 Continue straight ahead at Chimney Beach-
Snow Valley Peak junction

▶4 4.7 Turn left at Hobart Road junction

▶5 6.1 Marlette Lake Dam/Start of Flume Trail

▶6 10.5 Merge with Tunnel Creek Road

▶7 10.9 Tunnel Creek Station

▶8 13.0 Highway 28

🌿 OPTIONS Lake Tahoe Nevada State Park Bike Trails

Aside from the section of the Tahoe Rim Trail closed to bikes
between Spooner Summit and Tunnel Creek Road (Trail 37), options
for mountain bikers are many — a fine network of trails and roads
carpets the Marlette-Hobart backcountry. A full-color brochure, complete with map and showing all the possible routes, is available from
Lake Tahoe Nevada State Park.

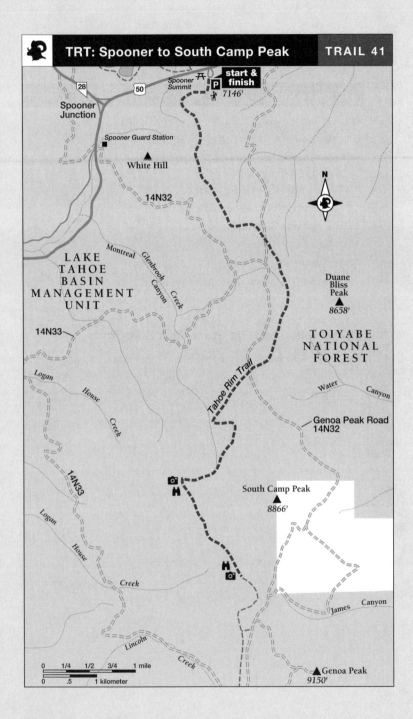

start & finish

Spooner
Summit

7146'

28

50

Spooner
Junction

Spooner Guard Station

White Hill

14N32

N

LAKE
TAHOE
BASIN
MANAGEMENT
UNIT

Montreal

Glenbrook

Canyon

Creek

Duane
Bliss
Peak

8658'

14N33

TOIYABE
NATIONAL
FOREST

Logan

House

Creek

Tahoe Rim Trail

Water

Canyon

Genoa Peak Road
14N32

14N33

Logan

House

Creek

South Camp Peak

8866'

James   Canyon

Lincoln

Creek

0   1/4   1/2   3/4   1 mile

0   .5   1 kilometer

Genoa Peak
9150'

Tahoe Rim Trail: Spooner Summit to South Camp Peak

Lake Tahoe is considered the premier natural wonder in northern Nevada and this trip to South Camp Peak may provide the quintessential view. Don't forget your camera, as even the most jaded photographer will be impressed by the vistas from the open slopes along the mile-long traverse of the peak. Getting there does require a 5-mile, 1875-foot climb along a waterless stretch of the Tahoe Rim Trail, but the scenic rewards are definitely worth the effort.

Best Time

Receiving roughly half the amount of winter snow that falls on Desolation Wilderness, trails in the Carson Range open sooner than their western counterparts. Consequently, in average years, hikers can hit the trail to South Camp Peak by June and continue through October before the first significant snowfall dusts the range.

Finding the Trail

Follow Highway 50 to Spooner Summit, 0.75 mile east of the junction with Highway 28. Park on the south side of the highway in the Spooner Summit picnic area (pit toilets).

Logistics

A couple of cautions are worth mentioning. Water is not available along the entire route of the trail—make sure you're carrying a sufficient amount for both the hike in and the hike out. Hikers should

TRAIL USE
Hike, Run, Bike, Horse
LENGTH
10.2 miles, 4-6 hours
VERTICAL FEET
±2100'
DIFFICULTY
– 1 2 **3** 4 5 +
TRAIL TYPE
Out & Back
SURFACE TYPE
Dirt

FEATURES
Dogs Allowed
Summit
Mountain
Wildflowers
Great Views
Photo Opportunity

FACILITIES
Restrooms

maintain a cautious eye while on the trail, as mountain bikes are permitted on this section of the TRT.

Trail Description

▶1 Leave the trailhead parking lot and make a stiff, switchbacking climb on sandy trail up the hillside south of Highway 50 through sagebrush, tobacco brush, currant, chinquapin, and manzanita, beneath scattered Jeffrey pines and quaking aspens that dot the slope. Eventually the roar of traffic from the highway is left behind, as you gain a ridge and follow a milder climb along the crest. Farther on, keen eyes will reveal that this area was selectively logged at some time in the past, the result of a bark beetle infestation that killed a number of trees in the early 1990s. This scattered forest of Jeffrey pines and red firs allows partial views of Carson Valley to the east and Lake Tahoe to the west, and provides enough sunlight for a fine array of early summer wildflowers, including mule ears, lupine, and paintbrush. Near the 1.5-mile mark, you climb to a knoll, where a very short use-trail leads to impressive views.

A stretch of mild descent, followed by a mild climb brings you to a crossing of a dirt road, 2.5 miles from the trailhead. A mildly rising traverse leads across the selectively logged slope below Duane Bliss Peak. At 0.25 mile past the first road crossing, you cross an abandoned road and climb to the crest again. A moderate climb along the ridge takes you just below a rocky knob, where a short use-trail leads up the knob to good views of the Carson Valley backdropped by the Pine Nut Range. You eventually leave the views behind, following a mildly graded descent into a mixed forest of western white pines, Jeffrey pines, and red firs to the signed crossing of the Genoa Peak Road (FS 14N32), 3

Water is not available along the entire route of the trail.

 Great Views

miles from the trailhead. ►2 This road is a major backcountry thoroughfare for not only the 4WD crowd, but mountain bikers as well.

A moderate climb away from the Genoa Peak Road passes through an area of selective logging and slash burning that is a bit unsightly, although this activity has produced a fine wildflower display in early summer. The long, steady climb reaches a switchback, beyond which the trail bends east before curving back toward the southwest. As you gain elevation, mountain hemlocks and lodgepole pines join the dense, mixed forest. Nearing the crest at the north end of South Camp Peak, approximately 1.3 miles from Genoa Peak Road, you suddenly break out of the forest into a sublime Tahoe vista. ►3 A short climb takes you up to the top of a rocky knoll, where an even better view awaits. Be sure you pack along a detailed map of the Tahoe Basin to help identify the bounty of landmarks visible from this exceptional viewpoint, from where a finer view of the lake is hard to imagine.

▲ **Summit**

The essentially flat-topped plateau of South Camp Peak stretches south for another mile, providing nearly continuous, stupendous lake views. The true summit is actually 0.7 mile east of the trail, hardly worth the extra effort of a cross-country journey. The high point along the trail is another 0.8 mile south, near where a conveniently placed log bench offers an excellent seat for perhaps Tahoe's best show. ►4

🚶 **MILESTONES**

►1	0.0	Start at trailhead
►2	3.0	Genoa Peak Road
►3	4.3	North edge of South Camp Peak
►4	5.1	South edge of South Camp Peak

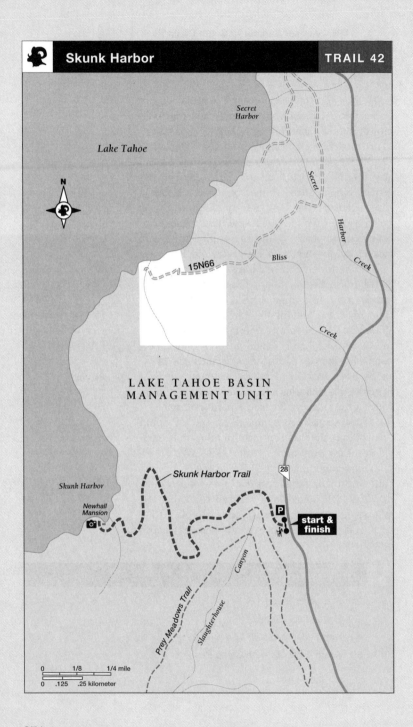

Skunk Harbor

Secret
Harbor

Lake Tahoe

N

15N66

Bliss

Secret

Harbor

Creek

Creek

LAKE TAHOE BASIN
MANAGEMENT UNIT

Skunk Harbor Trail

28

Skunk Harbor

P

*Newhall
Mansion*

start &
finish

Prey Meadows Trail

Canyon

Slaughterhouse

0	1/8	1/4 mile
0	.125	.25 kilometer

Skunk Harbor

Lake Tahoe is world renowned for the beauty of its exceptionally clear waters and sparkling sand beaches. Despite the name, Skunk Harbor confirms that reputation, beckoning swimmers, sunbathers, picnickers, and sightseers to visit the scenic, crescent-shaped shoreline. Along with the natural beauty, visitors will experience a bit of history from the Newhall Mansion, a preserved relic from Tahoe's resort period of the early 1900s. The 1.6-mile hike and limited parking at the trailhead insures that Skunk Harbor won't be as crowded as other Tahoe beaches. Nevertheless, don't expect to be alone.

TRAIL USE
Hike, Run, Bike
LENGTH
3.2 miles, 2-3 hours
VERTICAL FEET
±700'
DIFFICULTY
– 1 2 **3** 4 5 +
TRAIL TYPE
Out & Back
SURFACE TYPE
Dirt

Best Time

The lake level elevation insures a long hiking season, from April to November, but unless you're a card carrying member of the polar bear club, don't plan on swimming in the typically frigid waters of Lake Tahoe unless summer temperatures are prevalent.

FEATURES
Child Friendly
Shore
Great Views
Photo Opportunity
Historic

Finding the Trail

The trailhead is on the west shoulder of Highway 28 at a closed steel gate, 2.4 miles north of the junction with Highway 50.

FACILITIES
Restrooms
Picnic Tables
Water
Phone

Logistics

Reaching the trailhead may be the most formidable challenge of this trip, as the trailhead is unsigned, parking is extremely limited, and there is no mass transit service available.

Newhall Mansion

George Newhall built this rustic mansion in 1923 as a wedding present to his wife Caroline. The property served as a retreat and entertainment center for family and friends until its sale in 1937 to George Whittell. Eventually the property was acquired by the Forest Service and made accessible for public enjoyment. A number of plaques with photographs provide insights into the history of the area.

Trail Description

►1 From the highway, descend northwest on a paved road, which quickly turns to dirt, amid Jeffrey pines and white firs, with an understory of manzanita, sagebrush, chinquapin, rabbitbrush, buckwheat, tobacco brush and wild rose. Lupines and mule ears brighten the slopes in season. Soon the road curves above the head of Slaughterhouse Canyon and proceeds in a more westerly direction. Keen eyes may spy the old railroad grade hugging the hillside below the road. Built in 1875, the narrow gauge railroad hauled timber to sawmills near Glenbrook. The resulting lumber was primarily used in Virginia City and the mines of the

Comstock Lode. A half mile from the highway, the trail intersects the railroad grade. ▶2

Continue on the main road on a steeper, curving descent toward the lake. As you near the shoreline, cedars join the increasingly dense forest and the underbrush thickens as well. At 1.5 miles, you reach a three-way junction. ▶3 The road to the right leads to the north side of Skunk Harbor's sandy beach, which is bordered by a pile of large rocks. ▶4

Turning left, you cross a tiny stream and parallel the creek toward the lakeshore. Soon the roof and rear walls of the Newhall Mansion appear, along with a patio complete with outdoor fireplace. Granite steps lead down to the structure, and although the doors are locked, you can peer through iron screens over the windows for a view of the inside. The front porch overlooks the sandy beach and the sparkling clear waters of Skunk Harbor.

Keen eyes may spot the old railroad grade hugging the hillside below the road to Skunk Harbor.

🏠 **Historic**

🚶 MILESTONES

▶1 0.0 Start at trailhead
▶2 0.5 Junction with old railroad grade to Prey Meadows
▶3 1.5 Veer left at three-way junction
▶4 1.6 Reach Skunk Harbor

Side Trip to Prey Meadows

OPTIONS

The old railroad grade provides a gently descending route to Prey Meadows, a fine destination in late spring, when copious wildflowers are blooming.

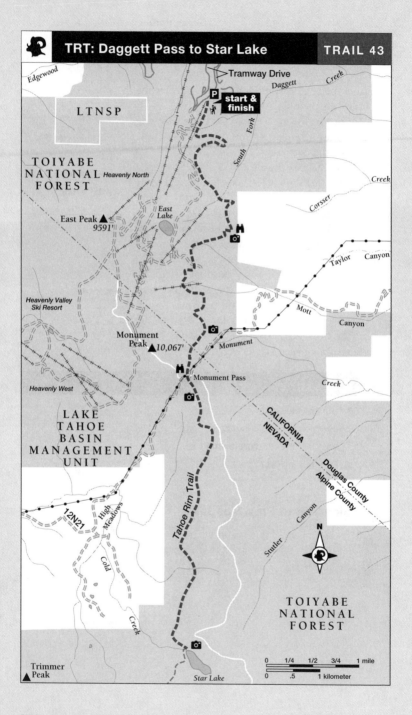

TRT: Daggett Pass to Star Lake

TRAIL 43

Tramway Drive

start & finish

Edgewood

Daggett

Creek

LTNSP

South Fork

Corsser

Creek

TOIYABE
NATIONAL
FOREST

Heavenly North

East
Lake

East Peak ▲
9591'

Taylor

Canyon

Heavenly Valley
Ski Resort

Mott

Canyon

Monument
Peak ▲ 10,067'

Monument

Monument Pass

Creek

Heavenly West

CALIFORNIA
NEVADA

LAKE
TAHOE
BASIN
MANAGEMENT
UNIT

Douglas County
Alpine County

12N21

High
Meadows

Tahoe Rim Trail

Stutler

Canyon

Cold

TOIYABE
NATIONAL
FOREST

N

Creek

Trimmer
▲ Peak

Star Lake

| 0 | 1/4 | 1/2 | 3/4 | 1 mile |
| 0 | | .5 | | 1 kilometer |

Tahoe Rim Trail: Daggett Pass to Star Lake

Although not the shortest route to lovely Star Lake, this trip offers fine views of Carson Valley and Lake Tahoe away from the crowds. The 17.6-mile round trip makes for a long day, but helps to reduce the number of people you're apt to meet along the way. Once you surmount the first half-mile of steep trail, the remainder is one of the most pleasantly graded sections along the entire 165-mile Tahoe Rim Trail.

Best Time

Hiking season begins in earnest once the winter snows have melted, usually by sometime in June. Mid-July through August will see the warmest temperatures, and would be the best time for a dip in lovely Star Lake. Cool but pleasant weather generally lasts from mid-September to the end of October, about when the first significant storm of the season drops snow on the mountains.

Finding the Trail

Drive on Highway 207, also known as Kingsbury Grade, to Dagget Pass and turn south onto Tramway Drive, which eventually becomes a one-way road that circles through the Nevada side of Heavenly Valley Ski Resort. Park your vehicle in the parking lot near the base of the Stagecoach Express ski lift, 1.5 miles from Highway 207. (No facilities.)

TRAIL USE
Hike, Run, Bike, Horse
LENGTH
17.6 miles, 10 hours
VERTICAL FEET
±3500'
DIFFICULTY
– 1 2 3 **4** 5 +
TRAIL TYPE
Out & Back
SURFACE TYPE
Dirt

FEATURES
Dogs Allowed
Mountain
Lake
Great Views
Photo Opportunity
Camping
Secluded

FACILITIES
Restrooms
Picnic Tables

Logistics

Star Lake is an excellent overnight destination and wilderness permits are not required.

Combining this trip with Trip 44 can create a nice point-to-point trip, although that requires a somewhat lengthy car shuttle.

Trail Description

▶1 Amid towering condominiums and ski area development, the route of the Tahoe Rim Trail begins alongside the base of the Stagecoach Express ski lift and follows a moderately steep climb of the ski slope. After an initial stretch of climbing, the grade eases momentarily at a saddle to cross some dirt roads and then quickly resumes a stiff climb along a road for 75 yards or so to where the TRT leaves the open ski slope and heads east. Now on a more pleasantly graded climb on single-track trail, you enter light, mixed forest, composed of Jeffrey pines, western white pines, lodgepole pines, and red firs. Reach a switchback and a partial view through the trees of Carson Valley to the east, the spine of the Carson Range to the north, and part of Lake Tahoe to the west. More switchbacks lead to a saddle, about 1.1 miles from the trailhead and directly southwest of peak 8331.

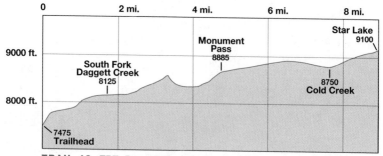

TRAIL 43   TRT: Daggett Pass to Star Lake Elevation Profile

View south *toward Freel Peak, Jobs Peak, and Jobs Sister*

Now through lighter forest, which permits a groundcover of pinemat manzanita, tobacco brush, and chinquapin, you follow mildly graded trail past an informal junction with a short spur to a ski area road and then pass below another chairlift and ski slope. Shortly past the ski slope, hop across the narrow channel of South Fork Daggett Creek, 1.7 miles from the trailhead. ▶2

A short, mildly rising traverse leads to a crossing of a jeep road and more views of Carson Valley. Back into the forest, a mile-long, switchbacking climb climaxes at a saddle near peak 8611, 3.0 miles from the trailhead, where the trail merges with a ski-area road from East Peak Lake. Just before the saddle you have a fine vista across an open slope of 10,057-foot Monument Peak, 1 mile south-southwest, and the more distant Freel Peak, Jobs Peak, and Jobs Sister.

Great Views

Descend very steeply along the road toward the bottom of Mott Canyon and curve around to where you'll be grateful as single-track trail resumes. A short way after the resumption of trail, step over trickling Mott Canyon Creek, which by late summer is usually is dry at this elevation, and pass below another Heavenly Valley chairlift. A moderate climb leads out of the canyon, followed by a rising traverse that follows the folds and creases of the topography before angling directly across a mostly open slope. Along the traverse you have expansive eastward views of the Carson Valley, and views to the south of Jobs Peak. Cross the unsigned Nevada-California border and continue the climb to the crest of the Carson Range at Monument Pass, 4.8 miles from the trailhead. ▶3 Aside from the power lines that run through the pass, the view of Freel Peak and Jobs Sister is quite dramatic, made even better by a short scramble to a neighboring rock outcrop.

≋ **Lake**

Now on the west side of the crest, follow sandy trail on an open, 2-mile traverse through widely scattered trees with good views down into High Meadows and across the lake to the Crystal Range peaks in Desolation Wilderness. On a nearly imperceptible descent, you eventually enter a light forest that obscures most of the views. At 7.7 miles, you encounter the flower-lined, refreshing brook of a Cold Creek tributary. ▶4 From there, slightly rising trail proceeds through western white pines, mountain hemlocks, and lodgepole pines toward Star Lake. Just before the lake, the trail curves east and then drops to a crossing of the outlet. ▶5

At 9100 feet, Star Lake is one of the highest lakes in the Tahoe basin, and therefore not one of the warmest. A number of passable campsites along the north shore lure overnighters.

Star Lake and Jobs Sister *(right)*

🚶 MILESTONES

▶1 0.0 Start at trailhead

▶2 1.7 South Fork Daggett Creek

▶3 4.8 Monument Pass

▶4 7.7 Cold Creek tributary

▶5 8.8 Star Lake

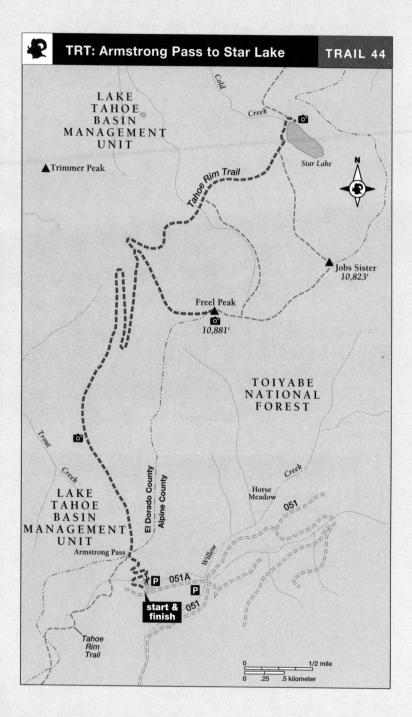

LAKE TAHOE BASIN MANAGEMENT UNIT

▲ Trimmer Peak

Cold

Creek

Star Lake

Tahoe Rim Trail

N

▲ Jobs Sister
10,823'

Freel Peak
10,881'

TOIYABE NATIONAL FOREST

Trout

Creek

LAKE TAHOE BASIN MANAGEMENT UNIT

Creek

Horse Meadow

051

El Dorado County
Alpine County

Armstrong Pass

Willow

051A

P

051

start & finish

Tahoe Rim Trail

0   1/2 mile
0   .25   .5 kilometer

Tahoe Rim Trail: Armstrong Pass to Star Lake

This trip leads to two excellent destinations, Freel Peak, the highest summit in the Tahoe basin, and Star Lake, one of the basin's highest lakes. A lightly used section of the Tahoe Rim Trail takes you all the way to the lake, and most of the way to the summit. The remainder of the climb to Freel Peak follows a boot-beaten path to the top, suitable for all but the most timid of trail hikers. Backdropped by the volcanic slopes of rugged Jobs Sister, the lake's setting is quite picturesque, luring both dayhikers and backpackers to the serene shores. The view from Freel Peak is stunning in both scenery and scope.

Best Time

The route along the TRT to Star Lake is often open by July 4th, but those wishing to climb Freel Peak will most likely find snowfields still covering the slopes below the summit at that time. Snow-free ascents of the peak are usually possible by the end of July. The high elevation of Star Lake insures chilly swimming throughout the season, but the warmer temperatures from mid-July through August will make the possibility of a lake dip more palatable. Although cooler temperatures prevail in autumn, you'll find less traffic on the trail. Snow returns to the area by late October.

Finding the Trail

From Highway 89, turn north onto Forest Service Road 051, 0.8 miles from the Highway 88 junction in Hope Valley and 1.8 miles from Luther Pass.

TRAIL USE
Hike, Run, Bike, Horse
LENGTH
11.6 miles, 6 hours
VERTICAL FEET
±2200'
DIFFICULTY
– 1 2 **3** 4 5 +
TRAIL TYPE
Out & Back
SURFACE TYPE
Dirt

FEATURES
Dogs Allowed
Mountain
Summit
Lake
Great Views
Photo Opportunity
Camping

FACILITIES
None

Follow dirt road roughly northwest for nearly 3.5 miles and turn left onto Forest Service Road 051F. This junction immediately follows the second bridge crossing over Willow Creek. Proceed on dirt road for a short distance to a flat area just before the rough road makes a steep climb up a hill. Unless you're driving a 4WD vehicle, park in the flat area off the road and start your hike from here. Follow the road for a half-mile to its end at a wide turnaround, where a TRT sign marks the official start of the trail.

Logistics

The dirt road into the trailhead is rough enough to advise the use of a sturdy vehicle with good clearance. You'll need a 4WD with high clearance to get all the way to the trailhead, but most road-worthy vehicles driven with a little care will get you close enough.

Trail Description

▶1 Start climbing moderately steeply on single-track trail, soon crossing a small tributary of Willow Creek. Beyond the crossing, switchbacks attack a hillside carpeted with sagebrush, currant, and tobacco brush and dotted with an occasional western white pine or juniper. At 0.4 mile from the official trailhead, the stiff climb ends at a T-junction

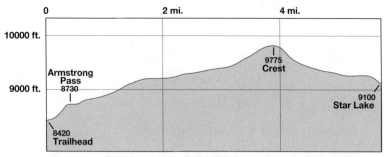

TRAIL 44 TRT: Armstrong Pass to Star Lake Elevation Profile

at Armstrong Pass, amid scattered red firs. ▶2

Turn right and follow the pleasantly graded Tahoe Rim Trail on a rising traverse below the west slope of the Carson Range crest. You quickly emerge from the scattered forest and walk across mostly open slopes past an occasional western white pine or juniper. Past a rock cliff known as Fountain Face you enjoy good views across the Trout Creek drainage of the meadows in Hell Hole and Fountain Place, and across Lake Tahoe of the Crystal Range. Continue the steadily rising traverse, hopping over a few tiny rivulets along the way. Near the 2.75-mile mark, the trail angles across the slope via the first of a pair of long-legged switchbacks. At 4.0 miles, amid scattered whitebark pines, the climb culminates at the crest of an auxiliary ridge of Freel Peak, at 9730 feet the high point of the trail to Star Lake (and the start of the side trip to Freel Peak). ▶3

Remaining on the TRT, descend from the ridge via some switchbacks to the floor of a cirque basin on the northwest side of Freel Peak. A short, moderate descent leads through open forest to the crossing of a thin ribbon of water from a tributary of Cold Creek. Beyond the stream, you follow a nearly mile-long traverse to the north ridge of Jobs Sister, and then make a short drop along the ridge to Star Lake. ▶4

At 9100 feet, Star Lake is one of the highest lakes in the Tahoe basin, and therefore not one of the warmest. Backpackers will find a number of passable campsites along the north shore with a nice view across the lake of Jobs Sister.

Before construction of the Tahoe Rim Trail, Star Lake was virtually inaccessible, as the only viable access crossed private property. Nowadays, not having a trail to this delightful cirque-bound lake is hard to imagine.

Great Views

🚶 **MILESTONES**

▶1   0.0   Start at trailhead
▶2   0.4   Turn right at TRT junction
▶3   4.0   Crest of ridge (start of Freel Peak climb)
▶4   5.8   Star Lake

Side Trip to Freel Peak

If you're bound for the summit of Freel Peak, leave the TRT at the high point on the ridge, 4.0 miles from the trailhead, ▶3 and climb a use-trail on the right-hand side of the ridge past some low rock outcrops. Eventually, the boot-beaten path gains the steep ridgecrest and follows it for a while before leaving the ridge to make an angling ascent across the gravelly northwest face of the mountain. The entire route is straightforward and, unless lingering patches of snow cover the slope, you should be able to follow a discernible path all the way to the top of Freel Peak.

In former days an array of communications equipment littered the summit, producing an annoying electronic hum that would irritate the ears of successful climbers. Thankfully, most all of the equipment has been removed except for a noiseless rectangular foundation. From the top of the Tahoe Basin's highest summit is a 360°, unobstructed view of the lake and surrounding terrain.

Peak baggers can easily add Jobs Sister to their list of accomplishments by following a mile-long path along the ridge between Freel Peak and Jobs Sister. Experienced cross-county hikers bound for Star Lake need not retrace their steps to the TRT, but rather can descend the stream gully between Freel Peak and Jobs Sister to the TRT, or the north ridge of Jobs Sister directly to the lake. ▶5

This side trip adds 2 miles round trip and 1150 vertical feet to the described trail.

Local Resources

Major Outfitters

Alpenglow Sports
415 North Lake Blvd., Tahoe City, CA 96145
530-583-6917

Back Country
690 North Lake Blvd., Tahoe City, CA 96145
530-581-5861

Back Country
11400 Donner Pass Rd., Truckee, CA 96161
530-582-0909

Recreational Equipment Inc. (REI)
2225 Harvard Way, Reno, NV 89502
775-828-9090   www.rei.com

Reno Mountain Sports
155 E. Moana, Reno, NV 89523
775-825-2855   www.renomountainsports.com

The Sporting Rage
4338 S. Carson, Carson City, NV 89701
775-885-7773   www.sportingrage.com

Tahoe Sports Limited
4008 Lake Tahoe Blvd., South Lake Tahoe, CA 96150
530-542-2000   www.tahoesportsltd.com

Tahoe Sports Limited
1032 Emerald Bay Road, South Lake Tahoe, CA 96150
530-544-2284   www.tahoesportsltd.com

Outlets

Patagonia
8550 White Fir, Reno, NV 89523-2050
800-543-5522 or 775-747-1887   www.patagonia.com

Sierra Trading Post
6865 Sierra Center Pkwy., Suite 200, Reno, NV 89511-2216
775-828-8050   www.sierratradingpost.com

Sportif
1415 Greg St., Suite 101, Sparks, NV
775-359-6400   www.sportif.com

Major Organizations

League to Save Lake Tahoe
955 Emerald Bay Road, South Lake Tahoe, CA 96150
530-541-5388

Tahoe Area Sierra Club
PO Box 16936, South Lake Tahoe, CA 96151
530-320-1795   www.sierraclub.org/chapters/laketahoe

Tahoe Rim Trail Association
DWR Community Non-Profit Center
948 Incline Way, Incline Village, NV 89451
775-298-0012   www.tahoerimtrail.org

Major Public Agencies

Department of Parks and Recreation (California State Parks)
1416 9th Street, Sacramento, CA 95814
800-777-0369 or 916-653-6695   www.parks.ca.gov/

Eldorado National Forest
100 Forni Road, Placerville, CA 95667
530-622-5061   www.fs.fed.us/r5/eldorado/

Lake Tahoe Basin Management Unit
35 College Drive, South Lake Tahoe, CA 96150-4500
530-543-2600   www.fs.fed.us/r5/ltbmu/

Lake Tahoe Nevada State Park
PO Box 8867, Incline Village, NV 89452
775-831-0494   www.parks.nv.gov/

Tahoe National Forest
631 Coyote Street, Nevada City, CA 95959
530-265-4531   www.fs.fed.us/r5/tahoe/

Tahoe National Forest, Big Bend Visitor Center
49685 Hampshire Rocks Road, PO Box 830, Soda Springs, CA 95631
530-426-3609

Tahoe National Forest, Truckee Ranger District
9646 Donner Pass Road, Truckee, CA 96161-2949
530-587-3558

Toiyabe National Forest
1200 Franklin Way, Sparks, NV 89431
775-331-6444
www.fs.fed.us/r5/htnf/

Toiyabe National Forest, Carson Ranger District
1536 S. Carson Street, Carson City, NV 89701
775-882-2766

Useful Books

Carville, Julie Stauffer. 1989. *Hiking Tahoe's Wildflower Trails.*
Edmonton: Lone Pine Publishing.

Graf, Michael. 1999. *Plants of the Tahoe Basin.*
Berkeley and Los Angeles: University of California Press, Ltd.

Hauserman, Tim. 2002. *The Tahoe Rim Trail.*
2nd Ed. Berkeley, CA: Wilderness Press.

Lekisch, Barbara. 1988. *Tahoe Place Names*.
Lafayette, CA: Great West Books.

Schaffer, Jeffrey P. 1998.
Desolation Wilderness and the South Lake Tahoe Basin.
4th Ed. Berkeley: Wilderness Press.

Schaffer, Jeffrey P. 1998.
The Tahoe Sierra: A Natural History Guide to 112 Hikes in the Northern Sierra.
4th Ed. Berkeley, CA: Wilderness Press.

White, Mike. 1998. *Snowshoe Trails of Tahoe*.
Berkeley, CA: Wilderness Press.

Maps

The introduction to each chapter describes Forest Service (USFS) and State Park maps for that area. Listed below, by chapter, are the names of U.S. Geological Survey (USGS) 7.5-minute quadrangles, plus which trails in *Top Trails Lake Tahoe* are shown on that map.

Chapter 1: North Tahoe USGS Maps

Trail 1	Independence Lake, Webber Peak
Trail 2	Hobart Mills
Trail 3	Independence Lake, Norden
Trail 4	Norden
Trail 5	Norden
Trail 6	Cisco Grove, Soda Springs
Trail 7	Norden
Trail 8	Granite Chief, Tahoe City
Trail 9	Granite Chief, Tahoe City
Trail 10	Granite Chief, Tahoe City
Trail 11	Mt. Rose
Trail 12	Mt. Rose
Trail 13	Mt. Rose, Martis Peak
Trail 14	Mt. Rose, Marlette Lake

Chapter 2: West Tahoe USGS Maps

Trail 15   Tahoe City, Homewood
Trail 16   Homewood
Trail 17   Homewood
Trail 18   Homewood
Trail 19   Homewood

Chapter 3: South Tahoe USGS Maps

Trail 20   Homewood, Rockboud Valley
Trail 21   Emerald Bay
Trail 22   Emerald Bay, Meeks Bay
Trail 23   Emerald Bay
Trail 24   Emerald Bay
Trail 25   Emerald Bay, Rockbound Valley
Trail 26   Emerald Bay
Trail 27   Emerald Bay, Rockbound Valley
Trail 28   Emerald Bay, Echo Lake
Trail 29   Echo Lake, Pyramid Peak
Trail 30   Echo Lake, Pyramid Peak
Trail 31   Echo Lake
Trail 32   Echo Lake
Trail 33   Caples Lake, Carson Pass
Trail 34   Caples Lake
Trail 35   Caples Lake
Trail 36   Caples Lake

Chapter 4: East Tahoe USGS Map Names

Trail 37   Glenbrook
Trail 38   Glenbrook
Trail 39   Glenbrook, Marlette Lake
Trail 40   Glenbrook, Marlette Lake
Trail 41   Glenbrook
Trail 42   Glenbrook
Trail 43   South Lake Tahoe
Trail 44   Freel Peak

Index

Author and Editor

Mike White

Mike was born and raised in Portland, Oregon. He learned to hike in the Cascades, and honed his outdoor skills while attending Seattle Pacific University. After college, Mike relocated to the high desert of Nevada, where he was drawn to the beautiful and sunny Sierra.

In the early 1990s, Mike began writing about the outdoors full time. He expanded Wilderness Press' *Trinity Alps*. He then authored *Nevada Wilderness Areas and Great Basin National Park*, followed by the *Snowshoe Trails* series, *Sequoia National Park, Kings Canyon National Park* and *Backpacking Nevada*. Mike also contributed to *Backpacking California* and has written for *Sunset* and *Backpacker* magazines and the *Reno Gazette-Journal*. He teaches backpacking and snowshoeing at Truckee Meadows Community College. Mike lives in Reno with his wife, Robin, and their two boys, David and Stephen, along with their yellow lab, Barkley.

Joe Walowski

Joe Walowski is the editor of *Top Trails Los Angeles, Top Trails San Francisco*, and *Top Trails Lake Tahoe*. By day, Joe is a strategy consultant to magazine publishers. An avid hiker and climber, he has spent many pleasant days on the top trails throughout California. A longtime resident of San Francisco, he now makes his home in Seattle.

Joe conceived of the Top Trails series as the definitive sampler of trails, the "must-do" hikes in the most interesting destinations. Feel free to e-mail feedback on Top Trails to joe@highpointpress.com